D0207549

B L A C K   S E A

PONTUS

Neocaesarea

Amaseia •   • *Lycus R.*

ys R.

• Ibora

Iris R.

• Sebasteia

ARMENIA

KINGDOM OF ARMENIA

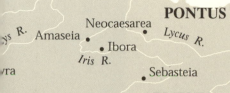

sa •

• Caesarea

PADOCIA

• Nazianzus

Sasima •

MTNS.

• Samosata

Tyana •

• Podandus

AURUS

CILICIA

Tarsus

• Seleucia

• Antioch

SYRIA

PERSIAN

EMPIRE

Euphrates R.

• Jerusalem

PALESTINE

LIBRARY

Gift of

Catherine E. Boyd

Professor of History
at Carleton 1946-1966

WITHDRAWN

Families and Friends

Families and Friends in Late Roman Cappadocia

Raymond Van Dam

PENN

University of Pennsylvania Press
Philadelphia

Copyright © 2003 University of Pennsylvania Press
All rights reserved
Printed in the United States of America on acid-free paper

10   9   8   7   6   5   4   3   2   1

Published by
University of Pennsylvania Press
Philadelphia, Pennsylvania 19104-4011

Library of Congress Cataloging-in-Publication Data

Van Dam, Raymond
   Families and friends in late Roman Cappadocia/Raymond Van Dam
      p. cm.
   ISBN 0-8122-3712-9 (cloth : alk. paper)
   Includes bibliographical references and index.
      1. Cappadocia (Turkey)—History. 2. Rome—Provinces—Turkey—
Cappadocia—History. I. Title
DS156.C3 V356   2003
275.64′02′092—dc21   *2002072882*

Endpapers: Asia Minor and the Eastern Mediterranean in the fourth century.

DS
156
.C3
V356
2003

03 2008-46

For Helen

"I saw a young hawk flying and my soul began to rise"
—Bob Seger, Roll Me Away

Contents

Acknowledgments

As students of classical rhetoric Basil and Gregory of Nazianzus hoped to internalize the eloquence of Greek culture so thoroughly that they would embody the books they had read as "living libraries." Modern historians face a similar seduction of identifying with the subjects they study. Gregory's immediate family might well have been the family I grew up in: a revered father, a beloved mother, a devout sister and her husband now with their own children and grandchildren, a distinguished older brother and his wife, and me, a slightly wayward younger son. Like Gregory, I also had the good fortune to spend my boyhood in the joyful company of cousins, uncles, aunts, and grandparents. This book about Cappadocian families provides an opportunity to thank my immediate and extended family, again, for their abiding love and support.

This book is also an invitation to remember friends. At the end of his life Gregory still dreamed about renewing his friendship with Basil. Their friendship had flourished during their years together as students, in particular at Athens. Not surprisingly, my closest friends too have often been fellow students. My memories of high school, college, and graduate studies, of starting out in an academic career as a research fellow and a young professor, always focus on the friends with whom I shared those happy times, in particular Bruce and Flossie Bode, Brent and Shauna Shaw, Dave Braund, Grace Mizen, John Heath, Andrew Cooper, and Jill Dupont. The dedication of this book celebrates one cherished friendship that first blossomed when we were graduate students at our Athens.

Introduction

"I will start my story a bit in the past." During his later years Gregory of Nazianzus was searching for meaning in his life. As he looked back, all he could see was grief for the loss of loved ones, dismay at unexpected misfortunes, and regrets for broken relationships and unwanted obligations. A good story could change all that. In his attempts at writing an autobiography he hoped to find a consistent trajectory of beliefs, commitments, and values that would link his past and his future life in a single unwavering arc. We modern historians should readily sympathize with this commitment to retrospection. Like Gregory, to move forward we must look to our own past. The introduction to a series of historical studies can preview their contents only by recalling their making.[1]

*   *   *

The lives of the Cappadocian Fathers and their known ancestors stretched from the later third century to the end of the fourth century. The grandparents of Basil of Caesarea and Gregory of Nyssa and the father of Gregory of Nazianzus were born in a Roman empire that was finally beginning to recover from the near breakdown of the mid-third century. Insecurity on the frontiers had led to political fragmentation and the rapid turnover of emperors. Christianity was still a minor religion in the Roman world, and Basil's grandparents in Pontus endured persecution under some of the last pagan emperors. The reign of a Christian emperor changed everything. Gregory of Nazianzus' father in Cappadocia was an obscure municipal magistrate, until he saw how the emperor Constantine patronized Christian bishops at the Council of Nicaea in 325. He quickly converted and soon became bishop of his hometown. Basil and Gregory of Nazianzus were born at about the time Constantine was dedicating his new capital of Constantinople, and Gregory of Nyssa at about the time of Constantine's death. All three Cappadocian Fathers were students of classical Greek literature and philosophy. All three served as bishops in Cappadocia. All three contributed extensively to the development of Christian theology. Basil died a few years before the Council of Constantinople in 381 reaffirmed the orthodoxy of Nicene Christianity. By the time Gregory of Nazianzus and Gregory of Nyssa died, the emperor Theodosius had declared orthodox Christianity the sole legitimate religion of the empire.

The renewal of the Roman empire, conversion, orthodoxy and heresy, Christianity and classical culture, the foundation of Constantinople as New Rome, the evolution of cities, the rise of bishops: the Cappadocian Fathers were participants in all these grand transformations, and the reigns of Constantine and Theodosius were the parentheses that enclosed their careers. Within their lifetimes the empire had gone from the first Christian emperor to a ruler with such a reputation for piety that he would be lauded as "less an emperor than a servant of Christ."[2]

A study of Cappadocia in late antiquity provides a vantage point from which to survey these consequential transformations. High on the plateau in central Asia Minor, cut off from the Mediterranean by rugged mountains, Cappadocia had long been a marginal region in the ancient world, dismissed as unruly and cold, maligned for its cultural backwardness, hardly registering in historical texts, seemingly little affected by the great political and social changes in the Mediterranean world and the Near East. The whole region seemed stagnant, almost petrified, as if it had been dipped in the mythical lake between Caesarea and Tyana that was thought to turn reeds into stone.[3]

During the fourth century, however, Cappadocia flourished. The three most important reasons for the sudden renown of the region were Basil, Gregory of Nazianzus, and Gregory of Nyssa. Their prominence made others take note of central and eastern Asia Minor, and they composed many sermons, treatises, letters, and poems. The writings of these Cappadocian Fathers were in fact so voluminous that coming to terms with them already then required a lifetime of disciplined commitment. As part of her ascetic regimen Melania the Elder read millions of lines of Gregory of Nazianzus and Basil, sometimes seven or eight times each week! Every scholar of late antiquity would like to have her as a research assistant.[4]

*   *   *

I started reading too. Today Melania would probably skim the ancient authors only once a week, in order to find time to cope with all the modern scholarship. Much of this scholarship on the Cappadocian Fathers and their era is magnificent. New editions, translations, and commentaries have made their texts more accessible and more readable. Some of the best of these editors and translators include Werner Jaeger (for initiating the ongoing edition of the writings of Gregory of Nyssa), Pierre Maraval (for his editions of Gregory of Nyssa), Paul Gallay (for his biography of Gregory of Nazianzus and editions of his letters), Jean Bernardi (for his study and editions of the orations of Gregory of Nazianzus), and Wolf-Dieter Hauschild (for his translation of and commentary on Basil's letters). For a historian of the Roman empire like myself this combination of extensive ancient writings and equally extensive modern scholarship about the Cappadocian Fathers and about central and eastern Asia Minor in general presented a unique opportunity to study culture, society, and religion in one locale during a short time period. In fact, it provided such a panorama for a series of regional studies that it motivated three books on different themes: *Kingdom of Snow*, on Roman rule and Greek culture; *Becoming Christian*, on the impact of Christianity; and this one on families and friends.

Some of my reading also left me a bit disheartened. The revival of the study of late antiquity has been one of the great success stories of the modern historical enterprise. One conspicuous monument to this success is the recent publication of a magnificent handbook whose subtitle is a subtle pun on our postmodern times: *A Guide to the Postclassical World*. But the seasoning of the field has come with a price. Increasingly, scholarship seems to be taking place in parallel universes that coincide but do not often overlap. Family history, gender studies, administrative history, prosopography and aristocratic careers, doctrinal studies, literary criticism, textual criticism, the history of asceticism and spirituality: the fragmentation of scholarship in the field begins to resemble the fragmentation of the later Roman empire itself. This segmentation of methods and interests has reduced the value of some of the scholarship on Cappadocia and the Cappadocian Fathers.[5]

The details require more scrutiny. So much of our basic chronology for the lives of the Cappadocian Fathers and our prosopographical identifications still rests on the "inimitable accuracy" of that "sure-footed mule," the eminent seventeenth-century antiquarian and church historian Louis Sébastien LeNain de Tillemont, in the ninth volume of his monumental *Mémoires pour servir à l'histoire ecclésiastique des six premiers siècles*. Tillemont's conclusions survive in common circulation, even if often unknowingly filtered through subsequent studies. These results now require updated examination; an excellent model is Marie-Madeleine Hauser-Meury's meticulous prosopography of the writings of Gregory of Nazianzus.[6]

At the same time, our methods and interests need updating to take into account both new research in Roman history and comparative studies from other fields. Some of the topics that have jumped forward in recent scholarship on Roman studies are demography and family, gender studies, body and society, literary analysis, rhetorical strategies, and authorial self-representation. The chapters in this book, as well as in the companion volumes *Kingdom of Snow* and *Becoming Christian*, hence try to combine some of the new interpretive approaches necessary for understanding the Cappadocian Fathers, with the patient erudition necessary for understanding their writings.[7]

Perhaps most important is the need to rid ourselves of the deference and piety that still inspire many studies of Church Fathers. Too often the study of early theology and theologians, or at least of orthodox theology and orthodox theologians, is muffled by a sense of delicacy and discretion, or a reluctance to discuss personal foibles and disagreeable behavior. We need instead to become more candid, more respectfully severe, in our evaluations of Church Fathers, their ideas, and their actions. Biographies in particular are often too reverential, too patronizing, to be successful critical studies. For all their reputations as bishops, theologians, or ascetics, churchmen and churchwomen were still men and women, hardly immune to the passions and frustrations of ordinary life.

In order to highlight these passions, my trilogy of books has focused on interpreting texts and understanding people. There are so many texts and people to investigate. Too often books, articles, and conferences have concentrated on one or another of the Cappadocian Fathers and reduced the others to occasional cameo appearances. Yet their mutual relationships were some of their most important personal and psychological influences. Basil and Gregory of Nazianzus were inseparable for decades, as fellow students, close comrades, and then uneasy former friends. Gregory of Nyssa felt dominated by his older brother Basil, but found consolation with Gregory of Nazianzus.

Not only should the three Cappadocian Fathers appear together, but they should also be studied in conjunction with some of their notable contemporaries, such as Libanius and Himerius, two of their teachers; Themistius, a famous orator at Constantinople who was a correspondent; Eunomius, a heterodox Cappadocian theologian who became a rival; Macrina, the ascetic sister of Basil and Gregory of Nyssa; Amphilochius, a cousin of Gregory of Nazianzus who became bishop of Iconium; and the emperors Constantius, Valens, and Theodosius. Perhaps the oddest acquaintanceship was with Julian, who was the same age as Basil and Gregory of

Nazianzus and who had likewise grown up as a Christian in Cappadocia. But once Julian became an emperor and an open supporter of pagan cults, he also became an upside-down reflection of the Cappadocian Fathers, a learned pagan contrasted to learned Christians, a Roman emperor opposed to Christian clerics. The Cappadocian Fathers typically presented and defined themselves through their relationships, arguing with rivals, interceding with magistrates, remembering lost friends. As sons and brothers and friends, as patrons and correspondents, as preachers and theological polemicists, they found their identities in their personal interactions.

The texts and the people coalesce in their self-representations. Authors talked about themselves directly in their letters and orations and poems. They also talked about themselves indirectly in treatises nominally about other topics. So many of their writings presupposed unspoken agendas and implicit objectives. Gregory of Nazianzus examined his love for his mother in an oration about his sister. Gregory of Nyssa commented on his relationships with his sister and his brother in a treatise about virginity. Basil contemplated the breakdown of his friendship with an admired mentor in a sermon about the Forty Martyrs. In all of their writings these men were representing themselves, presenting themselves before others, simultaneously preening and apologizing. Their willingness to imagine themselves provides a license for us to do the same.

*   *   *

The format of this book is a series of interlocking chapters, or rather of reinforcing layers of interpretation, that investigate various topics and themes that have become increasingly important for the social and cultural history of the Roman empire. *Families and Friends* uses the Cappadocian Fathers and other members of their families to apply some of the recent research that has revolutionized the study of the Roman family. That research has typically employed the techniques and evidence of prosopography (the close study of biographical data and personal alliances), Roman law, and statistical sampling. For specific examples it has regularly highlighted the writings, and often the families, of Cicero at the end of the Roman Republic and Pliny the Younger in the early empire. Because the writings of the Cappadocian Fathers now offer a rare opportunity for a close investigation of two provincial families side-by-side, the chapters in this book evaluate this research on other Roman families by focusing instead on personal and emotional experiences within the families of Basil and Gregory of Nazianzus.

The first section discusses fathers and sons. These chapters exploit the discrepancies between the expectations of demographic profiles and the restrictions of Roman law on the one hand, and the actual experiences of the Cappadocian Fathers and members of their families. Because his father died sooner than he might have expected, Basil spent his life searching for mentors and replacement fathers. Because his father lived much longer than anyone might have expected, Gregory of Nazianzus was constantly torn between his devotion to his father and his resentment at his father's meddling. Yet despite the tensions in their relationships with their fathers, both ended up assuming or imitating their fathers' careers. Basil and Gregory of Nazianzus were furthermore the oldest brothers in their respective familes, and both became substitute fathers for their younger brothers, such as Gregory of Nyssa. Since all three of the Cappadocian Fathers were at the same time pondering the theology of the Trinity, it is reasonable to speculate that their personal experiences might have influenced their thinking about God the Father and Jesus Christ the Son.

The second section discusses mothers and daughters. In both families the mothers were unconventionally strong figures, one because as a widow she controlled the family's patrimony, the other because her husband was so elderly and sometimes incapacitated. In Basil's family Macrina, the oldest sister, acquired a reputation for her ascetic piety. But despite their prominence, most of our information about these women is from texts composed by men, their sons or brothers. These chapters hence consider women as a medium, a rhetorical strategy, a means for men to reflect on themselves and their own concerns. They also consider the consequences of the heightened emphasis in Christianity on a life of asceticism and virginity. Choosing virginity was a statement about both religious preferences and social reproduction. Because sons might choose not to marry and produce more sons, entire families were extinguished. The families of both Basil and Gregory of Nazianzus ended with their generation.

The final set of chapters discusses friendships. Unlike family relationships, friendships were voluntary relationships based on personal choices. These decisions transformed friendships into conflicted relationships, simultaneously utilitarian and emotional. As a result, the letters that provide most of the information about friends essentially mimicked the relationships, since they too tried to combine deep feelings with the formalities of protocol. In their friendships with others Basil and Gregory of Nazianzus revealed their own, sometimes divergent, notions of friendship. Those contrasts were most apparent in their own friendship. As students sharing a passion for

Greek culture, they were fast friends, but when they became ascetics, priests, and bishops, their friendship collapsed. Classical culture had kept them together, and ecclesiastical affairs had come between them. In an odd reversal of expectations, Basil, the son of a teacher, privileged Christian concerns in their relationship, and Gregory, the son of a bishop, gave priority to familiarity with classical culture. Gregory was left baffled as he tried to make sense of their earlier intimacy. At the end of his life he still cried when he thought about Basil. Their friendship had been one of the great love stories of the fourth century.

* * *

Even though the Cappadocian Fathers and some of their distinguished contemporaries are the main actors, this book is primarily a study of the dynamics and the emotions of family relationships and friendships. As such, it is an attempt to link ecclesiastical concerns more widely with social and cultural history. Ecclesiastical texts provide so much information about so many aspects of Roman society in the Greek East that the later Roman empire is much better documented than the early empire. Yet patristics scholars and church historians, the scholars who are most familiar with the texts, are often not much interested in, or not much familiar with, social and cultural history, and social and cultural historians all too often still do not approach ecclesiastical texts with any systematic thoroughness. Theological studies and cultural studies need to find some sort of accommodation.

Covering so many topics and texts and people in this and my other two books about Cappadocia in late antiquity can be overwhelming, for both author and readers. This comprehensiveness is meant to encourage some sideways reading by specialists. In this volume, patristics scholars interested primarily in the Cappadocian Fathers might read about the implications of demographic simulations. Historians of the family might read about the connection between friendships and personal identity. In addition, even though the discussions in this trilogy highlight Cappadocian topics, the analytical models should be applicable to other regions and other interests. We will all benefit by trying to make connections between different topics, different approaches, and different texts. This comprehensiveness is furthermore an attempt to raise the level of scholarly discourse, in detail, in interpretation, and in intensity. People are in the details: we will all benefit again from readings of the ancient texts that are both multidimensional and more careful.

In the later fifth century one law student at Beirut asked a fellow student whether he had "the books of the great Basil and the illustrious Gregory and the other teachers." This student did indeed have a large library of Church Fathers, with editions of many of Basil's treatises, sermons, and letters as well as of some of the sermons of Gregory of Nazianzus. "I replied that I owned many of their writings." These young scholars were already trying to make connections, not only among the writings of the Church Fathers, but also between their own studies in Roman law and their interest in ecclesiastical affairs. We should follow their example. As historians it is our obligation to combine ecclesiastical texts with secular history, patristics with social history, theology with cultural studies, and meticulous erudition with interpretive speculation.[8]

Fathers and Sons

Modern studies of the Roman family have highlighted several approaches during the past half-century. One is prosopography, the close study of biographical details in order to interpret political behavior in terms of struggles over power and prestige among groups defined by family loyalties, personal friendships, or regional affiliations. Prosopographical interpretations presuppose that family members were loyal and supportive, and that men made friendships primarily to advance their careers and ambitions. As a result, prosopographical interpretations have typically transformed the dynamics of families into another aspect of imperial intrigues, political maneuvering for high offices, and, after the rise of Christianity, ecclesiastical factionalism. A second approach to the Roman family has been through the study of Roman law. Emperors, imperial magistrates, and jurists issued edicts and legal opinions about many aspects of the family, including marriage, divorce, the legitimacy of children, and the technicalities of wills and inheritances. Yet another, more recent approach is the use of statistical sampling to create a demographic profile of Roman society, especially in regard to fertility rates, ages of men and women at marriage, and life expectancy.

All of these approaches have contributed to the great success in reviving and modernizing our understanding of the Roman family. All of them also have limitations, some specific to each approach, others more generic. One shared shortcoming is their reluctance to discuss emotions. Prosopography assumes that political calculations and personal ambitions dictated behavior, and it leaves little room for marriages or friendships that were based largely, if not exclusively, on true love and devotion. Interpretations derived primarily from Roman law can outline the legal demands and structures, but provide little sense of how they might relate to the vagaries of habits of the heart. In this respect the interpretations follow the lead of their primary sources, since Roman law itself was often simply reactive and represented the imposition of prescriptive regulations against practices that somehow offended emperors or baffled jurists. Demography and statistics are similarly heartless, with little interest in the feelings that motivated marriages or the conception of children.

Another common limitation of all these approaches is a tendency toward blanket pronouncements and sweeping conclusions. In real life, however, experiences never quite matched these expectations. No particular family or individual lived up to all the anticipated intrigues of prosopography, the constraints of Roman law, or the profiles of demography. In the family of Gregory of Nazianzus, for instance, Gregory seemingly contradicted the assumptions of prosopography by insisting that he was not ambitious and by repeatedly trying to avoid clerical promotion. Because he began to assume responsibility for his family already during his father's lifetime, in particular by acting like a father for his own brother, Gregory challenged the restrictions of Roman law about paternal authority. And, to confound all demographic expectations, Gregory's father lived to be almost a centenarian. In Basil's family, the oldest sister and oldest brother helped their younger siblings and even became substitute parents for them. Yet the siblings also distanced themselves from each other, Macrina as an ascetic, Basil as a cleric and bishop at Caesarea, Naucratius as a solitary hunter, Gregory as bishop of Nyssa and briefly of Sebasteia, Peter as the baby brother of the family and then bishop of Sebasteia, their other sisters by going off to their husbands' families. For all their achievements and their reputations, the lives of these siblings never seemed to allow much interaction or mutual devotion. This was a family with seemingly little sense of being a family.[1]

One purpose of the chapters in this and the next section is to evaluate these tensions between general expectations and specific experiences. Since these discrepancies between expectations and experiences exposed deep emotions and passions, another purpose is to examine some of the emotional relationships within these two particular families. In contrast to austere discussions based on prosopography, Roman law, and demography, other recent studies have investigated the possibility of finding affection and love between spouses and between parents and children. Although this transformation of the Roman family into an arena of true feelings is a welcome development, it has sometimes made the Roman family a bit too saccharine by ignoring animosities and tensions. Patristics scholars in particular often seem reluctant to investigate the lives of Fathers of the Church, as if fearful of discovering less than pleasant aspects about them and their families. Some churchmen certainly did have difficult pasts to overcome, or just forget. Augustine of Hippo would have to live with memories of a domineering father, a long-suffering mother, a discarded mistress, and an abandoned son. But precisely because churchmen were so reflective about the proprieties of personal behavior, they were also often very candid about their own feelings. The writings of churchmen hence offer modern historians some of the best opportunities to investigate the inner dynamics of particular families in antiquity, "at a level of intimacy that is beyond reach for other Roman families."[2]

The chapters in the next section will discuss relationships with and among women in the families of the Cappadocian Fathers; the chapters in this section discuss primarily the relationships among the men.

One set of relationships involved oldest sons and their fathers. Basil was the oldest son and most likely the second oldest child in his family. His father was probably about thirty at Basil's birth, and even with the high mortality rates in the Roman empire he could have looked forward to mentoring his son well into young manhood. Gregory of Nazianzus was the oldest child in his family. But since his father was already about fifty or older at Gregory's birth, he would have been fortunate to see his son reach his teenage years. Basil could have anticipated growing into adulthood with his father, while Gregory should have become fatherless at a young age. The fates of both inverted expectations. Basil lost his father when a young teenager, and into his mid-forties Gregory was still caring for his aged father. These experiences, in part because they were unexpected, clearly affected their feelings about their fathers. Basil never mentioned his father and rejected anything that resembled his father's career. He also seems to have nursed deep painful yearnings for his father, and he longed for a fatherly mentor. Gregory revered his father for decades and consistently followed his father's lead. He praised his father's gentleness and serenity. Yet at least twice he thought of his father as a "tyrant," as if somehow his father's amiable reasonableness had itself become oppressive. Loss and longing, devotion and resentment: both Basil and Gregory had conflicted feelings about their fathers.[3]

Another set of relationships involved younger brothers, nephews, uncles, and cousins. Discussions of the Roman family rarely evaluate relationships among brothers and the differences in their experiences and expectations, or relationships with kin like uncles, cousins, and nephews. This is an odd omission in studies of the Roman family. For the later Roman empire it is an equally odd omission in discussions of politics and imperial rule. In place of the earlier pattern of family dynasties of successive emperors, during the fourth century the multiplicity of emperors had created family dynasties of co-emperors, brothers like Constantine's three sons or Valentinian and Valens, cousins like Constantius and Julian, and uncles and nephews like Valens and Gratian. Among the Cappadocian Fathers the oldest brothers are the best documented, but they always had to think about and deal with younger brothers, uncles, cousins, and nephews. The career of one younger brother, Caesarius, raised both anxieties and true regrets for Gregory of Nazianzus. Another younger brother, Gregory of Nyssa, became a distinguished theologian in his own right, but only after Basil's death. And Gregory of Nazianzus' cousin, Amphilochius of Iconium, was one of the few to survive Basil's prickly disposition.[4]

One final relationship was both a paradigm worthy of imitation and an idealized projection of actual experiences. Historians of the Roman family have used the techniques of prosopography and demography and scrutinized the evidence of Roman law, inscriptions, and literary texts. Debates over Christian doctrine are also important sources of information. The great theological controversies of the fourth century focused precisely on the relationship between God the Father and God the Son, and both theologians like the Cappadocian Fathers and ordinary believers struggled to articulate this relationship. For their analyses of Christian theology the personal experiences of churchmen were relevant and influential. To talk about the Father and the Son was also to think about their own fathers and themselves as sons.

Chapter 1

Adopting a Father:
Basil and Basil the Elder

Basil's grandparents had been Christians in Pontus and Cappa-docia. In their lifetimes Roman emperors had still been hostile to Christianity. Within a generation, however, everything would change. The emperor Constantine became a supporter of Christianity already during his rise to power in the western empire. Because he seized control of the eastern empire a few years before Basil's birth, Basil and his siblings grew up in a Christian Roman empire. Their father, Basil the Elder, had already become a successful teacher and advocate, and Basil and his brothers could look forward to choosing among various careers, either secular, as local teachers or imperial magistrates, or ecclesiastical, as clerics and bishops. Their futures were limitless. Yet Basil consistently preferred to define himself and his life in terms of a more restricted past when Christians had been marginalized and even persecuted. This perspective of oppression spilled over to affect his memories of his father. Basil lost his father when he was a young teenager. As he then searched for mentors to replace Basil the Elder, he seems to have been most attracted to men who reminded him of his grandparents and their generation that had survived the last persecutions.

Grandparents

Ancient accounts of early Christianity in Cappadocia and Pontus high-lighted persecutions and hostility. In the early second century a contagion of anonymous accusations had forced the imperial envoy Pliny to investigate Christians in Pontus and even sanction some executions, and at the end of the century a provincial governor mistreated Christians in Cappadocia because he was angry that his own wife had converted. In the early third century a series of earthquakes in Cappadocia and Pontus so terrorized the locals that they turned upon the Christians as scapegoats, apparently with the support of the governor. In the mid-third century emperors took the initiative first in ordering all Roman citizens to sacrifice to the pagan gods, then in imposing penalties specifically on Christian bishops and clerics. One victim was Gregory Thaumaturgus, bishop of Neocaesarea in Pontus, who saved himself only by fleeing to the mountains. Shortly afterward members of Basil's father's family became guardians of legends about the life of Gregory Thaumaturgus, carefully collecting and preserving some of the saint's sayings. For Basil's grandparents perhaps the most meaningful of these traditions were the stories about Gregory's success at surviving this persecution. They would soon face the same threat.[1]

The heroic exploits of their grandparents were the earliest events of family history known to Basil and his siblings. All four of his grandparents had apparently suffered at the beginning of the fourth century during what was later known simply as "the time of the persecutions." Diocletian and other emperors in the Tetrarchy, the "gang of four" that ruled during the late third and early fourth century, had issued edicts that repressed Christianity, and in both Pontus and Cappadocia horrific tortures accompanied these persecutions. In Cappadocia Basil's maternal grandfather had been executed because of "imperial displeasure" and his possessions dispersed to other owners; his maternal grandmother had also died, either during the persecutions or shortly afterward. His paternal grandparents had spent seven years hiding in the mountains of Pontus during the reigns of the eastern emperors Diocletian, Galerius, and, in particular, Maximinus. Maximinus had become an emperor in the East following Diocletian's retirement, and once he acquired control over Asia Minor, he had insisted that municipal councils should expel Christians from their cities. Even though some of Basil's grandparents had survived these persecutions, they had still earned the right to be called "living martyrs."[2]

These traditions about persecution and martyrdom were certainly noteworthy within Basil's family, and subsequent generations passed them on. When he was a young boy growing up in Pontus, his paternal grandmother, Macrina the Elder, had told him about the deeds and sayings of Gregory Thaumaturgus. Presumably she had also told him, and his siblings too, about her and her husband's experiences. Macrina the Younger, the oldest of the children in Basil's family, eventually became the keeper of these traditions. In her dying days she again recited all that she knew about their family's history to a younger brother, Gregory of Nyssa, "in sequence, as if in a book." Gregory then recorded some of those memories, and Gregory of Nazianzus, a friend who had most likely heard stories from Basil or Gregory of Nyssa or even from Macrina herself, recorded others. Tombstones were one important means for individuals and families to immortalize their achievements and preserve an enduring record. In Pontus one son commemorated his parents' virtues on their tombstone: "they possessed a wholesome and moderate life, they venerated and yearned for God with purity and glory, and in life they had a mutual love and shared their activities." A woman likewise thought that a tombstone would honor the "eternal memories" of her husband. Yet there were limits to the effectiveness of tombstones. Although the stones themselves may have been permanent markers, without the veneration of descendants these ancestors were easily forgotten. So rather than relying upon only a lapidary account, members of Basil's family in addition preserved its traditions in their memories as "breathing tombstones."[3]

Oral traditions often included the exploits of just three generations, since the most memorable memories were those that young children could hear directly from the participants, their grandparents and parents. These particular traditions about Basil's grandparents took on an added resonance after Christianity acquired the support of emperors. Their heroic deeds made explicit that here was a family that had not only been Christian before the reign of Constantine and his patronage for Christianity, but that had doggedly preserved its beliefs in the face of persecution. This family now had a pedigree for the future. Other families continued to flaunt their descent from notable aristocrats and Roman magistrates, or even from mythological ancestors. In contrast, in the new Christian society of the mid- and later fourth century Basil's family could now claim to include sons and daughters of the Christian revolution. Lest anyone forget this heritage, their family tomb was in a shrine dedicated to the Forty Martyrs, other famous victims associated with the persecutions of the early fourth century.[4]

Throughout his life Basil revealed a natural affinity for his grandparents' heroic exploits. In part this attraction reflected a sense of temporal displacement. Basil always seemed to be older than his age. Among the Cappadocian Fathers an entire epoch seems to have separated Basil from Gregory of Nazianzus, his slightly older friend, and Gregory of Nyssa, his younger brother. Physically Basil suffered from poor health that afflicted him early on with the infirmities of old age. He himself wryly acknowledged that, as in a Greek tragedy, impending calamity loomed over any of his plans for the future. His episcopal career magnified his comparative seniority. By the time he became metropolitan bishop of Caesarea his suffragan bishops included men from his father's generation, such as his own uncle, as well as a distinguished peer of his grandparents, Gregory the Elder. His physical frailness and his episcopal authority combined to make Basil appear to belong to an earlier generation.[5]

His stern demeanor also made him sympathetic to his grandparents' experiences. Basil had a knack for generating opposition and hostility, and then for exploiting that antagonism to his advantage. Like his grandparents, Basil would be a survivor. But by interpreting contemporary events in terms of his grandparents' experiences of persecution and martyrdom, Basil again identified himself with an earlier, pre-Constantinian generation. Gregory of Nazianzus could always sense the discrepancy. "Who likewise possessed the wisdom of old age even before becoming old?"[6]

Basil the Elder

Basil's father had also survived the persecutions. Basil the Elder had been born before the outbreak of persecution in the early fourth century, perhaps already during the later third century. As a boy he would therefore have endured the persecutions with his parents. But despite his father's experiences, Basil never credited him as a member of this generation of founders. Instead, Basil seems to have wanted to ignore, even forget, his father.

Basil the Elder had benefited from the new tolerance for Christianity under Constantine and his fellow emperor Licinius. He acquired a prominent position in local Pontic society, and by the time of his marriage to Emmelia he already possessed a considerable reputation that he had built up as a schoolteacher, an advocate in the courts, and a local landowner. This combination of owning land, pleading in courts, and teaching boys from the region was widespread among provincial aristocrats throughout the Roman empire, and could earn some of them special distinction.[7] All of Pontus, according to Gregory of Nazianzus in a later oration, had hailed Basil the Elder as the "common teacher of virtue." Basil the Elder was furthermore reputable enough to attract students from neighboring regions such as Armenia who subsequently went on to study at Athens. Another of his students was Basil, his firstborn son, whom he would have taught as a young boy perhaps during the later 330s and early 340s.[8]

Arranging suitable teachers for their sons was an important concern for families. Later in his life Gregory of Nazianzus assumed some responsibility for a niece's sons. To safeguard their interests Gregory once reminded a rhetorician of his obligations: "you are teaching my blood and the blood of my closest relatives." Teaching within families would seem to be the safest solution. Yet this particular relationship between Basil and his father as student and teacher was perhaps more stressful than reassuring, for several reasons.[9]

First, Basil had had an isolated childhood. In the years following his birth his mother had given birth to more children perhaps biannually or even almost annually, and there seems to have been no space for the young Basil to grow up within his immediate family. Relatives substituted for his parents and siblings. Initially he was raised by a wet nurse, a relative Basil later remembered with great affection as his "substitute mother." He also remembered with fondness two youthful playmates, both relatives, one this woman's son whom he subsequently considered to be his foster brother. After he became a bishop Basil had the opportunity to assist both of his childhood chums. When he recommended one to become a bishop, memories of his own childhood may have invoked one striking comment in his endorsement, because he made a point of emphasizing how this man's patronage for others had created a situation that reminded him of "a young child's dependence on his mother's breast." His paternal grandmother, Macrina the Elder, also assisted in his upbringing, "molding and shaping me in the teachings of piety when I was still young."[10]

Basil's early minding hence came from a wet nurse, who then seems to have become his nanny, and from his grandmother. Late in his life Basil would also concede that his mother had helped shape his early ideas about God. In contrast, not only did he not associate his father with his memories of his childhood, but in all his extant writings he never mentioned Basil the Elder directly. Only once did he refer to some action by his father, but then merely as one of his "parents." Even more telling was the context for this reference to his parents' behavior, which was their payments for Basil to live with his wet nurse and foster brother. Basil's only allusion to his father involved the arrangements for his removal from his immediate family.[11]

Basil had most likely had limited contact with his father, and perhaps with the rest of his family, before becoming his father's student. His return now to his immediate family was a reversal of the usual sequence. Typically the children of respectable families received their first instruction at home from private tutors before going on to a grammarian's school; their departure for secondary education hence often marked an initial break from the restrictions of their families. Basil, however, because he had been raised outside his family by a foster mother, was now taking a step back into his family and toward a relationship with his father.

Yet this pedagogical context was precisely another factor that could readily warp this new relationship. Teaching and learning were highly competitive pursuits. Teachers competed with each other through public displays of eloquent virtuosity and by trying to recruit the best students. In Cappadocia one referred to a rival who was about to filch a student as a "charlatan and sorcerer"; his opponent responded with "words that were more deadly than spears." Students not only competed with each other, but also evaluated their teachers and discussed their merits and weaknesses. This relationship could easily become confrontational, because in order to improve their standing young men would challenge older teachers and orators, and sometimes even their own teachers. One eminent orator had been both impressed and a bit unnerved upon listening to a young advocate perform. "He makes my heart skip a beat and my head ache when I hear how many people praise him." When the future heresiarch Aetius was a young man studying with a grammarian in Cilicia, he was so taken by his own intelligence that he publicly embarrassed his teacher for his ignorance and misinterpretations. As a result, this teacher banished Aetius from his house.[12]

In their classroom Basil the precocious student and his father the experienced teacher were likewise always challenging each other, and the intense intellectual diligence required for teaching and learning could lead to an emotional friction that would have hampered the development of a loving relationship. Mastering correct speech and acquiring an intimate familiarity with the classical canon required years of disciplined effort. The first years of formal schooling focused on the study of grammar, "which polishes speech and smoothes out barbarian sounds, and which is the best sentinel of the noble language of Greece." In his role as grammarian Basil the Elder appeared both as a generous benefactor offering access to cultural polish and social advancement and as a strict enforcer of the diligence required to achieve linguistic brilliance. As a "guardian of language and tradition" he could become a beloved teacher or a feared disciplinarian, "with his texts in one hand and his cane in the other." When Basil once described the consequences of ignoring God's teaching, he seemed to be drawing upon personal memories. "Young boys who are careless about their lessons become more attentive after their teachers and tutors use their canes. Instructions that were ignored before a beating are heard and remembered after blows from a cane." The sternness required of Basil the Elder as a teacher would have made it difficult for Basil to see him as an affectionate father.[13]

Even without the encumbrance of a pedagogical relationship, fathers and sons might compete over their familiarity with classical literature. In a loving relationship such a rivalry remained supportive. Gregory of Nyssa once complimented a son for his friendly rivalry with his father over "primacy," and noted that the father himself was hoping that his son would surpass his "father's reputation." Sometimes, however, fathers and sons clashed over their assessments of the value of higher education and each other's competence. In Phrygia a father personally taught grammar to his young son. As a teenager, however, the son became more interested in adopting a life of Christian asceticism, and he finally left home after his father beat him. In Cappadocia a father sent his son to be educated in Greece. When his son returned, the father was ready to disown him because he thought his son's interest in philosophy made him useless. During the later fourth century another father in Cappadocia would disinherit his sons because he thought they did not measure up to his standards. Vitalianus belonged to a prominent family and was renowned for his generosity and hospitality. Yet he eventually became so angry at his two sons that he banished them from his home and forbade them from attending their sister's wedding. Petrus, the older son, was reticent in describing the cause for their banishment and merely insisted that Vitalianus was not the only father with disobedient and presumptuous children. Since Petrus noted that he was an experienced poet and had hoped to compose songs for his sister's wedding, perhaps his father felt threatened by his son's abilities. Another possibility is that Vitalianus was embarrassed by his son's inadequacies, since Petrus also admitted that he was sometimes tongue-tied and inarticulate. By the end of his attempt to mollify Vitalianus, however, Petrus explicitly associated his father's anger with his pride, his unwillingness "to concede first place in appearance and in greatness to anyone." "The only misdeed among your sons is that we appear to be worse than a better father." In this family comparisons between a father and his sons had led to scandal, almost a feud, and learning, either too much familiarity with it or not enough, had caused estrangement.[14]

Basil had grown up in isolation from his parents and his immediate family; when he resumed contact with his father, he had had to cope in addition with the highly competitive and confrontational atmosphere of the classroom. Since Basil the Elder was apparently one of Basil's first formal teachers, a final factor encumbering memories of their relationship was comparisons with subsequent teachers. Basil the Elder had been content with his local celebrity: "distinction in his homeland had been attractive to him, and his reputation did not exceed Pontus." He had carried on with his teaching and his service as an advocate in local courts. His assistant was the young man whom he had selected as the prospective husband for Macrina, his oldest daughter. Since this young man came from a notable family and had recently finished his education, it is likely that he had once been a student of Basil the Elder. If so, then he had returned to help his former teacher and future father-in-law as a local advocate and orator.[15]

In contrast, Basil would go on to study at Caesarea in Cappadocia and then at Constantinople and Athens, and at each stop his teachers became more reputable and more remarkable. One rhetorician in Cappadocia was known as "a distinguished teacher, the father of many orators." At Constantinople Basil studied with Libanius, and at Athens with Proaeresius and Himerius. Libanius may at the time have been at the beginning of his teaching career, but in his public orations at the capital he already displayed "the charm of Aphrodite." Proaeresius was so distinguished that he was considered "the image of Hermes, [the patron deity] of culture." Himerius simply equated culture with life itself. As young men studied with increasingly more notable rhetoricians and philosophers, they tended to downplay and forget their earlier studies with mere grammarians. As Basil advanced his education, his father's reputation could not but suffer in comparison with the memorable rhetoricians and philosophers he would meet at larger cities.[16]

Initially Basil the Elder was a remote figure, someone Basil would have known primarily by reputation as a notable at Neocaesarea. After he reappeared in his son's life, he was more a strict teacher than a loving parent. Basil's opportunity to benefit from this reintroduction to interaction with his own immediate family and this newly revived relationship with his father was brief, however, because sometime during the early 340s, when he was still a young teenager, his father died.[17]

His father's death was not altogether unexpected; demographic simulations based on assumptions about age at marriage and mortality rates suggest that in Roman society sons, even firstborn sons, would often lose their fathers while they were teenagers. Nevertheless, even though freedom from their fathers' formal power may have implied legal and financial independence for sons, from a social and emotional perspective freeing themselves from the legacy of their fathers' examples was more difficult. Sons measured themselves against the achievements and expectations of their fathers and other ancestors. Even though Basil had had limited interaction with his father, and even though he then spent several years overseas, the loss of his father had a lingering impact. His return to his homeland seems in particular to have conjured up memories of and comparisons with the father he had lost over a decade earlier.[18]

In a region such as Cappadocia that was noted for its extensive ranches, good breeding was a self-conscious obsession among local aristocrats, and scrutiny of a man's pedigree was no less important than checking the bloodlines of "the best bred and most honored horses." At the end of her life Macrina the Younger would remind her brother Gregory of Nyssa that their parents' worldly renown had allowed them and their siblings to boast of their ancestors and their own bloodlines. In his retrospective commemoration of Basil's life, Gregory of Nazianzus would claim that Basil the Elder had indeed served as a formative trainer for his son, who "ran alongside his father with the friskiness of a colt." By the time of his return from Athens in the mid-350s, however, Basil more closely resembled an "unbroken colt that threw to the ground those whom it had previously exalted"—a comparison that Basil himself later used for a mentor whose friendship had gone sour.[19]

In particular, Basil's advanced schooling and growing reputation seem to have gone to his head. Basil was so impressed by his own "lengthy education in the schools and his training in culture" and by his "skill in oratory" that he was unable to conceal his disdain for the other notables of the region. When his brother Gregory of Nyssa later described the life of Gregory Thaumaturgus, he included a story about the comeuppance of an arrogant young man from Athens who had mocked the plain oration of a bishop from Pontus for its lack of "Athenian refinement." Basil could have been that impertinent young man. In a later, rather rueful letter Basil seemed to be talking about himself when he wrote in the name of a young rhetorician who had been accustomed to linger in the public arena, "indulging himself in words": "I was seduced by [the pursuit of] prestige, and it was not easy for me to renounce pride in myself." An embassy of municipal councilors from Neocaesarea tried to recruit Basil to become a teacher for its young men: "What did they not offer? What did they not promise?" Basil refused, and instead seems to have taught briefly as a rhetorician at Caesarea. Although his father had been a local teacher, most likely a grammarian, in Pontus, Basil seems now to have decided that his father's occupation, perhaps even his father's very job at Neocaesarea, was no longer good enough for him. In the studied phrasing of a rhetorician who had politely declined an invitation to teach in his hometown, "the nightingale does not sing in a small cage." Like another young rhetorician with high expectations, Basil too was "determined not to hide himself in a small city and sink to the level of that city." Having been educated at Constantinople and Athens, if Basil was to teach in his homeland, it would only be as a rhetorician at Caesarea, a "metropolis of culture."[20]

Yet if Basil now declined the possibility of assuming his father's career in Pontus, his subsequent behavior nevertheless reflected a deep sense of loss and yearning for a father. For all his presumptuous arrogance Basil was still searching for guidance, in particular from mentors and teachers. Like another young man who had been trained as a rhetorician and an orator, he felt he needed "a reputable and experienced teacher." His quest for a mentor involved more than simply furthering his education or his career, because in one letter Basil conceded that teachers assumed the role of fathers. In this perspective, his ongoing search for mentors was also a search for substitute fathers, men whom he could "classify as fathers and treat as guides of my soul."[21]

Roman law allowed fathers to acquire new sons through adoption, but there were no similar legal provisions for the adoption of new fathers. For paternal guidance fatherless sons hence had to look to relatives such as uncles or grandfathers, or to older brothers, or to mentors such as teachers or bishops. Through a series of substitutes Basil spent a lifetime trying to reconstruct a fatherly love and a filial relationship he had hardly known.

Mentors in Pontus

Basil had of course already studied with several distinguished teachers who he might have assumed would naturally become his mentors and patrons. He certainly talked about Libanius with his brother Gregory, and he maintained some contact with his former teacher through letters. Of his teachers at Athens, Proaeresius was almost a generation older than Basil's father. His family was from Armenia, although he himself was a "Cappadocian" of sorts, having grown up in Caesarea. Once he became an official teacher at Athens, the young men who came from Asia Minor naturally studied with him, and Proaeresius acquired a reputation for treating each student "as if he were a true son." Himerius was a decade or more older than Basil, and he likewise had contacts with Asia Minor, since he was a native of Bithynia and owned estates in Armenia. Both Proaeresius and Himerius had extensive connections with imperial courts and imperial magistrates. At the conclusion of their studies Himerius may well have lauded Basil and Gregory in an oration that already resembled a letter of recommendation. "Our wealth [consists of] these young men who are in the prime of their development and peaking in their maturity. They are intimidating in their demeanor, with their heads held high because they are begotten from the center of

Zeus' heart." Because of his teachers' connections, Basil might have expected to benefit from their patronage. His fellow student Gregory of Nazianzus was certainly aware of how famous teachers could help their students: "whoever knew of Athens knew of our teachers, and whoever knew of our teachers knew of us." Yet in his extant writings Basil never mentioned his former teachers at Athens.[22]

As a student at Athens, Basil had not been happy. Other students had seemingly failed to concede his innate superiority by challenging his intellectual competence, and he had perhaps struggled to separate the literary and philosophical aspects of classical culture from its association with all the famous temples and statues of pagan deities that decorated the city. Back in Cappadocia his abortive attempt to establish himself as a prominent orator and rhetorician was another indication of his lingering ambivalence about his classical education and his uncertainty whether it would directly shape the contours of his future career or mark simply a negligible phase in his past. Whatever he would decide, however, he did not allow his former teachers to become his patrons and mentors.[23]

Instead, he now attached himself to Eustathius, already or soon to become bishop of Sebasteia. Eustathius was of the same generation as Basil's father, perhaps a few years younger, and by the mid-350s he already had a reputation for promoting Christian monasticism in northern and eastern Asia Minor. After his own brief tenure as a teacher in Caesarea, Basil became increasingly attracted to a life of renunciation and philosophical asceticism. So he now tried to meet Eustathius. His first attempts were unsuccessful, even though he followed Eustathius around the eastern Mediterranean as far as Syria, Palestine, Mesopotamia, and Egypt. Eventually they visited often and even traveled together. Eustathius and Basil could have talked about more than the promotion of an ascetic lifestyle, however, because Eustathius too had once clashed with his father. One tradition claimed that he had been expelled from the clergy by his own father, a bishop, for wearing a robe that was inappropriate for the priesthood. Having already resolved not to duplicate his father's teaching career, Basil may now have decided to make a similar public statement of rejection through his apparel. At the monastic retreat that he soon established on his family's property in Pontus, Basil imitated other ascetics he had seen in Cappadocia by dressing in a thick cloak and rugged sandals. After adopting this flamboyant austerity, he and his friend Gregory of Nazianzus enjoyed frequent conversations about theology with Eustathius.[24]

Eustathius had become a model for Basil after his return to Pontus and

Cappadocia. In Basil's mind Eustathius even seems to have replaced his father as his first teacher, because although Basil was already in his late twenties when they first met, he later described himself as still a "boy" when he had become Eustathius' supporter. With this concession Basil could effectively erase his years in Athens by making his ascetic life in Pontus appear to be the natural extension of a boyhood tutelage under Eustathius' direction. Eustathius' teaching about asceticism had the additional advantage of reviving memories of Basil's grandparents' experiences, because with his withdrawal to the Pontic countryside Basil was able to imagine himself as an imitator of his grandparents' seclusion in the mountains during the persecutions. Eustathius therefore had a double claim on Basil's memories and yearnings. Since Eustathius was both a substitute for his father and a mentor who revived the legacy of his grandparents, it is no surprise that Basil's relationship with Eustathius endured for almost two decades.[25]

Basil's devotion to Eustathius and his teachings seems furthermore to have been intertwined with the decisions that he would have had to make about resuming relationships with his family and relatives after his return to his home region. In Basil's absence his sister Macrina had become an increasingly important influence in the family. She herself may have already come under Eustathius' spell, and she may have informed Basil about Eustathius' ideas while he was still in Athens. His brother Gregory of Nyssa would later claim that their sister Macrina had furthermore been the one to turn Basil from his vain pursuit of worldly celebrity to a new life of poverty and philosophical asceticism. At about the same time Macrina had persuaded their mother to share her ascetic life on a family estate in Pontus. Their ascetic residences were near enough that Basil would take Eustathius to visit his mother, and presumably Macrina, "in the opposite village." If Macrina had indeed transformed Basil's thinking by dissuading him from the pursuit of secular fame, it is all the more striking that Basil never acknowledged her influence. In fact, in his extant writings he never mentioned his famous sister. However he learned about Eustathius and whatever the motives for his withdrawal, Basil preferred to present himself as a self-made man with few, if any, obligations to his family.[26]

This isolation on a family estate in Pontus was also a telling indication of Basil's lack of a wider impact in his home region. As the oldest son of a distinguished family that owned several estates in the region Basil might have been expected to assume a prominent role in Pontus; and since he had many brothers and sisters, a series of favorable marriages would have enhanced both his and his siblings' standing. In fact, few of his siblings married, and Basil was not able to presuppose much support from his family in Pontus, either from members of his immediate family or from his relatives. Basil's father may have found a fiancé for his oldest daughter, but after this prospective groom had died young, Macrina had never married. Although their mother, Emmelia, was apparently responsible for arranging marriages for her other daughters, by then going to live with their new husbands' families they seem to have effectively disappeared. None of them attended their mother's funeral. If his sisters were not of much help in extending Basil's local influence, he might have anticipated leaning on his brothers' support. As an interpreter of dreams had put it, "the shoulders are brothers to one another." At Amisus in Pontus, for example, one man set up a dedication that commemorated his brothers as well as his wife and their children. Of Basil's brothers, however, Naucratius died young and Peter lived with his mother and sister Macrina before becoming a cleric; only Gregory of Nyssa may have married. Basil and his brothers had hence not created alliances with other local families through advantageous marriages.[27]

Relatives were other potential supporters, including uncles, aunts, and cousins. A dedication at Amaseia in Pontus, for instance, pointedly illustrated the importance of relatives by mentioning a woman's uncle and aunt on her father's side and two cousins on her mother's side as well as her parents. As a young boy Basil had been raised with some of his father's relatives in Pontus. Yet later in his life he was estranged from his relatives, in particular at Neocaesarea.[28]

During his episcopacy Basil never had good relations with Neocaesarea. In his laudatory eulogy for Musonius, the recently deceased metropolitan bishop of Neocaesarea, he tried to save face by arguing that Musonius had once told him that he had been unable to assist Basil's pursuit of ecclesiastical harmony because of "some prior commitments." Musonius' successor was Atarbius, and although he was a relative of Basil, their relationship too was wary. Even though Basil was older, he humbled himself by initiating correspondence with the new bishop and practically begging for his support. Part of their uneasiness was a consequence of differing theological interpretations about the correct formulation of the doctrine of the Trinity. Some of their mistrust seems also to have been personal. In 375, when Basil hoped to talk with him at Nicopolis, he was miffed to learn that Atarbius had instead avoided a meeting by hastily departing in the middle of a council that he had himself convened. Basil then began to refer to Atarbius as a slanderer and instead tried to find support from others at Neocaesarea and in Pontus. In the next year he put his case directly to the people at

Neocaesarea and requested a public hearing before bishops. He furthermore wrote directly to the other bishops of Pontus and suggested that they behave like neighbors, and to the clerics of Neocaesarea to defend his particular liturgical practices in Cappadocia. Later in that year Basil visited his brother Peter in Pontus, where he wrote again to the people of Neocaesarea and warned them against subverting the true faith. At some point during his episcopacy he even tried to recruit the support of a governor of Pontus Polemoniacus, the province for which Neocaesarea served as capital. Basil's opponents in Neocaesarea were meanwhile not inactive, since they pleaded their cause by letter to Anthimus, the bishop of Tyana who had recently become Basil's rival metropolitan bishop in Cappadocia.[29]

Basil's single-minded focus on the rightness of his own theology had hence intersected with his troubled relationship with his father's family in Pontus. In his estimation, "blood relations" should have led to harmony in his dealings with Neocaesarea. Instead, his doctrinal insistence had only exacerbated a long-standing estrangement from his relatives in Pontus. A theological disagreement had become first a scornful confrontation between two metropolitan bishops who were relatives, and then a generalized regional antagonism between Pontus and Cappadocia.[30]

During this dispute the bishop and people of Neocaesarea appealed to the corroboration of Gregory Thaumaturgus, their patron saint. Basil responded by associating himself with the saint too. His special relationship was first of all part of his father's family legacy, since he explained to the people of Neocaesarea that he had initially learned about the saint from his grandmother Macrina the Elder, "a blessed woman who was descended from you." He furthermore suggested that because he had adopted Gregory Thaumaturgus as one of his "spiritual fathers," his own life had closely followed the saint's career. During his early years Basil may indeed have been strongly influenced by the example of the life of Gregory Thaumaturgus. In his oration about the saint Gregory of Nyssa would claim that, after returning to his homeland from his studies overseas, Gregory Thaumaturgus had initially rejected invitations to share his learning in "public assemblies." Instead, he had abandoned "the bustling of the market place and the affairs of the city" and adopted a life of ascetic seclusion. Only in this way, according to Gregory of Nyssa, could Gregory Thaumaturgus avoid being "consumed by a love of prestige." Basil seems to have consciously mimicked the seclusion of Gregory Thaumaturgus, since later in his life he would claim that he too, upon his return from his studies overseas, had wanted to avoid the "uproar of the city" by fleeing to seclusion in Pontus. Because of his family's special intimacy with the traditions of Gregory Thaumaturgus and his own imitation of the saint's life, Basil could imply that he should still have influence in the saint's homeland of Pontus.[31]

Yet Basil could push this implicit comparison of himself with Gregory Thaumaturgus only so far, because while the saint had eventually emerged from his solitude to become bishop of Neocaesarea, everyone knew that Basil had scorned an invitation to teach there. During his episcopacy Basil's appeals to the patronage of Gregory Thaumaturgus hence seemed a bit hollow and willfully confrontational, and at one point in his dispute with the bishop and clerics of Neocaesarea he was reduced to warning them not to misinterpret the saint's words. In one of his theological treatises Basil would mention that it was possible to verify his own loyalty to the ideas of Gregory Thaumaturgus by visiting Neocaesarea: "not much effort [is necessary] for someone who travels a short distance to find confirmation of these statements." Basil himself, however, no longer made that trip. Instead, "Neocaesarea" became shorthand for a bungling failure in his episcopal career, a situation so embarrassing that it made his friends feel awkward about writing to him at all. Since the standoff involved a relative who had become a rival bishop, the episode also represented yet another example of Basil's clumsy relationship with his father's family and relatives in Pontus.[32]

Eventually, as his estrangement from Neocaesarea persisted, Basil even decided to abandon his claim of a special bond with Gregory Thaumaturgus. When he again wrote to the bishops of Pontus, he invited them to attend the annual festival for St. Eupsychius and St. Damas, two martyrs from Caesarea. If the bishops of Pontus were unwilling to invite him to a public hearing or even to the festival of Gregory Thaumaturgus, then he would approach them instead in the name of Cappadocian martyrs. By now he was himself a "Cappadocian."[33]

Mentors in Cappadocia

Even though Basil had been raised in Pontus and had retired there again soon after his return from his overseas studies, his rejection of his father's teaching position at Neocaesarea, and later his dispute with a relative who had become bishop of Neocaesarea, estranged him both from his father's family and relatives and, more generally, from the bishops and clerics in Pontus. Instead, Basil would make his career in Cappadocia. Because Caesarea, its metropolitan capital, was one of the most prominent cities in Asia

Minor east of Ancyra, it offered opportunities for ambitious outsiders to prosper. As a newcomer from Phrygia had once exclaimed, "I flourished at Caesarea." Basil, of course, started with some advantages. He had already been a student at Caesarea, he had relatives in the region because his mother was a native of Cappadocia, and he soon acquired the support of various influential churchmen.[34]

An uncle named Gregory, most likely his mother's brother, was probably one of his first sponsors. One likely moment for the beginning of their mentoring relationship was Basil's arrival to study at Caesarea, at about the time of his father's death. Maternal uncles had a common reputation for their concern and affection for nephews. Uncle Gregory became more than a guardian for his fatherless nephew, however, since Basil later admitted to his uncle that "from the beginning you have been in the place of a father." "Throughout my entire life you displayed more care for me than was expected from our kinship." Uncle Gregory had become a surrogate father for Basil.[35]

Another early mentor was Dianius, bishop of Caesarea since at least 341. Basil received his baptism from Dianius, perhaps at the time that he decided to take up an ascetic life in Pontus, and at some point Dianius ordained him into the clergy, probably as a reader, perhaps instead (or subsequently) as a deacon. Since uncle Gregory would be a bishop in Cappadocia during the early 370s, he may now already have been a cleric; and since clerics often selected junior clerics on the basis of kinship, uncle Gregory too may have been involved in the recruitment of Basil into the clergy. Dianius openly indicated his support by including his new cleric in his entourage when he attended a council at Constantinople in early 360. During the immediate years after his return from his overseas studies, Basil had hence reacquainted himself with his mother's family in Cappadocia, and the respected bishop of Caesarea had become his patron. A decade later he still recalled the affection he had felt for Dianius "from my earliest youth."[36]

Yet as Basil became more involved in ecclesiastical service and in theological controversies, these relationships too fell apart. Basil was so deeply upset that Dianius had subscribed to the creed issued by the council at Constantinople that had endorsed the mere "similarity" between God the Father and God the Son, that he returned again to his retreat in Pontus. On his deathbed in early 362 Dianius confessed to Basil that he had accepted this doctrinal formulation only because of "the simplicity of his heart" and not because he had rejected the earlier creed of the Council of Nicaea. Even though Basil claimed that he had then revived his communion with

Dianius, this rift was a preview of Basil's obsession for privileging his notions of doctrinal purity or ecclesiastical harmony at the expense of a personal relationship. In this case he had distanced himself from the ecclesiastical mentor who had baptized and ordained him.[37]

When he became bishop of Caesarea, his relationship with his uncle also sputtered. Basil's consecration as bishop was contested, and his opponents included some bishops in Cappadocia. Among them was his uncle Gregory, who was still miffed at Basil for some unspecified "old mistakes," and who was perhaps in addition now dismayed at finding himself a suffragan of his nephew, the new metropolitan bishop of the province. Initially Basil maintained a sullen silence and hoped his uncle would suggest a meeting. Finally he took the initiative in writing to end this "feud with relatives."[38]

Dianius and uncle Gregory were not the only bishops in Cappadocia with whom Basil had awkward relationships. Already upon the death of Dianius Basil seems to have been considered as a potential replacement as the new bishop of Caesarea. Even though he was then only in his early thirties, Basil's credentials were impressive, because he was already serving as a cleric and his supporters included the local monks. Despite Basil's talents, one group of citizens finally insisted instead upon the consecration of Eusebius, a local notable. Basil and Eusebius seem immediately to have shared a mutual antipathy. Eusebius had no experience as a churchman. In fact, not only had he not held any prior clerical office, but at the time of his selection he was not yet even baptized. Although Eusebius apparently tried to win Basil over by ordaining him as a priest, this nominal promotion seems to have made Basil even more sour. By now it was increasingly common for teachers to move sideways into the ecclesiastical hierarchy. But whereas grammarians typically became priests, rhetoricians often became bishops. Apollinarius the Elder, for instance, was a grammarian who had become a priest; his son Apollinarius was a rhetorician who became bishop at Laodicea. Because Basil had taught briefly as a rhetorician at Caesarea, he might well have perceived his ordination to the priesthood as an insult, an insensitive failure to acknowledge his skills. Not only was he now serving under a bishop with no clerical experience, but his own new clerical office was beneath his qualifications.[39]

Basil's responses were both typically self-serving and equally typically self-reflective. One reaction was the delivery of some public sermons. In one sermon Basil discussed Proverbs. Verses from this Old Testament book had become contentious texts in the intramural theological debates about defining the relationship between God the Father and God the Son. During his consecration at Antioch only a few years earlier, for instance, bishop Meletius had outraged his detractors, among them the emperor Constantius, by publicizing his doctrines in a sermon on a verse from Proverbs about "wisdom" and its role in God's act of creation. Even though Basil was now invited to comment only on the first few introductory verses of Proverbs, he nevertheless took the opportunity to cite and analyze many biblical texts. He also included a few subtle allusions to current events. At one point he noted that for an "infant," someone who had recently been reborn in baptism, the teachings in Proverbs offered "pure milk," "an understanding of the present and thoughts about the future." At another point he offered advice about "steering": "a helmsman needs a keen and straightforward intelligence." With this propaedeutic sermon Basil had effectively usurped the prerogative of a new bishop to articulate his theology. He had furthermore neatly reversed their roles by offering Eusebius candid advice about governing, and he had implicitly reminded the audience that their novice bishop was himself one of those new catechumens who would benefit from reading Proverbs. This sermon was quietly subversive of Eusebius' standing and influence.[40]

In another sermon Basil spoke about envy, a naturally contentious topic among local worthies obsessed with their reputations and sense of dignity. Even death did not end their grudges, since men took their resentments to their graves and were quick to attribute any unexpected deaths to "hateful envy." Basil's general argument that envy destroyed people's souls was unexceptional, and so was his use of examples from the Bible. The subtext of his sermon was more intriguing, however, since Basil seems to have hinted that he was himself another, unfairly maligned, target of envy, in particular because of his learning and his oratorical skills. In his estimation, envious people were unable to appreciate "skillful oratory that is adorned with majesty and grace." One of his examples described reactions to a talented young man whom an envious rival "praises [only] after his death, when with innumerable panegyrics he extols his beauty, his learning, and his sweeping skills. But while that young man was alive, he never favored him with even a kind word."[41]

Basil was one such young man still looking for respect and acknowledgment of his abilities, and at a moment when he thought himself to have been improperly overlooked, he used his vast rhetorical skills to skewer his adversaries. Yet Basil seems to have realized that he too was susceptible to the blighting corrosion of envy, and at the end of his sermon he was perhaps talking about himself. "If you desire fame above all and therefore cannot endure being second, transform your pursuit of prestige into the acquisition of virtue." A few years earlier Basil had arrogantly indulged his pursuit of prestige by delivering public orations and teaching as a rhetorician, before retreating to ascetic seclusion. In this case, at a moment of open disappointment Basil was unable to resist another rather petulant display of his rhetorical skills in these sermons, before following his own advice. Basil's second reaction to his ordination as a priest at Caesarea was to disappear again to his retreat in Pontus.[42]

Both Eusebius and Basil were to blame for this confrontation. Like some teachers apprehensive about the success of their gifted students, like some fathers concerned about their sons' intellectual promise, an insecure bishop too might indulge in cheap shots against a talented junior cleric. Gossip in circulation at the time still alleged that over a century earlier the bishop of Alexandria had engineered the condemnation of the priest Origen not because of his doctrines, but because his opponents "could not endure the glory of his eloquence and his knowledge. When Origen spoke, everyone else was thought to be tongue-tied." Basil and Gregory of Nazianzus would have known about Origen's illustrious career, since during their ascetic retreats they had compiled an anthology of long extracts from his writings. Recollection of Origen's experiences may have influenced both Basil's disdain for his new bishop and Gregory's brusque evaluation of their relationship. A few years after Basil's ordination Gregory would compare Eusebius to a man who patted someone on the head with one hand and slapped him across the cheek with the other; his advice was for Eusebius instead to show the "usual flatteries" to Basil. Eusebius was apparently still feeling a bit bruised, because his response was to accuse Gregory of insolence.[43]

In 365 Eusebius did finally request Basil's assistance in confronting the emperor Valens, a proponent of a heterodox version of Christianity who was then traveling through Cappadocia. By conceding that it was time to set aside "smallmindedness," Gregory seems also to have been speaking on behalf of Basil, whom he then convinced to offer his help. Basil returned on his own terms, however. Gregory had invited him to combat "the wild beasts who were ravaging the church," that is, the emperor and his supporters; Basil instead returned as "the lion tamer who controlled the lion," that is, bishop Eusebius. At Caesarea Basil had now become "the leader of the leader of the people."[44]

During the period from the later 350s to the early 370s Basil's mentors included bishop Dianius, bishop Eusebius, and his uncle Gregory in Cappadocia, as well as bishop Eustathius of Sebasteia. Eustathius had encouraged his interest in asceticism, Dianius had baptized him and ordained him into the clergy, Eusebius had promoted him to the priesthood, and uncle Gregory had become a patron and even a substitute father. Yet, whether gradually or quickly, Basil ended up estranged from all these mentors. These examples strongly suggest that Basil consistently had difficulties sustaining relationships with men of his father's generation. Perhaps it is possible for modern historians to speculate about the displacement of repressed hostility toward a father who had abandoned him prematurely. Even as Basil sought out and needed these mentors for their guidance and support, he seems eventually to have rejected their authority and leadership. "A son who has repressed his hostile feelings towards his father may express these hostile feelings against other symbols of authority." In contrast, the two men with whom Basil did develop long-standing relationships belonged to or conjured up an earlier generation that Basil associated with the exploits of his grandparents.[45]

Gregory the Elder and Eusebius of Samosata

The one churchman in Cappadocia who supported Basil and whom Basil consistently venerated in return was Gregory the Elder, father of Gregory of Nazianzus. Basil had most likely first met Gregory the Elder in the early 340s when he had gone to study at Caesarea. One of his fellow students there was Gregory of Nazianzus, who would have introduced Basil to his father. Gregory the Elder was already bishop of Nazianzus; he was furthermore already quite elderly, certainly as old as Basil's grandparents. Basil would have resumed his acquaintance with Gregory the Elder after he and Gregory of Nazianzus returned from their overseas studies. At the time, Basil the haughty young rhetorician and Gregory the Elder the long-serving pious bishop were almost complete opposites. In fact, during the later 350s and early 360s, as Gregory of Nazianzus vacillated between his devotion to a life of ascetic seclusion with his friend and his concern for his elderly parents, Basil and Gregory the Elder neatly personified his conflicting desires.

Despite this potential for rivalry, Basil did not end up estranged from Gregory the Elder. Instead, he became a protégé of his friend's father, and at each moment when he faced the sort of situation that had led to a falling out with one of his other mentors in Cappadocia, he remained loyal to Gregory the Elder. Although Basil had become annoyed when bishop Eusebius ordained him as a priest, he accepted advice about his new priestly duties from his friend Gregory, whom Gregory the Elder had ordained as a priest shortly before. Although Basil had severed communion with bishop Dianius after he had signed a questionable creed, he may have used his influence with monks in order to help end their hostility at Nazianzus toward Gregory the Elder because of his endorsement of a suspect creed. In 370 Gregory the Elder strongly supported Basil's selection as the new bishop of Caesarea. In one letter Gregory the Elder presumably relied upon his own firsthand experience in recommending Basil for his "purity in life and doctrine." In another letter he lobbied the enclave of bishops on behalf of Basil. In the end, in order to ensure Basil's selection he shrugged off his old age and illness and hobbled to Caesarea to participate in Basil's consecration. Unlike Basil's uncle Gregory, who was opposed to his nephew's selection as bishop, Gregory the Elder now readily accepted Basil as his new metropolitan bishop.[46]

Doctrinal controversies, ordination as a priest, consecration as a bishop: each of the flash points that had led to estrangement from other mentors served only as an opportunity to reaffirm his relationship with Gregory the Elder. As a result, Basil always acknowledged his devotion for Gregory the Elder. In 374, even though Nazianzus was then no longer within his ecclesiastical province, Basil attended the funeral service for Gregory the Elder. In his commemorative oration Gregory of Nazianzus noted that his father had not only served as a fellow pastor with Basil. In his summation, even though as a metropolitan bishop Basil had had higher clerical rank, Gregory the Elder had nevertheless also become a "father" for Basil, his "son in grace."[47]

Another mentor who became a surrogate father for Basil was Eusebius of Samosata. Eusebius had been serving as bishop of Samosata since at least the early 360s, possibly even the late 340s, and so he too belonged to the generation of Basil's father. His long-lasting relationship with Basil was hence an unexpected contrast with the failure of Basil's relationships with other mentors of his father's generation. By the later 360s when they began to correspond, Basil had matured. Then he was no longer the callow young man flushed with his overwhelming skill as an orator and a rhetorician who, when first introducing himself to a champion of ascetic values like Eustathius of Sebasteia, would nevertheless set a tone of shared intellectual prowess by addressing Eustathius as "your Eloquence." Nor was he the new priest who had confronted, abandoned, and then returned to dominate his own bishop. In his earlier sermon about Proverbs Basil had stressed the importance of "wisdom" in its different guises, including a "human wisdom that entails acquaintance with the events of life." At the time, that sermon had contributed to Basil's disdain for Eusebius, his new bishop at Caesarea.

A few years later, however, when Basil introduced himself to Eusebius of Samosata, he wrote as a deferential priest to an esteemed bishop. In his estimation Eusebius of Samosata personified human wisdom, and Basil hoped to be filled with the treasures of "your wisdom." By now Basil preferred wisdom to eloquence.[48]

Basil's first letter to Eusebius of Samosata was solemn and obsequious, half of it, in fact, filled with those reliable icebreakers for conversational small talk, banal comments about the weather and his own health! Basil and Eusebius soon met. Eusebius was apparently already an acquaintance of Gregory the Elder, who in 370 strongly encouraged him to go to Caesarea and support Basil's candidacy for the vacant episcopal see. After his consecration Basil wrote to thank Eusebius for his visit and hoped that he would visit again. He also began to ask Eusebius for advice on family matters. After his mother died, Basil lamented to Eusebius about becoming an orphan. A few years later he consulted Eusebius about Gregory of Nyssa, who had clumsily attempted to mediate the dispute between Basil and uncle Gregory and who Basil thought was now meddling in theological disputes. Since Eusebius was one of the few correspondents from whom Basil solicited advice about his family, they certainly shared a deep emotional bond. And since Eusebius was probably about the age of Basil's father, he was also one of the few men from his father's generation with whom Basil sustained a long-term mentoring relationship. It is not surprising that in his letters Basil acknowledged his emotional dependence on Eusebius by addressing him as "father."[49]

Becoming a Father

Coming to terms with his feelings about his father was one of the primary motivations in Basil's life and career. In Greek society the expectation for a son to surpass the achievements of his father was common, since only so could a family indicate the progress it was making in improving its standing and reputation. An epitaph in Cappadocia commended a father for his children's prominence: "you have left children who are better than their parents." At Antioch the orator Libanius once praised the emperor Julian for having surpassed his ancestors: "although you have distinguished models in your family, you have demonstrated that even the most distinguished are insignificant [in comparison] to your own [accomplishments]." As a landowner, advocate, and teacher Basil the Elder had become successful and reputable by conforming to local norms, and he had surpassed his ancestors by reestablishing the family's prominence after the persecutions. Gregory of Nazianzus certainly thought that Basil had likewise fulfilled the expectation of surpassing his father in turn, since in his estimation Basil the Elder "had been prevented from obtaining primacy only by his son alone."[50]

Basil himself, however, had simply declined to compete directly with his father, or to imitate his father's life and career, or even to mention his father directly in his writings. Yet his father's example was constantly in Basil's mind, and he commented on his father's life and career indirectly. One commentary was through the trajectory of his own life. Not only did Basil reject his father's career, he also effectively bypassed middle-aged adulthood altogether. Upon his return from Athens, after all his years as a student he was expected to outgrow his boyishness. As Gregory of Nazianzus recalled the moment, "from beardless boyhood we passed into manhood, and we approached our ascetic life with more manliness." In fact, ascetic seclusion and austerity kept Basil in a condition of extended adolescence. By not marrying, not having children, and not accepting a position as a municipal magistrate or a teacher, Basil declined to take on the usual obligations of male adulthood in Greek cities. His friend Gregory of Nazianzus had adopted a similar life, although with one important difference, since he had assumed responsibility for looking after his elderly parents. As the oldest son, Basil might have been expected likewise to look after his mother. Instead, Macrina, who never married, exonerated Basil by staying with and caring for their mother. Well into his mature years Basil effectively presented himself as a kind of adult waif.[51]

Only when he became a priest and then a bishop did Basil finally assume roles of leadership and responsibility. By then, however, he thought of himself as an old man. Basil became a priest in his early thirties, and bishop when he was about forty. His letters from his episcopal years were nevertheless full of complaints about his debilitating poor health, and he described himself as so wasted by cyclical fevers that he was "as delicate as a spider's web," even "thinner than myself." Soon he began to refer to himself as one of "the old men." In one of his sermons Basil would describe the phases of life by noting the fluctuations in a man's body as he grew from infancy to become a young boy, a teenager, an adult "at the peak of manhood," and finally a decrepit old man. Basil himself seems to have missed the peak of this cycle. In his representation of himself he had gone directly from an extended adolescence to an early old age, and he had skipped the vigorous middle-aged adulthood personified by what he remembered of his father's career as a local teacher and advocate.[52]

Basil's notion of himself as an old man reinforced a second indirect way of commenting on his father's life, which was his abiding affinity for his grandparents' behavior and reputation. Memories of their experiences during the last great persecution seem to have contributed to the strength of his relationships with Eusebius of Samosata and Gregory the Elder. Eusebius too had once defied an emperor. In 361 he had declined to surrender a document, even after the emperor Constantius had threatened to cut off his hand. Another bishop who had confronted an emperor was Gregory the Elder, who had stood his ground in 362 in the face of intimidation from the emperor Julian. The behavior of both Eusebius of Samosata and Gregory the Elder hence recalled the defiant resistance of Basil's grandparents.[53]

Even though his grandparents' opposition to imperial persecution had forced them to become fugitives, their experiences were obviously congenial to Basil's prickly personality. When describing Basil's own confrontations with the emperor Valens and his magistrates, Gregory of Nazianzus conjured up a memory of these grandparents' earlier persecutions by referring to Basil's opponents as "Tetrarchs." Basil would certainly have appreciated being hailed at his own funeral as a "martyr." In his letters Basil liked to compare his and others' tribulations to persecutions. "The crowns of martyrs await you," he wrote to the people of Alexandria; "remember the saints of old." To cope with his current ordeals Basil looked to past hardships, "some of which the historians recorded in writing, others of which we learned about through the unwritten memories of eyewitnesses." Those eyewitnesses would have included his grandparents. The historical context that he preferred to provide for his own times was hence not the recent period of acceptance and benign toleration that had made his father's career possible, but an earlier era marked by persecutions and martyrdom. "In our time the churches have suffered more afflictions than those remembered since the proclamation of Christ's gospel." To survive the current persecutions Basil needed mentors and exemplars who were unlike his father. Perhaps it was precisely because Eusebius and Gregory the Elder reminded Basil of his grandparents and their resistance during the earlier period of imperial persecutions that he was able to sustain his relationships with both bishops.[54]

In 374 Basil lost these substitute fathers too. Gregory the Elder died in spring, and later in the year the emperor Valens forced Eusebius to go into exile in Thrace. By then Basil had begun to assume some paternal responsibilities himself. He sent letters appealing on behalf of various relatives, and his position as a cleric, and especially as a bishop, had given him a general "fatherly standing" for members of his congregation. Widows hailed him as their protector, and orphans as their father. Eventually he became close enough to one of his relatives to think of him "in place of a son for me." He was also able to initiate a successful mentorship of Amphilochius, a cousin of Gregory of Nazianzus. After Basil had strongly supported his selection as bishop of Iconium, Amphilochius repeatedly consulted with Basil and asked for advice. Becoming a bishop did not, of course, completely soften Basil's rigidness and pedantry. One distraught woman bitterly complained that although Basil should have "comforted her like a father," he had instead been "indifferent to her calamity and had used the misfortunes of others to spout philosophy." Even though it was clearly not an easy role for him, as a bishop Basil was seen as and acted like a father.[55]

Basil also could not avoid his destiny as a teacher. Every now and then he slipped into a grammarian's pompous posturing of philological nit-picking. In his controversy with Neocaesarea he had claimed that the man-uscript of a treatise by Gregory Thaumaturgus contained "many mistakes of the copyists, as I will demonstrate from the readings." In his refutation of some heretical teachings he had supported his position by citing "other exegetes who had investigated the sense of the Hebrew text more critically." In a sermon about the first chapter of Genesis he discarded a sentence in the Greek translation of one verse because other interpreters did not include it and because it did not fit with "the usage of the Hebrews": "the accurate versions of these copies are marked with an obelisk, and the obelisk is a sign of rejection."[56]

At these moments of grammatical and stylistic pedantry Basil came closest to imitating his father and reliving their classroom experiences. That was all his father had ever been to him, a schoolmaster, an exegete of texts, an enforcer of scholastic exactitude and grammatical discipline. As a bishop Basil made himself responsible for people's morals rather than their gram-mar, an austere figure seemingly more concerned about their behavior than their feelings and emotions. But as he found faults, corrected slips, and insisted upon exactness, in his severity he would have resembled his father in his role as pedagogical disciplinarian. Having rejected his father's occu-pation and job, having supposedly turned his back on his classical education by becoming a cleric, Basil still grew up to become his father's son.

Chapter 2
"Sigh like a Lover, Obey like a Son": Gregory of Nazianzus and Gregory the Elder

Basil was of course not the only young man who became estranged from his father, nor even the only Church Father who looked for mentors and substitute fathers. Although Basil eventually claimed Gregory Thaumaturgus as a model for his interest in ascetic seclusion and his theology, the comparisons between their early lives were also significant. Gregory Thaumaturgus had lost his father when he was only fourteen, about the age when Basil had lost his father. A brother-in-law, a distinguished jurist who was assisting the provincial governor of Palestine, then invited Gregory to escort his sister as she traveled to join her husband. If Macrina had married the fiancé selected by Basil the Elder, then Basil too would have had an older brother-in-law who served as a legal advocate. Like Basil, Gregory left his hometown of Neocaesarea and his homeland of Pontus to study overseas. Although he started to study Roman law at Beirut, he ended up studying Christian doctrines with the illustrious theologian Origen, who had recently begun to teach at Caesarea in Palestine. He was certainly not the only student from eastern Asia Minor who visited Origen in order to "improve his knowledge of the divine." But Gregory now found in Origen more than a teacher. As he finally prepared to return to "my father's house" in Pontus, he emphasized the difficulty of leaving "the house of our true father." While this spiritual language suggested his regret at departing from God's presence in the pedagogical paradise he had discovered during his studies, it also hinted at Gregory's sadness at having to leave his teacher. Origen had effectively become a substitute father for Gregory Thaumaturgus.[1]

Gregory Thaumaturgus in the early third century and Basil in the mid-fourth century had hence found mentors outside their families. In contrast, Gregory of Nazianzus grew up in a much different environment, with different memories, traditions, and expectations. Most obviously, as he conceded in an oration about his brother, he had never had to look for models and mentors outside his family. Until Gregory was middle-aged, the dominating figure in his life was his father, Gregory the Elder.[2]

Father and Bishop

Born during the late 270s, well before the reigns of the Tetrarchs, Gregory the Elder belonged to the generation of Basil's grandparents. Unlike them, however, he did not experience hardships during the last persecutions. His family was apparently well-off, although undistinguished until he acquired "a position second to none in the city," a vague remark probably imply-ing that he had been a municipal councilor and held some magistracy at Nazianzus. He and his family were furthermore not Christian, and Gregory later described his father at this time as a "wanderer." Gregory the Elder belonged to a sect of Hypsistarians, "worshippers of the Most High," who had apparently combined some Jewish attitudes and practices with notions of a pagan monotheism into a syncretistic religious system by venerating fire and lights but rejecting images and sacrifices, and by observing the Sabbath and dietary regulations but declining circumcision. Like thousands and thousands of other nondescript local elites, Gregory the Elder had served on the municipal council and joined a local cult.[3]

For Gregory the Elder, it was not the persecution of Christians but rather their subsequent success under Constantine that changed his life. Sometime before 325, perhaps after the death of a previous wife, he had married Nonna.[4] Nonna represented more than a marriage with another locally prominent family, however. With this marriage Gregory the Elder seems to have had instinctively appreciated the growing role of Christianity in local society, because his new wife came from a family that was already Christian. For all her deference to her husband, Nonna was insistent about the preservation of her faith. Already before the birth of Gregory she had decided that she would raise their first son as a Christian. Gregory was raised at home, and not contracted out to a wet nurse. In contrast to Basil, who had received some of his first catechism from his grandmother, Gregory received his first "teaching in the faith" from his mother. In addition, Nonna began to pray for the conversion of her husband. In subsequent evaluations Gregory credited the "drops" of his mother's prayers with eventually wear-ing down the "rock" of his father's resolve.[5]

In fact, Gregory the Elder converted to Christianity only after two premonitions, one in a vision and the other from watching current events. In a dream he once saw himself reciting a verse from Psalms: "I was glad when they said to me, 'Let us go to the house of the Lord!'" Psalms was course important for Jewish communities, and presumably also among semi-Jewish sectarians like Gregory the Elder and his fellow Hypsistarians. Christian communities likewise held Psalms in esteem for its wisdom: "the book of Psalms remembers history and prophesies the future." Nonna now provided a Christian interpretation for this verse from her husband's dream, and by considering this vision to be confirmation of her prayers she urged her husband to act upon it.[6]

Gregory the Elder finally conceded her interpretation of his dream only after direct observation of the new patronage that a Christian emperor now extended to Christian bishops. During the winter of 324–325 the emperor Constantine traveled through Asia Minor on an abbreviated trip to the East. Soon after, or perhaps during, his visit a council met at Antioch to discuss ecclesiastical and doctrinal disputes, and among the participants were bishops from Cappadocia. In late spring of 325 hundreds of bishops and lesser clerics traveled to Nicaea to participate in a huge council at which the emperor himself planned to preside. Bishops from Cappadocia again attended, and many of the churchmen from the Levant would have traveled overland across Asia Minor through Cappadocia. After seeing the emperor's generosity to churchmen, after watching the activities of local bishops from Cappadocia and their attendance at councils convened by the emperor, Gregory the Elder moved with the times. Even though he was already about fifty years old, he abandoned his successful career as a municipal notable. As his son put it, he now became a "friend of Christ," and he had himself instructed as a catechumen by Leontius, then the metropolitan bishop of Caesarea. At his baptism the bishop of Nazianzus was inspired to proclaim him as his successor; and in 329 Gregory the Elder did become bishop of his hometown.[7]

At the time this was still a bold move. Not only was the rise of Christianity to dominance still decades in the future, but at Nazianzus itself the Christian community was inconsiderable. Even though Gregory the Elder's episcopal predecessor may have had a "marvelously angelic disposition," he had apparently not been very successful, since the church the new bishop inherited was "wild and rustic," a description perhaps implying that it was outside the urban center. In contrast to his inept predecessor, Gregory the Elder now advertised his new prominence and enhanced the reputations of himself and his hometown in time-proven style by financing the

construction of a new church. The appearance of this "beautiful and celestial" church was as traditional as its meaning was innovative. The church
was quite elaborate, constructed from marble in the shape of an octagon,
surrounded by two perambulatories, and topped by a dome. With its dis-
tinctively angular cone shape this church would have resembled another
church in the region whose octagonal silhouette had earned it the popular
name of "birdcage." Gregory the Elder's church was certainly a prominent
"memorial to his generosity"; it was also a concrete realization of the vision
of "the house of the Lord" that had initially motivated his conversion. With
the construction of this church he had both satisfied the displays of muni-
ficence that citizens anticipated from their local aristocrats and honored his
religious heritages, both old and new. In one of those ironic gyrations that
make the rise of Christianity such a compelling historical transformation,
Gregory the Elder had now fulfilled as a Christian bishop the teachings of
the Psalm that he had most likely learned earlier as a member of his semi-
Jewish cult. In fact, if he followed the common custom of having a biblical
verse inscribed on the portal of his new church, perhaps he memorialized
the very verse from the Psalm that he had recited in his dream.[8]

In comparison with his new episcopal peers Gregory the Elder may
have been only a "smalltown bishop," but through his generosity it become
possible for his son to indulge in some hyperbole by imagining that under
his father's leadership Nazianzus was as small and insignificant as . . .
Bethlehem, "the metropolis of the world"! Because of his new standing as
bishop and as benefactor people furthermore acknowledged Gregory the
Elder as the "father and teacher of orthodoxy," and he now came to represent paternal authority within his community. So his son would later
remind the congregation at Nazianzus that this new church was also a
public affirmation of their bishop's "love for his children."[9]

Gregory the Elder's life hence divided into two contrasting careers. His
affiliation with the semi-Jewish Hypsistarians and his service as a municipal notable corresponded with the generation of Basil's grandparents, and
his second career as a Christian bishop synchronized with the generation of
Basil's parents. But while Basil's grandparents had endured persecution,
Gregory the Elder had not suffered for his religious affiliation, and his early
career had prospered under the persecuting emperors. And while Basil's
father had remained a conventional landowner and teacher, Gregory the
Elder had been quick to take advantage of Constantine's new patronage
for Christianity. In a remarkable display of time-honored opportunism,
Gregory the Elder had significantly improved the standing of both himself

and his family, and his success at reinventing himself as a bishop represented in miniature the ongoing general transition from a pre-Christian to a Christian society.

Although his son had certainly heard stories about his father's earlier activities, that part of his life had become the stuff of legends, a mere preamble to his later clerical career. One of Gregory's few slight nods to that earlier life was his tendency to recall the ancient history of the Jews by comparing his father to illustrious figures from the Old Testament like Noah and, especially, the elderly patriarch Abraham. Gregory's own first-hand experiences included only his father's career as a bishop. Because his father had furthermore become the "common father" for the congregation at Nazianzus, as far back as Gregory could remember his father's paternal guidance had merged with his spiritual authority. In Gregory's family "father" and "bishop" were interchangeable roles.[10]

As a young man Basil had been attracted to a career as a high-powered rhetorician as a way of surpassing his father the grammarian. In the end, rather than trumping his father the teacher he differentiated himself by adopting an ascetic lifestyle and entering clerical service. At one time, Gregory too seems to have contemplated a career as a rhetorician. He had most likely first met Basil when they studied together as teenagers at Caesarea, the capital of Cappadocia. Gregory had then studied at some of the great intellectual centers of the eastern Mediterranean world, including Caesarea in Palestine, Alexandria, and Athens. Gregory adored his years of study at Athens, and in order to delay his departure he may perhaps have been offered one of the endowed positions for teaching rhetoric there. Upon his return to Cappadocia he gave a display of his rhetorical brilliance for his friends; according to Gregory, even Basil had to acknowledge his superiority in learning and rhetoric. Gregory apparently also taught briefly, perhaps as a rhetorician, in Cappadocia.[11]

But Gregory had never considered his education and rhetorical skills as a means of competing with his father. That would anyway have been an unfair competition, since he readily admitted that his father had been a latecomer to study of the Bible and that his preaching did not resort to the "artificial techniques" of "today's pundits." In his respectful phrasing, Gregory the Elder had compensated for his deficiencies in oratory with his piety. Nor did Gregory adopt a flamboyantly affected appearance, like Basil when he advertised his preference for asceticism. Instead, Gregory admired his father's unadorned demeanor and lack of affectations, "no limply bent neck, no relaxed voice, no lowered eyes, no long beard, no closely barbered head."[12]

Gregory admitted that he was "in love with solitude." Yet to indulge that passion completely would have required leaving his parents. Throughout his life Gregory faced this dilemma again and again, and each time, sometimes with reluctance, his commitment to his parents took priority. When choosing between his passion for intellectual reclusiveness and his devotion to his parents, Gregory always sighed like a lover and obeyed like a son. Leaving his beloved Athens was the first of many indications of his devotion. Years later he claimed that he had returned to Cappadocia out of concern for his parents, who were "worn down by old age and the years." Soon after his return he had joined Basil at his ascetic retreat in Pontus. There they intended to rejuvenate their friendship and their intellectual pursuits by studying Christian writings. Despite the attractions, Gregory was nevertheless hesitant about staying with his friend. Once again his concern for his elderly parents was more important: "the law that demands caring for parents surpasses the law of intimate companionship."[13]

Back in Nazianzus during the winter of 361–362, Gregory was ordained as a priest. Decades later in one of his retrospective poems Gregory was still conflicted about his father's role in his ordination. He conceded that his father had wanted to honor him by promoting him to "the second throne," and he admitted that Gregory the Elder had been motivated by "paternal love." Yet Gregory also implied that, in the face of his father's episcopal authority, he had had little say: "love combined with power is fearsome." The most disconcerting aspect was not the ordination itself, but rather his father's disregard of his son's preference for a reclusive life: "my father was very well aware of my thinking." As Gregory later put it, a son's trust in his father had to be matched by a father's respect for his son. In this case, however, Gregory concluded that his father had acted "with force," and he was embarrassed that the only word he thought appropriate to describe his father's action was "tyranny." Gregory's immediate reaction was to leave town and rejoin Basil in Pontus.[14]

Gregory returned in the spring and delivered some sermons explaining his abrupt disappearance and his equally sudden return. By then he had come to terms with his ordination. He still complained that he had been a victim of "tyrants," among them the members of the congregation in his audience, but he was now prepared to concede that in fact it had been a "beautiful tyranny": "at the moment I am adding this qualification." So Gregory complimented himself for his hesitation and contrasted his deliberateness with the unseemly eagerness of other new clerics. He then explained his return in terms of two concerns. One was "my longing for you," the people in the audience. With this admission Gregory accepted responsibility for the Christian community at Nazianzus; in fact, he now even felt confident enough to scold his audience for being so eager to have him ordained but so tardy to attend his sermon. His second concern was "my obligation, my duty," to care for his aged parents. Despite his father's role in imposing this unwanted priesthood, Gregory could not deny his love for his parents. Years later his retrospective evaluation of his ordination was just as bittersweet about his devotion to his parents, and especially his father. While Gregory the Elder had only wanted his son to honor his "last gasps," Gregory himself had worried that "my father's love for me would disintegrate into a denunciation."[15]

As Gregory now returned to Nazianzus to assume his priesthood, he described himself as a "staff." This was a common characterization of a junior cleric. When Basil would finally return to Caesarea to assume his duties as a priest, Gregory would describe him as a "staff" to support bishop Eusebius in his old age. Given the open tension between Basil and Eusebius, however, their relationship could never be more than a politely mannered recognition of the protocol of ecclesiastical hierarchy. In contrast, Gregory had a much more personal relationship behind his description of his new role, and he seems to have seen himself not so much as a junior cleric buttressing his bishop, but as a devoted son supporting his beloved parents. In one of his retrospective poems he described the attractions of such a relationship: "Blessed Christ, you have allowed people to have children as a sturdy aid and to place them as a staff beneath their trembling limbs." As a result, in addition to assisting his father in his episcopal duties Gregory also took over leadership and responsibility in his family. His duties as a priest could now complement his obligations as a son.[16]

Son and Priest

Three episodes within the next few years highlighted Gregory's image of himself primarily as a son helping his parents rather than merely as a priest helping his bishop. The first involved the emperor Julian. During the summer of 362 Julian passed through Cappadocia on his way to Antioch. At Caesarea he intervened in a quarrel between the provincial governor and Eusebius, the new metropolitan bishop, and he threatened the city with various penalties for having destroyed a local pagan temple. The emperor relented on his threats only after a direct challenge from Gregory the Elder.

Soon afterward Gregory commemorated this defiance in a sermon nominally about the martyrdoms of the Maccabees. Because of his father's earlier association with the semi-Jewish cult of the Hypsistarians, Gregory may have thought the example of the celebrated Jewish family of the Maccabees to be particularly appropriate, since long ago, during the second century B.C., they had led the opposition to the Seleucid king Antiochus Epiphanes, who had desecrated the Jewish Temple at Jerusalem. In fact, Gregory proceeded to use other stories, since he described not the activities of the Maccabees, but Eleazar's defiance of this king and the martyrdom of seven brothers during the period of the Maccabean revolts. In his version, Eleazar was an elderly priest whose seven sons were "students of Moses' law." Their mother was just as impressive, because she had "the soul of a man in the body of a woman." Since in the original version in the Old Testament the story of Eleazar had been distinct from the story of the seven brothers and their mother, Gregory was clearly allowing himself some license by turning Eleazar into a father and husband. His revisions were presumably deliberate, because as a result Gregory had essentially transformed the opposition of this priest, the seven brothers, and their mother into a collective family affair. His audience at Nazianzus could readily have made the appropriate comparisons with their own elderly and intrepid bishop and his wife, Nonna, and even with Gregory himself, especially since he put a long defiant speech into the mouth of one of the sons. At the conclusion of the oration Gregory reminded his audience to imitate "clerics and mothers and sons." Rather than preaching as a priest highlighting only the boldness of his bishop in facing down the emperor, as a son Gregory had refashioned the confrontation into a promotion of both of his parents and their worthiness as paradigms for the congregation.[17]

A dispute with schismatics provided another opportunity for Gregory to support his father. During the confrontation with Julian the congregation at Nazianzus had remained united, in particular with regard to its theology: "we share a soul, we think the same, and we cause no damage to the Trinity." Soon afterward, however, a schism appeared as a reaction to Gregory the Elder's endorsement of a suspect creed. The exact identification of this creed is uncertain. One possibility is that it was the creed proposed in early 360 by the council of Constantinople that had insisted upon the mere "similarity" between God the Father and God the Son. If so, then Gregory the Elder had endorsed the same creed that had misled Dianius of Caesarea, his metropolitan bishop. Another possibility is that it was a creed proposed by a council that met at Antioch in the autumn of 363. Even as this new creed reaffirmed its acceptance of the creed issued by the famous Council of Nicaea, it diluted that earlier Nicene creed's doctrine that the Son was "identical in essence" with the Father to mean that the Son was merely "similar in essence." Many bishops signed this new creed, among them Eusebius of Samosata, an acquaintance of Gregory the Elder. Whichever questionable creed he had accepted, Gregory the Elder was in good company.[18]

In later orations Gregory would explain his father's support for this creed in various ways. Because some bishops were being deposed or exiled, other bishops were so intimidated and dismayed that they were "shaken by fear, enslaved by opportunism, ensnared by flattery, or hijacked through ignorance." Gregory's father in particular, since he had a reputation for plainness and faultless integrity, had been misled by the "clever words" of this creed. Yet Gregory did not want to offer mere excuses for his father's innocent behavior, because his goal was to reconcile the dissidents. Gregory described them as "a group that for a long time joined us in chanting hymns to God, until it suddenly changed its mind." This "more fervent faction of the church" consisted most likely of monks, perhaps of local clerics. In 364 Gregory delivered a sermon at Nazianzus in which he predictably highlighted the importance of peace and harmony for the community. Although he analyzed different examples of unity and harmony, Gregory kept returning to the significance of parents and families. Even the natural elements proclaimed this familial devotion. "Without peace there ceases to be a cosmos. The earth and the air together support all living creatures, one through nourishment, the other through breathing. By sustaining life in these ways, do they not imitate the tender love of parents?"[19]

In this sermon Gregory hence adopted a perspective that subtly moved the dispute from the setting of a religious community to the setting of a family. Gregory explained that he had remained silent during this period of schism because he had wanted to "purify himself through the practice of philosophy." If these dissidents included monks, then Gregory was pointedly claiming that he was one of them, since ascetics often identified their lifestyles with the pursuit of philosophy. Gregory furthermore associated himself with these dissidents by referring to them repeatedly as "brothers," a title which may have been the common designation for monks but which in this context also conjured up a personal relationship. As he then described their austere behavior and appearance and demeanor, presumably they would have remembered that Gregory too had spent time at Basil's ascetic retreat. At the end of the sermon Gregory could finally invite them, "brothers," to approach Gregory the Elder, "this common father with his distinguished white hair, this gentle and mild shepherd," and admit they were his off-spring. "Look around," they were to say to Gregory the Elder, "and see your assembled children." Just as two years earlier Gregory had returned from his flight to Pontus to help his father, so these dissidents should now reconcile themselves to their episcopal father. By stressing the significance of parental love for everything from sustaining the cosmic order to restoring harmony in communities, Gregory had effectively transformed the reconciliation of the dissidents into a family reunion.[20]

"The violent storm became a gentle breeze." A decade later when Gregory recalled this schism he complimented his father for the purity of his theology. He was also proud that he had been able to support his father as a "partner in his piety." As a priest, Gregory of course had assisted his bishop, but his most effective contribution had been to recast the dispute as a family disagreement. As a son, he then preferred to reconcile his schismatic "brothers" by having them acknowledge Gregory the Elder as their father. "Brotherhood" was perhaps a pressing issue on Gregory's mind, because at the same time that he was helping in these disputes involving the emperor Julian and the local dissidents, he had yet another opportunity to assist his father, this time with regard to his own brother.[21]

Caesarius was a bit younger than Gregory and had been serving as a doctor at the imperial court at Constantinople. Even after Julian emerged as the sole emperor in late 361 and began to demonstrate his hostility to Christianity, Caesarius stayed. Back in Nazianzus his brother was dismayed: "I have been very embarrassed about you." Two concerns prompted Gregory's alarm, both involving their parents. One was the impact on their father's effectiveness as a bishop. People were already gossiping, and some were openly wondering about Gregory the Elder's authority. "Now the son of the bishop is serving at court. How can the bishop admonish someone else not to be swept away by the times and not to associate with idols? How can he rebuke other delinquents when he does not have full authority in his own house?" Gregory's other concern was for their parents' emotional health. Although he had so far been successful at keeping their mother ignorant, their father was so depressed upon hearing the news that he considered his life wearisome. By reminding his brother of his responsibility to their parents, Gregory convinced him to leave Julian's court.[22]

A few years later the new emperor Valens recruited Caesarius back into the imperial administration. Caesarius served as a treasurer responsible for imperial revenues in Bithynia until his death in late 368 or early 369. His death had troublesome consequences for Gregory and their father. Not only were some of Caesarius' possessions distributed improperly, but some men claimed to have loaned money to Caesarius and now demanded repayment. Gregory again took the lead in trying to resolve these disputes. Initially he tried to satisfy these creditors without complaint. As the dunning continued, however, he appealed for assistance to friends and imperial magistrates. His friend Basil wrote letters to magistrates who were also, not so coincidentally, fellow Cappadocians and longtime friends. Gregory himself wrote to one of these friends who was an important magistrate at the imperial court of Valens. In his letter he bemoaned the fickleness of human affairs and appealed to this friend's own grief: "O ruthlessness, O cruelty!" He also asked him to restore hope to "the living," that is, to himself and his parents. His brother's death and the subsequent squabbling had left Gregory completely distraught, almost unable to cope with the "dogs" feeding on his brother's estate: "the pain makes me groan." Over a decade later Gregory admitted that he had considered fleeing yet again, until he remembered his devotion to his father. "It was necessary to endure everything, good and bad, with my noble father." So this time he stayed.[23]

During the 360s his family and his father's episcopacy had merged together in Gregory's thinking. He realized that the behavior of the sons, his own flights to seclusion and Caesarius' service at Julian's court, had the potential to undermine Gregory the Elder's authority as bishop. After Gregory the Elder had successfully confronted Julian in Cappadocia, Gregory concluded that his father, as well as his mother (and perhaps their sons too), had become exemplary paradigms for the community. Gregory was then able to convince Christian dissidents to reconcile by having them think of Gregory the Elder as their loving father. And he was able to rise above his own anguish over his brother's death in order to help his parents cope with their grief. Gregory's reluctant adoption of his priesthood had hence marked not just his assumption of a clerical career, but more importantly his overt acceptance of his familial responsibilities.

Gregory's familial perspective on his priesthood is one important key to understanding his dismay over his consecration as a bishop in spring 372. Gregory had already once rejected the offer of an episcopal see from Basil after his friend became bishop of Caesarea. A few years later, however, when faced with the loss of subordinate bishops and revenues through the division of his ecclesiastical province, Basil insisted that Gregory become bishop of the small village of Sasima. Because his own aged father joined his closest friend in consecrating him, Gregory was doubly distraught: "nothing is more powerful than old age or more venerable than friendship." At the time, and still years later, Gregory attached most of the blame to Basil and complained that he had betrayed their friendship. He also responded in typical fashion by referring to his consecration as another example of "tyranny" and by fleeing briefly to seclusion.[24]

Gregory's reaction to his father's role in his consecration was more conflicted and more poignant. Initially Gregory the Elder made an effort to settle his son at Sasima, and at first Gregory resigned himself to serving at his new see. As he later remembered the moment, he had been afraid of his father's anger. Then, as his frailness became more debilitating, his father changed his mind and asked Gregory to assist him at Nazianzus. In his retrospective account of a decade later Gregory was probably only too happy to recall his father's entreaty. "Dearest son, your father begs you; the aged father makes a request of the young man. This is a proper request. Even if it is not, it is a father's request." Gregory was elated: "my soul broke free from its weight, just like the sun from a cloud." Consecration as a bishop had certainly raised many concerns for Gregory. One was the loss of the benefits of occasional seclusion, the "tranquillity of body and soul"; getting stuck in the mud at Sasima was another. Gregory's most pressing concern, however, had been separation from his parents, and especially from his father. In the sermon that he delivered upon taking up his duties at Nazianzus later in 372 Gregory openly acknowledged that he was now his father's heir. "I agree to share my beloved father's responsibilities, like a young bird soaring high next to a great eagle." When faced with episcopal consecration Gregory had hence objected in part to serving as a bishop at all, but even more to the prospect of leaving his father and mother. As a result, Gregory never served as bishop at Sasima. Instead, he would become essentially an adjunct bishop with his father.[25]

During their shared tenure Gregory assumed more and more of his father's episcopal tasks. He participated in the consecration of a new bishop elsewhere in Cappadocia. At Nazianzus he became both a comforter and an admonisher. When severe winds and a hailstorm ruined an entire harvest, Gregory the Elder was unwilling, or perhaps unable, to address his congregation. In his place Gregory tried to console the people. In his sermon he explained that his new standing as "chief shepherd" allowed him to substitute for his father. To reassure his audience Gregory requested God's mercy for deliverance from these plagues. He was also more pointedly practical, because at the end of his sermon he severely criticized those who were capitalizing from this misfortune by seizing others' land, offering exorbitant loans, and hoarding grain. In another sermon Gregory directly addressed an imperial magistrate on behalf of a petition presented by the congregation. Gregory argued that because this magistrate had received his sword, the insignia of his rule, from Christ, "the law of Christ subjects you to my authority and my throne."[26]

Although Gregory had now become the new champion and patron at Nazianzus, he consistently backed up his reassurances and his admonitions by appealing to his father's long experience. To the end Gregory remained respectful and deferential toward his father. In the spring of 374 Gregory the Elder died. Later in the year Nonna died too. Years later Gregory hinted at pressure from people who had worried that in the absence of a bishop many would die unbaptized, and so for a while, despite the loss of his parents, he carried on with his episcopal duties at Nazianzus. He also felt obligated to represent the congregation before a local tax assessor. At the same time, however, he was asking the other local bishops to choose a new bishop for Nazianzus. When they procrastinated, Gregory took the initiative. Already in his sermon addressed to an imperial magistrate he had hinted that he preferred to resume a life of seclusion. In 375 he left for Seleucia, in the province of Isauria on the south coast of Asia Minor. Gregory's clerical service had effectively ended with his parents' death. Since he no longer had responsibilities as a son, he would no longer serve as a priest or a bishop at Nazianzus.[27]

A Family Man

For several years Gregory was alone. Within the previous six years he had lost his brother, his sister, his father, and finally his mother, and his friendship with Basil had disintegrated in a flurry of recriminations. A few years later, when he was remembering his aching despair, all he could do was echo the words of a Psalm: "my father and my mother have forsaken me."[28]

In order to cope with all these losses Gregory resorted to his usual solution of going to live in isolation. In this instance he also seemed to retreat into a happier time from his own past. Decades earlier, as a young man, Gregory had left his home region to study overseas. He had eventually settled at Athens, where he had been delighted to remain as a student for several years: "while searching for eloquence I found happiness." At Athens he would certainly have visited the famed Acropolis and its collection of ancient shrines. The most illustrious monument was of course the Parthenon, the celebrated temple in honor of the virgin goddess Athena. At Seleucia Gregory now went to stay at another virgin's shrine. In a later autobiographical poem he would mention his extended residence at the shrine of St. Thecla only in passing. "I immediately went as a fugitive to Seleucia, the shrine of the glorious virgin Thecla." Yet it is clear even in this brief notice that Gregory had linked this interlude in Seleucia with his earlier joyous years at Athens, because the term he used for the saint's shrine was *parthenon*. At the shrine of St. Thecla, Gregory was now imagining himself to be reliving the one earlier period in his life when he had been separated from his parents for a long period. Presumably he was also trying to revive the happiness that he had felt then at Athens. The only aspect missing during his years in Seleucia that would have completed the illusion was his parents waiting for him at home. Such a homecoming now existed only in his memories. "My mother, you met me in fields of flowers as I returned from a foreign land." He could still hear his mother greeting him as she "shouted out 'Gregory!'"[29]

"I stayed there a long time." Gregory eventually emerged from his hibernation, first to return briefly to Cappadocia, then to go to Constantinople to serve as leader for a small struggling community of Christians still devoted to Nicene theology. He also returned in order to reclaim his links with and assist his extended family.[30]

Like Basil, Gregory too had had a prominent maternal uncle in Cappadocia, and he had for decades been involved with this uncle and his family. Amphilochius the Elder had once been a fellow student with the illustrious rhetorician Libanius, and he too had become famous for his familiarity with rhetoric. As a teacher and a legal advocate, Amphilochius the Elder was an equivalent in Cappadocia of Basil the Elder in Pontus. Gregory in fact had once studied with his uncle. His uncle's children included Euphemius and Amphilochius. Both sons had been students of Libanius at Antioch and had followed their father's lead in their careers. Euphemius had become a rhetorician and a poet, as noted for his Latin poems as for his Greek verses, and Amphilochius had become an advocate and orator, possibly in Constantinople. In some respects both had become other younger brothers for Gregory, and Gregory had responded to them in the same way he had responded to his brother Caesarius. When Euphemius died just as he was about to marry, Gregory had deeply mourned his death. In the later 360s, when Amphilochius become entangled in an accusation involving money, Gregory had written on his cousin's behalf to important imperial magistrates.[31]

Gregory had become concerned over aspects of his brother's career in part because he had been worried about their father's reactions. Years later he had found himself in the middle of a similar disagreement between another father and son, this time his uncle and his cousin, over another career choice. By the early 370s Amphilochius was living with and caring for his father in Cappadocia. During the winter of 373–374, however, Basil had recommended Amphilochius to become bishop of Iconium, the new capital of the recently created province of Lycaonia. Basil knew that this appointment would take Amphilochius away from his father, since in an earlier invitation to visit he had suggested that Amphilochius break "the chain of caring for his father": "urge your father to allow you to leave him for a short time." Amphilochius the Elder had become predictably distraught over his son's departure to assume his new episcopacy, and he seems to have blamed Gregory for neglecting him. Gregory had defended himself by noting that he had gone to talk with Amphilochius the Elder when his son was being considered for the episcopacy, and that after Amphilochius' selection he had been unable to console his uncle because he had been too preoccupied with his own father's funeral.[32]

When Gregory had left for the shrine of St. Thecla in 375, he was trying to cope with more than the recent loss of his parents. The recriminations of his uncle had been another burden. In addition, he too had been distressed over the departure of his cousin Amphilochius. After the breakdown of his friendship with Basil and his father's death, Gregory seems to have relied increasingly upon the support of Amphilochius, whom he had considered to be "my only prop, my only good advisor, my only companion in piety." Perhaps it is possible to speculate that Gregory was furthermore upset because he had hoped that Amphilochius, if he were to become a bishop, would have replaced Gregory the Elder at Nazianzus. In that case Gregory could have retired gracefully from his role as acting bishop, and Amphilochius the Elder would still have had his son nearby to care for him. Instead, Basil's intrigues had intervened. Just as a few years earlier when he had almost separated Gregory from his father, so now Basil had interfered yet again in the episcopal administration at Nazianzus, this time because his recommendation had sent Amphilochius to become bishop in another province. When Gregory the Elder died shortly thereafter, Amphilochius had already become a bishop elsewhere. Gregory probably shared his uncle's dismay over the unavailability of Amphilochius. Even as he insisted that Amphilochius the Elder not hold him responsible for his son's selection, he also hinted, not surprisingly, that his uncle should instead blame others, "common friends whom you think to be only benefactors."[33]

Amphilochius the Elder died as an old man. Since Gregory noted that his uncle had died "outside his fatherland," perhaps he had gone to live with his son at Iconium. For several years some of the senior men in Gregory's extended family were living outside Cappadocia, bishop Amphilochius in Iconium, Gregory in Isauria and then at Constantinople. In 381 Gregory finally returned to Cappadocia for good. Back in his native province Gregory again had the opportunity to reassess trying events and to reinterpret broken relationships from his past. He delivered a laudatory oration about Basil on one of the anniversaries of his friend's death. He composed several long retrospective poems that noted his reactions to earlier difficult events in his life. For about a year, from after mid-382 until the spring or summer of 383, he even served again as acting bishop of Nazianzus.[34]

This renewed episcopal service was quite surprising, especially since Gregory had always been a reluctant bishop and since he was now complaining about so many physical infirmities. One important incentive was his commitment to the well-being of his hometown. Other bishops were pressuring him, and Gregory was certainly sensitive to complaints that he was ignoring the Christian community at Nazianzus. His most compelling motivation, however, was, as usual, his "respect for his father." By early 382 Gregory was completing another of his long autobiographical poems, in which he remembered and recorded his relief at having avoided episcopal service at Sasima. Versifying that memory had also reminded him of his father's earlier request for assistance. In 372 Gregory the Elder had finally asked his son to help in his episcopal see of Nazianzus; ten years later Gregory effectively agreed to do so once again.[35]

These renewed familial obligations were influential outside his episcopal service too. At Constantinople, Gregory had already resumed contact with another cousin. In the capital he had once taken refuge in "a pious and devout house belonging to relatives in body and in spirit." He was most likely alluding to the household of Theodosia, a cousin who was a daughter of Amphilochius the Elder. Theodosia had moved to the capital perhaps because of a marriage into a distinguished aristocratic family, and she had become a tutor, or even guardian, for the famous heiress and benefactor Olympias.[36]

Once back in Cappadocia Gregory became a champion and an overseer for other members of his extended family. He again relied upon his cousin Amphilochius, Theodosia's brother. During an illness he thanked Amphilochius for his prayers, and later he thanked him again for having defended a fellow bishop. Gregory furthermore petitioned imperial magistrates, the bishop of Constantinople, and a local bishop to assist various relatives, although he also castigated one of these relatives for bringing some women to live on his estate. The family members with whom he had his closest relationships after his return to Cappadocia were a niece, her husband, and their children. Just as uncle Gregory had once helped Basil, just as Amphilochius the Elder had once assisted Gregory himself, so Gregory now assumed his responsibilities as a maternal uncle.[37]

Alypiana was a daughter of Gregory's sister. In the mid-360s Alypiana had married Nicobulus the Elder, who was wealthy, a member of a reputable family, and a veteran of military service during campaigns against the Persians. At the time Gregory was a priest at Nazianzus. Since he was then assuming more responsibility for his own family, he had begun to look out for his new nephew's welfare by appealing for assistance from his cousin Amphilochius and from imperial magistrates. After Gregory returned to Cappadocia for good in 381, Nicobulus became his caretaker. Gregory showed his gratitude for Nicobulus' assistance by again representing his concerns before bishops and magistrates, and by taking an interest in the education of his sons. When Nicobulus died a few years after Gregory's return, Gregory continued to look after his family. Since Nicobulus' sons were apparently not quite yet adults, Gregory took the initiative in writing to a governor in Cappadocia on behalf of his niece, who was now unfortunately a "premature widow," and her "distinguished and remarkable household."[38]

Gregory had left Cappadocia in 375 after losing his parents, the last members of his immediate family. Upon his return to Cappadocia in 381 he had finally found another family by reviving his interactions with his relatives. In one poem he explicitly linked his care for his parents in the past with his concern for the next generation: "your reward is to be a prominent and gracious father and to have pious children in the spirit." Gregory always had a tendency to embrace his relatives by referring to them with close degrees of affinity that were strictly incorrect but hence more intimate. Earlier in his life, when his own father had still been presiding over his family, Gregory seems to have thought more about additional siblings, and he had been ready to refer to both his cousin Amphilochius and his nephew Nicobulus as his "brother." During the 380s, however, as he reestablished his relationships with his relatives, Gregory adopted a more paternal perspective. Now he preferred to refer to both Amphilochius and Nicobulus as his "son" and his niece Alypiana and other relatives as his "daughter." In return, Gregory's relatives treated him as the patriarch of the family. By becoming Gregory's "staff," Nicobulus assumed the same filial role that Gregory had once played for his own father.[39]

Others likewise supported Gregory. For a while Gregory seems to have looked to Gregorius, who was probably a grandnephew, to care for him in his old age, although he had to abandon that hope when Gregorius died young. Another longtime aide was the deacon Gregorius, a former slave in Gregory's household whom he had designated in his will as "my heir who has faithfully served me." In these Greek families it was apparently common for first-born sons (like Basil and Gregory) to receive their father's name. Gregory himself of course had no children of his own. But in this make-shift family that he now assembled from his relatives and freedmen, there were namesakes who assisted him and became his heirs. Yet another relative who helped him was another cousin, Eulalius. During Gregory's tenure as acting bishop at Nazianzus Eulalius served as an adjunct bishop, much as Gregory himself had once assisted his father. When Gregory soon stepped down, Eulalius finally ended almost a decade of uncertainty over the epis-copal leadership at Nazianzus by becoming the new bishop. Just as Gregory the Elder had once requested help from his son, presumably with the hope and expectation that Gregory would then become his successor, so Gregory himself, according to a later tradition, now consecrated Eulalius as bishop of his hometown. In the end, even though Gregory had declined to become bishop, Nazianzus remained a family see.[40]

Offspring

After his return to Cappadocia Gregory increasingly presented himself as the head of an extended family, both the successor of his parents and the guardian of the next generation. During his later years he continued to link his actions explicitly with the fulfillment of the plans of his parents, "to ignore whose intention I consider disrespectful and disloyal." In an epitaph for his father Gregory had Gregory the Elder announce the two most im-portant achievements of his legacy: "I constructed a church for God, and I provided Gregory as a priest." Gregory himself seems to have finished the construction of his father's church. This church was a conspicuous memo-rial to his father's success as bishop, and its completion established it as a permanent reminder of the ongoing prominence of his family at Nazianzus. In addition to completing this family heirloom, Gregory acknowledged that he was his parents' heir, the son destined to preside in this church, by dis-regarding his reluctance and ignoring his infirmities to serve once more in his father's job as bishop of Nazianzus. Now he no longer sighed at the

demands of family. By again honoring his mother's vow about clerical service and his father's request for episcopal assistance, Gregory had fulfilled
his parents' legacy.[41]

Since Gregory left neither a son nor his own church, his legacy was
instead his literary heritage. Gregory understood that his writings were his
offspring. "The father always appears in his writings, just as in a noble
son." In addition, the collection and promulgation of his writings reinforced
Gregory's standing in his family, since various relatives took the initiative
in helping. One grandnephew was able to motivate him to put together a
collection of his letters, and his cousin Eulalius edited a collection of his
orations. Gregory's literary patrimony had become a family enterprise.[42]

For all his love of solitude and ascetic isolation, Gregory had always
remained a family man. Basil had rejected his father's vocation as a teacher
in order to become an ascetic and finally a bishop. In the process, he had
estranged himself not only from his father's family in Pontus, but also from
his siblings and other relatives. Although Gregory had likewise been reluctant to imitate his father's career as a cleric, he had never distanced himself
from his parents, his family, and his relatives. His devotion to his father in
particular was always a dominant influence in his life. Even in his final years
he continued to follow Gregory the Elder's lead, first as acting bishop and
patron for the congregation in his hometown, then as the patriarch of an
extended family.

Chapter 3
Forgotten Brothers

After Nicobulus the Elder's death, Gregory of Nazianzus continued to look after his widow and their children. One of these children became "the most important of the relatives I care about." This favorite was Nicobulus the Younger, the oldest child. Nicobulus the Younger had studied with his father, with Gregory himself, and with various local teachers in Cappadocia. He then hoped to study overseas. In support of this ambition Gregory composed a poem from the boy's viewpoint in which Nicobulus the Younger revealed his wishes to his father: "O father, I desire this one [goal] before all others, excellence in speaking." The model for Nicobulus the Younger's proposed advanced education overseas was, not so surprisingly, his great-uncle, Gregory himself. "Behold my mother's prominent uncle. Father, I turn my eyes to him." Nicobulus the Elder agreed with his son's request and suggested that he might consider studying at Alexandria, at Beirut, or even at Athens. Alexandria was noted for the study of medicine, Beirut for the study of Roman law, and Athens as the "nursery of eloquence." Egypt, Palestine, and Greece were also the regions in which Gregory himself had studied overseas. After further training at one of these great educational centers Nicobulus the Younger could have anticipated a successful career as an imperial magistrate or an illustrious teacher.[1]

In contrast, his younger brothers were not going to be so fortunate. While Nicobulus the Younger was dreaming of advanced training in "the fiery force of rhetoric" outside Cappadocia, Nicobulus the Elder had sent his other sons to learn shorthand at Tyana. For boys from Christian families an education that combined the study of biblical texts such as the Psalms and the Gospels with the acquisition of competence in "fast writing" was now increasingly common. These boys received an education that was not rhetorical or even very classical, but was certainly both pious and thoroughly practical. Even as Nicobulus the Younger hoped to use his rhetorical training to make a name for himself "both in assemblies and in court," his younger brothers were apparently being groomed for lesser careers as secretaries at the imperial court or in one of the departments of the provincial administration.[2]

Basil and Gregory were likewise firstborn sons whose prominence overshadowed the careers of their brothers already then and often continues to do so in modern accounts. Gregory had one younger brother, Basil three. Of these younger brothers, two had markedly different careers, one by serving in the imperial administration, another by becoming a famous hunter. Although the other two did become bishops, their experiences and thinking nevertheless separated them from their oldest brother. During the fourth century provincial notables promoted themselves in many different ways, as teachers, imperial magistrates, military commanders, or bishops. The activities of these younger brothers demonstrate that different careers, clerical and nonclerical, could appear even within the same family, and that even when men did follow the lead of an older brother, they might prefer to keep their distance. Not only did oldest sons sometimes want to distinguish themselves from their fathers, but younger brothers preferred to differentiate themselves from their older brothers.

Caesarius

Caesarius was not much younger than Gregory. They grew up together and eventually studied together at Caesarea in Cappadocia. Their departure for study overseas marked "the first time we had been separated from each other." Gregory went to Caesarea in Palestine, while Caesarius went to Alexandria, where he studied a more scientific curriculum of geometry, astronomy, mathematics, and medicine. Alexandria had a reputation as "an esteemed workshop for all sorts of learning," and some of the teachers and practitioners of medicine there even had contacts with emperors and the imperial court. After the doctor Zenon had been exiled from Alexandria, he would have his rank restored by no less than the emperor Julian. Magnus had been a student with the famous doctor Oribasius, who would become Julian's companion. Magnus himself had such a reputation as a healer that he was thought to be able to raise the dead from the underworld. As a teacher at Alexandria he was so celebrated that he had his own school.[3]

With these sorts of examples and contacts Caesarius could dream about acquiring a position in the imperial administration or at the court. After his own studies in Palestine, Gregory had visited his brother in Alexandria, before proceeding on for further study at Athens. Caesarius, in contrast, had different ambitions. Gregory went to the home of ancient classical culture, Caesarius to the seat of new political opportunities. After his studies at Alexandria he went to Constantinople.[4]

During the 350s Constantinople was a boom town. After being dedicated as the new capital of the eastern empire, Constantinople was now expanding its municipal aristocracy by attracting notables from the eastern provinces. Men from local aristocratic families were needed to become members of the city's new senate and to fill positions in the palatine ministries. Caesarius was now enticed to stay by being offered public honors, a marriage into a family of notables, and membership in the senate, and a delegation went to request that the emperor Constantius appoint him as doctor for the new capital. Caesarius declined these honors, however, primarily because of his brother's influence. Gregory had arrived at Constantinople on his way back from Athens. By appealing to their parents' beseeching, their homeland's needs, and his own longing, he was able to convince his brother to return with him to Cappadocia. Gregory was pleased: "Caesarius preferred me rather than the emperor himself."[5]

Although Gregory was content to return to his homeland, Caesarius clearly was not. Gregory claimed that he was now able to "shrug off ambition, as if it were a harsh despot or a debilitating illness." In contrast, Caesarius tried to persuade his brother about the advantages of "a desire for glory." His goal was "to obtain the foremost place with an emperor." Caesarius soon became the leading doctor and a "friend" of the emperor Constantius, apparently after returning to Constantinople, and seemed destined to acquire greater honors from the emperors, now Constantius and Julian. After Constantius' death in late 361 Caesarius remained at the court of Julian in Constantinople. Service at the court of an emperor who was by now openly antagonistic to Christianity was distressing for Gregory, their father, and the entire Christian community at Nazianzus. In their hometown people complained that "the bishop's son was now serving at court, that he was coveting secular power and glory, and that he was a hostage to money." In a candid letter Gregory again reminded his brother of their parents' dismay and begged him to reconsider. In his estimation, Caesarius had to choose between "desiring honor" or "remaining a true Christian."[6]

Caesarius may in fact still have been a member of Julian's court when the emperor passed through Cappadocia in the summer of 362 on his way to Antioch, and some of this murmuring at Nazianzus may have been a reaction to the humiliating sight of the bishop's son in the emperor's entourage. In the face of this grumbling Caesarius again retired. According to

Gregory, his brother declared "in a loud and clear voice" that he was a Christian, and then left imperial service. Once again Caesarius had listened to his brother's advice, and once again Gregory could preen himself that his brother had chosen him over an emperor. Yet Caesarius was still not content with living in his homeland, and after Julian's death he again served in the imperial administration. The new emperors Valentinian and Valens reputedly competed for his friendship, and soon he became a treasurer responsible for imperial revenues in Bithynia. Caesarius looked again to be on an upward track to higher offices and honors, until he abruptly changed his mind. Even though his brother had been nagging him for years about the impropriety of his imperial service, Caesarius only recanted after a cataclysmic disaster. In the autumn of 368 he survived an earthquake that leveled Nicaea and destroyed some of his own possessions. According to Gregory, this earthquake was "the most devastating in memory," and it finally rattled Caesarius' ambitions. Both Gregory and Basil wrote to suggest that Caesarius learn from his experience, and according to his brother, Caesarius did indicate that he had decided to give up his imperial service. Soon thereafter, however, later in 368 or in 369 but before he finally left the imperial administration, Caesarius died from an illness.[7]

Caesarius' career represented more to Gregory than a brother who he thought had gone astray. For all his devotion to his parents and his commitment to serving as a priest at Nazianzus, during the 360s Gregory had had to convince himself over and over that he had made the right choices. His brother's career exemplified one of the alternatives he had rejected. In particular, Caesarius had been ambitious. Just as his father had taken advantage of imperial patronage for Christianity to enhance his local standing by becoming a bishop, so Caesarius now took advantage of the proximity of an imperial court and the expansion of Constantinople to make a career in the imperial administration. Gregory was both proud and dismayed that his brother had become the "shining morning star at the imperial court." Even though Caesarius had occasionally punctuated his career by returning to Cappadocia, he had consistently pursued the opportunities of acquiring honors at the new capital or of serving in the imperial administration. He had furthermore been flexible enough to serve under three emperors, Constantius, Julian, and Valens, who each had different religious preferences. The disapproval of his parents, the criticism of his hometown, the entreaties of his brother, even the advice of an upstart priest like Basil had diverted him only momentarily from the pursuit of his ambitions. In the face of this aggressiveness and this success Gregory did not quite know how to react. Even as he tried to dissuade his brother from pursuing this career, Gregory also conceded that Caesarius had been helpful as an imperial magistrate, in particular through his "protection for relatives in trouble." After Caesarius' death Gregory continued to struggle with two, somewhat conflicting, reactions to his brother's career.[8]

One reaction was to suggest that it was possible to hold secular offices and acquire worldly fame while still living as a proper Christian. Gregory himself was not immune to this temptation. At the beginning of his funeral oration for his brother he noted that some in his audience were there simply to "feast their ears and find enjoyment," hoping that Gregory would turn his grief into an entertaining display of his rhetorical prowess. Gregory had to admit that once upon a time, "when I was ambitious about oratory," he might have done just that. But now that he had rejected ambition and adopted a life of "philosophy," he thought that "the most trivial rank with God was better than the foremost rank with an emperor here." Despite his own choice, however, Gregory was still reluctant to censure his brother for having adopted instead the "second life": "he does not deserve criticism." According to Gregory, Caesarius had not succumbed completely to the allurements of serving at an imperial court, since he had not charged fees for practicing medicine and he had eventually refuted Julian's arguments against Christianity. Gregory then went so far as to claim that Caesarius had in fact practiced "philosophy" even while serving at the court. In his estimation, his brother had only hidden his "philosophic soul," until he finally decided to devote himself to service to God. Shortly before his death Caesarius had publicly demonstrated his new devotion by announcing his intention to leave his possessions to the poor.[9]

This defense of a secular career allowed Gregory to justify his brother's life to an audience of mourners that included his parents and the congregation of Nazianzus, who had earlier all been skeptical about Caesarius' choices. In the end, even though it had taken him a decade longer, Caesarius had made the same decision as Gregory about renunciation and duty. This public explanation was also an important rationale within Gregory's extended family, since his cousin Amphilochius pursued a career as an advocate at Constantinople before returning to care for his father in Cappadocia and then to become a bishop. Yet in subsequent, more private reflections on his brother's career Gregory was more severely judgmental. By then he had also experienced the upsetting consequences of his brother's death.

The distribution of Caesarius' possessions was controversial. Although Gregory and his parents wanted to disburse them to the needy, men came forward to demand repayment on loans. Eventually Gregory could no longer endure their relentless dunning and requested resolution from the imperial treasury. A year or two later he recounted this trying experience in a long autobiographical poem. He first reminded himself of the ambitions he had rejected, marriage, luxuries, service at an imperial court, great influence in cities, even a reputation for learning, and then of the obligation he had assumed, looking after his parents. His brother's death had upset his equilibrium between renunciation and duty, since Gregory had had to endure the "barking dogs" scavenging over Caesarius' property. This emphasis on his own personal grievances hinted at another reaction to his brother's death. Even as Gregory mourned for his brother, he seemed to be blaming him, as if somehow Caesarius was the cause of his current misfortunes. His most important concern was not the loss of his brother, but the loss of his serene life of contemplation: "I mourn for my own soul." Gregory knew that listing his spiritual afflictions might seem laughable to others, but the loss of Caesarius was simply the latest in a long litany of trials that now threatened to overwhelm him. Gregory was close to reprimanding his brother for his own distress, first because Caesarius' career had taken him away from Cappadocia, then because his death had removed a prop for his parents and Gregory himself. At the end of this poem Gregory acknowledged that there was no one to console him, no wife, no children, no siblings: "I am the only child left."[10]

Envy at Caesarius' success, and dismay over his abandonment of his family and hometown: in part these conflicting reactions reflected different audiences and different circumstances. In a public oration at Caesarius' funeral Gregory justified his brother's career, but in a private poem a year or two later he despaired over its consequences and seemingly resented his brother for having pursued secular honors. Yet Gregory's mixed emotions were also an indication of his own inner searching. Caesarius' career had raised almost too many questions for his older brother. Gregory had always been somewhat passive, reclusive, more interested in studying than in doing, reluctant to assume positions of leadership, always prepared to justify his preference for solitude as the choice of a higher life of contemplation. A younger brother who was aggressive, sometimes even defiant and headstrong, was a challenge, the opposite to Gregory not just in career choices but also in temperament. Caesarius may well have respected Gregory like a father, especially since his own father was old enough to be his grandfather, but by the traditional standards of honor and prestige he had nevertheless surpassed his older brother by initiating a career in the imperial administration. Throughout Gregory's life this same pattern would emerge again and again, as other peers and younger contemporaries seemed to exceed him with their ambition. Gregory's friendship with Basil, for instance, would a few years later collide with the same obstacle of the pursuit of prestige.[11]

Given this sort of uneasiness about his brother's career, at the end of his funeral oration Gregory almost seemed relieved. His brother's life had now become a lesson in the vanity and transience of human affairs. Caesarius himself would never have to endure the bitter aftertaste of envy and the disappointment from being caught up in the race for wealth and power. Perhaps most important for Gregory was the realization that Caesarius would never again leave. "The illustrious Caesarius has been returned to us. His precious dust, his celebrated body, has been escorted to the shrine of the martyrs." Having been welcomed by both his parents and the community, Gregory's brother had finally returned to Nazianzus to stay. Concern over the consequences of his brother's secular career, possibly even regretful envy over his brother's success and honors, would no longer distract Gregory from serving as a priest at Nazianzus and looking after his parents. They were all together again.[12]

Naucratius

In Basil's family, in contrast, the oldest son became the most prominent of the brothers, although in part because he had also become aloof and disengaged from his family's affairs. In his absence, and as long as they kept their distance from him, his brothers flourished. The one brother who stepped completely out of Basil's shadow was Naucratius. The second oldest son, Naucratius was a few years younger than Basil and seemed to be his opposite. Even their personalities and appearance were different. Naucratius was noted for "the cheer of his disposition, his beautiful body, his strength, his swiftness, and his aptness at everything." Basil had a dour personality, almost surly sometimes, and he was sickly throughout most of his life; as he once confessed to some bishops, "you certainly know how serious a sickness has afflicted me from my earliest adulthood to my current old age." Naucratius furthermore seems to have stayed in his homeland of Pontus, where he acquired enough of an education to give public performances of his own writings. With his cheerful personality, handsome appearance, classical education, and local connections, he seemed destined for a golden career.[13]

Then, in the early 350s when he was still in his early twenties, Naucratius suddenly abandoned any possibility of further participation in municipal affairs, the imperial administration, or the law courts. Instead, he and a loyal companion adopted a life of seclusion and settled in a deep forest near the Iris River. According to his younger brother Gregory of Nyssa, Naucratius undertook two vocations. One was to provide for some elderly poor people by hunting; the other was to care for their mother. For five years Naucratius "made his mother happy through his own lifestyle." Then, unexpectedly, while still a young man, he was killed with his companion in a hunting accident.[14]

Since Basil was away from Cappadocia and Pontus until the mid-350s, he probably knew very little about his brother's life. Some implicit connections are nevertheless reasonable. During his years of seclusion Naucratius became a notable hunter. Various districts in Pontus were renowned for their abundance of wild animals, and earlier kings had kept hunting parks in the region. Hunting big game could make a reputation worth remembering even after death. In Pontus one tombstone had commemorated a man as a "hunter of wild animals in the high mountains," and another had honored a young man for his "distinction in hunting." With his hunting Naucratius was doing more than enhancing his own renown and helping some poor people, however. His roaming over the mountains and through the forests of Pontus would have recalled the experiences of his grandparents, who had had to live in the wild during earlier periods of persecution. Memories of these grandparents were clearly influential in the family. Once Basil departed for Caesarea in Cappadocia and then for his overseas study, Naucratius would have been the oldest son left with the family in Pontus. Eventually he too rejected his father's example of teaching and service in their native city. Instead, in his own way he chose to imitate the experiences of his grandparents.[15]

Basil had himself never been trained as a hunter. When Gregory of Nazianzus later described his friend's education, he noted that Basil had never learned "to shoot hares or chase fawns or hunt deer." Yet Naucratius' hunting camp may well have been an inspiration for Basil's own retreat on his family's lands near the Iris River soon after his return to Cappadocia. In fact, Basil's retreat was so isolated that he himself admitted that his only visitors were hunters. Both he and his brother had gone to the mountains to prove themselves, Naucratius as a provider and Basil as an ascetic. To do so, they had to distance themselves from the cities that were the usual arena for the pursuit of prestige and acclaim and take up residence in the untamed wilds. There they could prove their mettle by killing wild animals or harnessing nettlesome ambitions. "Only the hunter and the ascetic saw solitude and wilderness as positive values." A rough life would be a guarantee of their new commitments. Soon after Basil moved to his retreat, Gregory observed that "the wild animals sanction your faith."[16]

Naucratius' life as a hunter revived memories of his grandparents and anticipated the decision of his older brother. Yet Basil never mentioned Naucratius. His brother's lifestyle was perhaps too overtly rugged and vigorous for him to appreciate or imitate. Another factor that separated Basil from his brother may have been the influence of Macrina. According to their brother Gregory of Nyssa, Macrina had considered Naucratius to be the most beloved of her brothers. Since Basil had few ties with his sister, perhaps as a result he also kept his distance from Naucratius, or at least from admiring his brother's precedent. Just as he would not acknowledge his sister as a mentor, he would not recognize a younger brother as an exemplar.[17]

Gregory of Nyssa and Peter

Gregory of Nyssa and Peter also grew up under Macrina's influence. Peter was the youngest child in the family. Since Basil the Elder had died at the same time as his son's birth, and since his mother, Emmelia, was then distracted by grief and her growing piety, Peter was effectively an "orphan." Macrina was considerably older than her youngest sibling, old enough to have had children of her own if she had been married. She now took over her young brother's parenting and much of his education too. As their brother Gregory of Nyssa later recalled their relationship, Macrina became Peter's "father, teacher, tutor, mother, and confidant."[18]

Under Macrina's guidance Peter's education was quite practical, since he acquired a reputation for his handicrafts, and it seems to have emphasized biblical studies but not included much study of "outside culture." In his one surviving letter Peter plainly indicated the limits of his education by using many biblical citations but no allusions to classical literature: "a treatise is tasteless unless it is seasoned with the most spicy of God's words." This limited education was not surprising, since Peter would eventually live with his sister and their mother at their retreat in Pontus and become the head of the community of men there. Even though Basil was living off and on at a nearby retreat and occasionally visited his mother, and even though he eventually ordained Peter as a priest, his older brother remained a distant presence. Peter did not study with Basil or make a clerical career in Cappadocia. When in the later 360s Basil was trying to cope with the effects of a severe food shortage in Cappadocia, Peter instead organized the distribution of food from the family's resources in Pontus. Unlike Basil, who eventually lost contact with his father's family, Peter remained in Pontus and continued to live in a small house near Neocaesarea. Peter grew up primarily under the influence of his older sister Macrina and his mother, and at his mother's death he received her final blessing.[19]

Basil was not present when his mother died, although Gregory of Nyssa may have visited or attended the funeral. As one of the middle siblings in a family of nine or ten children, Gregory was effectively caught between generations, and while growing up he seems to have had little contact with his parents. In a later treatise he remembered vividly how grammarians would teach young boys who could still barely talk. "The grammarians inscribe an *alpha* on a wax tablet and then the other letters in sequence, they instruct [the boys] to recognize the names of the letters, and they guide their hands in shaping the forms. Next they proceed with syllables, and then they teach the pronunciation of words." Even if one of Gregory's first teachers had been his father, their acquaintance would have been brief, since Basil the Elder died when Gregory was still a young boy. Gregory's relationship with his mother was also limited, seemingly focused primarily on spiritual piety. In a later sermon he recalled how his mother had once insisted that he attend the celebration of a festival in honor of the Forty Martyrs. As he remembered the incident, he ruefully conceded that he had been a headstrong young man. But at the time he had been miffed, even a bit resentful that her obsessive devotion took priority over his own studious preoccupation with "many thoughts."[20]

Gregory too relied upon some substitute mentors, and in his later memories he highlighted the roles of his oldest sister and his oldest brother. Gregory referred to Macrina as "my mother after my mother," "the cherished replacement for my mother." As with Peter, Macrina seems to have guided his early education, and in his later writings Gregory called her "my teacher." Although Gregory eventually acquired a reputation for his familiarity with higher learning, he never explicitly discussed his subsequent education. He was especially reticent in mentioning any teachers. When he wrote to the eminent sophist Libanius, he was almost apologetic: "know that there is nothing distinguished in a list of my teachers." In fact, Gregory mentioned only one of his teachers, Basil. After his brother returned to Cappadocia from his overseas studies, Gregory apparently studied with him at Caesarea during the short period when Basil was flaunting his rhetorical skills before leaving for his retreat in Pontus. In terms of his intellectual development Gregory thereafter considered Basil to be "the guardian of my oratory." Gregory also thought of Basil as more than his brother, however. Although Basil had once studied briefly with his father, he subsequently seemed almost embarrassed by his father's lowly standing as a grammarian. Gregory now studied with Basil for just as brief a period; but perhaps because Basil had taught as a rhetorician, Gregory established a bond that went beyond their studies. In his writings not only did Gregory call Basil "my teacher," he also referred to him as "my father." As his teachers Basil and Macrina had furthermore become Gregory's substitute father and mother.[21]

Gregory of Nyssa did not have the sort of education at the illustrious overseas centers of learning that Basil, Gregory of Nazianzus, and Caesarius had indulged in for so many years. His education was both local and largely dictated by the interests of older siblings. In subsequent years he was acutely aware of his vulnerability to accusations of cultural inadequacy. Even late in his career Gregory was perhaps not simply indulging in false modesty when he once conceded that he had "exposed his rustic speech by using his native language." This concession was all the more startling because he included it in his longest and most learned theological treatise.[22]

One response to his feelings of inadequacy was to emphasize all the more his familiarity with classical culture by bloating his writings with allusions to philosophy, literature, science, and even medicine. Another was to present himself as a rhetorician. Gregory had thought about going to join Basil on his ascetic retreat, and he seems to have started on a clerical career by becoming a reader. Then he had second thoughts. During the 360s Gregory of Nazianzus once chided Gregory of Nyssa for his obsession with the pursuit of prestige: "why not hear candidly from me what everyone else is whispering?" According to Gregory of Nazianzus, his friend had abandoned "the sacred books that you once read to the people" and now preferred to be called "a rhetorician rather than a Christian." Gregory of Nazianzus advised Gregory of Nyssa to reconsider, and also hoped that his friend would not indulge in any "clever rhetorical arguments" by claiming that he could be both a Christian and a rhetorician. As usual, in this letter Gregory of Nazianzus was talking as much about his own situation as about his friend's decision. Because Gregory of Nazianzus was himself still trying to resolve his own contradictory feelings about Christianity and classical culture, his advice was a bit disingenuous. In fact, he effectively undermined his own recommendations by soaking his letter with allusions to classical poets and philosophers. Since Gregory of Nyssa admired authorial flair, he was probably more appreciative of the rhetorical flourishes than of the advice. As he would later admit to the famous orator Libanius, "I spent my time reading your writings with great enthusiasm, and I became a lover of your brilliance and never lost that love."[23]

Gregory of Nazianzus was ambivalent about rhetorical studies because he had received such a fine education that it threatened to overwhelm his devotion to his parents and distract him from his Christian piety. In contrast, Gregory of Nyssa was trying to compensate for his feelings of inadequacy about his homespun education. But if he was already insecure about his education, then it must have been especially hard when the brother and sister he considered to be his teachers also began to doubt him. After Basil became metropolitan bishop at Caesarea, he still faced some opposition from suffragan bishops. One of these reluctant subordinates was his uncle Gregory. Gregory of Nyssa now tried to appease his brother by delivering letters of reconciliation from their uncle. Basil was pleased, until he discovered that none of the letters was authentic. Then he was so angry that he accused his brother either of forging the letters himself or of passing on letters fabricated by other bishops. In either case, Basil concluded, "you are a thoroughly unreliable broker in such affairs." In his annoyance Basil castigated his brother for his "complete naiveté" and his "simplicity." A year or two later, however, as part of his scheme to extend his influence in Cappadocia, Basil insisted that Gregory become bishop of Nyssa. Even then Basil remained dubious about his brother's competence and support. He soon accused him again of naiveté in arranging some councils, and he was reluctant to send him as an envoy to Rome because of his "total inexperience in ecclesiastical affairs."[24]

Macrina seems to have shared this unflattering estimation of Gregory's abilities. Shortly before her death Gregory visited his sister at her retreat in Pontus. As he told her about the hardships he had endured during the reign of the emperor Valens, Macrina interrupted to praise their father's sterling reputation in Pontus. She then conceded that Gregory had acquired such a wide reputation among "cities and peoples and regions" that churches requested his intervention as a mediator. Yet the discouraging conclusion to this compliment was to remind her brother that he owed his achievements almost entirely to his parents. "The prayers of your parents are raising you to such heights, because you yourself have little or no aptitude for such success."[25]

As a younger sibling in a family with such dominant older children, Gregory could barely acquire any recognition for his own accomplishments. Not only did he himself acknowledge the important roles that Macrina and

Basil had played in his upbringing and education, but he also had to endure slighting remarks from both older siblings and sometimes heartless involvement in his brother's schemes. His early writings furthermore reflected their influence. One treatise, perhaps his earliest, was an encomium on the attractions and rewards of virginity. Already at the beginning of this treatise Gregory was modest enough to concede that only one person was capable of providing proper instruction, "the most pious bishop, our father," and he also admitted that he was writing at Basil's request. In some respects the composition of this treatise on virginity marked Gregory's public affirmation of the influence of both Basil and Macrina. Gregory acknowledged that he himself could no longer participate in a life of virginity, since he had already made a different choice. "My familiarity with the blessings of virginity is insignificant and useless. Blessed are those who can still choose the better life and who have not been walled off by already choosing the common life. I, for instance, have been separated from the glory of virginity as if by an abyss. It is not possible for a man who has once directed his footsteps toward a worldly life to return to virginity." This confession seems to suggest that Gregory, in addition to abandoning his clerical career, had also married. Now, however, Basil's invitation to write this treatise had provided him with an opportunity to admit his own mistake and extol instead the ascetic life of his older siblings. At the end of the treatise Gregory was hanging his head in contrition. "Who can list all the blunders someone is swept into by a refusal to submit to those who are esteemed by God?"[26]

This encomium on virginity was hence in part an admission that his attempt at differentiating himself from Basil and Macrina by becoming a teacher in his own right and by rejecting their asceticism in order to marry had been a mistake. Into his early forties Gregory remained in the shadows of Basil and Macrina.

Narrating a Brother's Life

Gregory was haunted by a painting of the patriarch Abraham and his son Isaac. This painting depicted Isaac bound and kneeling before his father, who already had his arm raised to strike his son with a sword. Gregory could not help but admire the ruinous devotion of both, one prepared to sacrifice his son out of love for God, the other prepared to die out of obedience to his father. He also seems to have sensed that this painting represented the conflict in his relationship to Basil. "Many times I gazed at a representation of this anguish in a painting. I could not pass by this sight without crying." To rescue himself, he would have to challenge his substitute father.[27]

After Basil's death Gregory finally came into his own. Gregory now inherited, or simply appropriated, some of his brother's projects and some of his influence and reputation. In fact, he was so successful at mimicking his brother's activities that Gregory of Nazianzus thought he had become an exact reflection of Basil: "I see his concerns in you, as if in a mirror." Within his extended family Gregory of Nyssa wrote to a provincial governor on behalf of a relative. Within the church he elaborated on Basil's sermons about creation, and he assumed the obligation of responding to the most recent attacks on his brother by the heresiarch Eunomius. He may have tried to mediate the old doctrinal conflict between Basil and the bishop of Neocaesarea, and delegations from Ibora and Sebasteia requested his assistance in selecting new bishops. After the ecumenical council that met at Constantinople in 381, the emperor Theodosius issued an edict that declared Gregory one of the arbiters of orthodoxy. The council itself commissioned him to visit Arabia and restore order to the churches. On his return the "leaders of the churches" invited him to arbitrate a conflict at Jerusalem. Basil had acquired his reputation primarily through his letters and treatises and rarely traveled outside central and eastern Asia Minor; Gregory now extended his reputation in person throughout the eastern empire from Constantinople to Jerusalem.[28]

His brother Peter too now achieved some wider prominence. When Gregory had worried that his reply to Eunomius was too reckless and indignant, Peter had encouraged him to publish it anyway: "the passion displayed in your treatise offers the pungency of salt for the taste-buds of the soul." Peter also attended the council at Constantinople in 381, and he eventually became the bishop of Sebasteia. Both Gregory and Peter certainly acknowledged the need to continue the legacy of "our father" Basil, and Peter even complimented his brother for having become a paradigm of "how sensible sons behave toward virtuous fathers." But just as sons were expected to replace and surpass their fathers, so Gregory in particular now seems to have been eager finally to have the opportunity to take the lead from his imperious older brother.[29]

Macrina had died within a year after Basil's death. Once liberated from the direct influence of his domineering older siblings, not only did Gregory began to expand his reputation by participating more widely in ecclesiastical affairs. He also became the guardian of his family's legacy. In the past Macrina had served as the keeper of the family's memories and traditions. Just before her death she and Gregory had had one final conversation about their family, in which she had reminisced about their parents and shared some memories about Basil. After her death Gregory seems to have assumed her responsibility of preserving and transmitting the family's memories, and one of his first objectives was to blend his older siblings into these ancestral traditions.

Gregory's writings about his family's memories formed a trilogy. For Macrina he composed a long biography that essentially combined her stories with his own memories and experiences into an extended history of the family. In this biography Gregory was able to praise his sister and analyze his emotional attachment to her. But since Basil had lived apart from his family for much of his life, and since he had been somewhat estranged from his older sister, a history derived from and focused on Macrina did not have much to say about Basil. Gregory hence became the keeper, and sculptor, of two separate legacies, one revolving around Macrina, the other around Basil. To collect his thoughts about his older brother he composed two other works.[30]

One was an oration about Gregory Thaumaturgus, the bishop of Neocaesarea in the mid-third century whose traditions had become closely linked with Gregory's family. Although in this panegyric Gregory never mentioned his brother directly, drafting an account of the life of Gregory Thaumaturgus allowed him to provide an oblique meditation on the career of Basil, another native of Neocaesarea who had also become a local bishop. Through these implicit comparisons and contrasts Gregory could comment indirectly on his brother's life and career. He also used this oration to comment on his own relationship with his brother.

One commentary took the form of silence. Some traditions had claimed that Gregory Thaumaturgus had had a brother named Athenodorus, who had joined him as a fellow student under Origen and who had become a fellow bishop in Pontus. Gregory of Nyssa never mentioned this brother. Instead, in one story he claimed that Gregory Thaumaturgus' companion in his studies had been Firmilianus, "one of the aristocrats in Cappadocia" who would himself later became bishop of Caesarea in Cappadocia. This version of Gregory Thaumaturgus' life suggested a parallel with Basil's life. Just as Gregory Thaumaturgus had studied with a friend from Cappadocia, so Basil, another native of Pontus, had studied with his friend Gregory of Nazianzus, another native of Cappadocia. Basil had selected a friend as his companion, rather than his brother. Another commentary was an unstated implication. In another story, Gregory of Nyssa mentioned a challenge to Gregory Thaumaturgus from a young man who questioned his teachings.

Gregory Thaumaturgus' response had been to exorcise the demon that controlled this young man. In Gregory of Nyssa's telling of his life, Gregory Thaumaturgus had not had a brother, and he had miraculously healed an insubordinate young man. These stories may well have had personal significance. Perhaps Gregory of Nyssa thought of himself in the same way, as the rebellious young man whom Basil had had to restore to an ascetic life, as the forgotten brother.[31]

Gregory offered another evaluation of Basil's career in an encomium that he delivered to mark an anniversary of his brother's death. Although this oration was directly about Basil, it too was quite vague and imprecise. Unlike the commemorative panegyric by Gregory of Nazianzus, which included many biographical details about Basil, this oration by Gregory of Nyssa had few specific details about his brother. Instead, Gregory supplied Basil with an alternative biblical genealogy by making him the spiritual descendent of Abraham, Moses, Samuel, Elijah, John the Baptist, and the apostle Paul. In his estimation, Basil was himself the equivalent of a distant biblical figure, so remote that "his family was his kinship with the divine." The Basil described in this oration might as well have been a member of a different family.[32]

Gregory's oration furthermore had few personal touches. Gregory of Nazianzus used much of his panegyric to analyze the intimate details of his friendship with Basil; Gregory of Nyssa never even hinted that Basil was his brother. Only once did he mention a specific episode from Basil's life. According to Gregory, when Basil was once very ill during his youth, Basil the Elder had had a dream in which he saw the Lord telling him that his son would survive. This story about Basil and his father might readily have been a parable about the relationship between Gregory and his brother. Even though Basil had never directly acknowledged any emotional relationship with his father, this story implied that his father had truly loved him. It also seems to have hinted at what Gregory had always hoped for from his substitute father, an overt indication of affection and concern for his younger brother.[33]

Instead, Gregory could imagine Basil only as his aloof teacher, and that image merely reinforced his feelings of inadequacy. Basil had surpassed his father the grammarian; Gregory could not imagine himself surpassing his brother the rhetorician and the metropolitan bishop. At the end of this oration, when Gregory boasted of Basil as his teacher, he essentially conceded that he would never replace him. At best he thought he might be able to embody his brother's teachings. But he could never be more than his brother's understudy.[34]

Chapter 4

"The Father Was Always the Father"

Every father is a son, but not all sons become fathers. None of the Cappadocian Fathers or their brothers became a father. Within their families their roles had always been primarily as sons and brothers, secondarily as nephews, cousins, and uncles (and, in the case of Gregory of Nyssa, a husband). One oldest brother was estranged and separated from his family, seemingly so embittered about being abandoned at an early age by his father's death that he never mentioned him, but also still so full of longing for a father figure that he tried to recreate a filial relationship with various older mentors. Another was so devoted to his parents that he declined other opportunities, even pursuits he preferred, in order to care for them in their old age. Basil rejected his father's occupation, and Gregory of Nazianzus sometimes felt "tyrannized" by the constraints of his devotion to his father; yet feelings for their fathers, whether repressed or overt, shaped both of their lives and careers. Of the younger brothers, one upset his family by becoming a doctor and pursuing a career in the imperial administration, another abandoned urban society in order to become a hunter, and another lived with his sister on an ascetic retreat until finally becoming a bishop. Another younger brother had an outwardly distinguished career as a rhetorician, bishop, and theologian, but always felt inadequate in comparison to the accomplishments and learning of his oldest brother. These sons had endured an absent father, a dominant father, an uncle as an acting father, and an older brother as a substitute father. The lives of the Cappadocian Fathers and their siblings represented many different experiences and notions of fatherhood, sonship, and brotherhood.

Three of these sons became prominent theologians. Given that one of the important issues in theological controversies during the fourth century was precisely the definition of the relationship between God the Father and Jesus Christ his Son, it seems reasonable to wonder whether personal experiences might have influenced their doctrinal formulations. The biblical language of "begatting" and "birth" had from the beginning shaped discussions of the origins of Jesus Christ. Both in its emerging theology as canonized in the New Testament and in the celebration of its liturgy, early Christianity had long since accepted the idea that the divine Trinity included a "Father" and a "Son." Basil noted, for instance, that the traditional invocation at baptism had acknowledged "Father and Son and Holy Spirit" as the source of salvation, and that it was necessary to preserve "the teaching of baptism in the profession of faith." Yet the precise articulation of the intimacy between Father and Son remained contentious. During prayers with his congregation Basil "recited the full doxology to God the Father in two forms, one 'with the Son together with the Holy Spirit,' the other 'through the Son in the Holy Spirit.'" Not everyone appreciated Basil's subtlety about the distinct Persons of the Trinity, or perhaps his sense of accommodation: "some of those in attendance complained and said that I had used unfamiliar words that were in addition inherently contradictory."[1]

A few theologians went further and tried to avoid using these familial terms. One bishop at Antioch repeatedly mumbled the doxology, so that his congregation could not make out his words. Eunomius, a rival Cappadocian theologian, preferred to discuss Father and Son by highlighting the equally influential biblical language of "creating" and "making." In his treatises he used more abstruse terms by replacing "Father" with "highest and most powerful essence," and "Son" with "another essence through that essence, after that essence excelling over the others." Gregory of Nyssa ridiculed these convoluted formulations. "The reason for this new nomenclature is obvious to everyone, because all men upon hearing the names 'father' and 'son' immediately understand the proper and natural relationship to each another [implied] by the names themselves." In fact, Gregory then tried to refute Eunomius' distaste for calling God "Father" by using a direct comparison with "your father," that is, Eunomius' own father.[2]

Modern discussions of early Christian theology tend to become abstract and philosophical. Like prosopography and demography and studies of law, theology avoids analysis of emotions and affections. This is a puzzling omission, since love was at the heart of the relationships both among the three Persons of the Trinity and between God and His believers. In addition, early Christian theologians were fully aware of the intimate connection between their doctrines and their ordinary lives, and they consistently clarified their doctrines by using analogies based on the family and personal relationships. At Constantinople a churchman once greeted the emperor Theodosius with respectful deference but addressed his young son Arcadius as "child" and caressed him with his hand. The emperor was outraged at this apparent disrespect of his son; but once he realized that this bishop was only demonstrating the practical implications of the theological doctrine that God the Son was inferior to God the Father, he rejected this heretical doctrine and became a firm supporter of orthodox theology. In Cappadocia people directly connected fatherhood and Godhood in their everyday lives. A son appealing for his father's forbearance might equate his father with God: "O father, whom the unbegotten and immortal God has given to me now as a begotten and mortal god." A son might furthermore use God's generosity as a reminder for his father to be magnanimous: "Father, become a god instead of a man for your son." Theological doctrines, once formulated, may have served as a source of instruction for relationships between fathers and sons, but the actual behavior of fathers and sons, and their accompanying feelings, had shaped the original template for imagining and defining God the Father and God the Son.[3]

Family relationships were both modeled upon divine relationships and the model for them in rhetoric and theology. Orators and theologians could not avoid thinking about their fathers when they argued about a divine Father. An illustrious sage had once pointedly told a young man to forget about composing a panegyric about Zeus, "the father of men and gods," because it was a topic that "exceeded human comprehension." He had instead recommended that the young man speak about his own father, "whom you know as well as you know yourself." Basil would have agreed with this advice. "How is it possible to grasp the concept of God the Father," he asked in one of his letters, "if we do not understand fatherhood?" As a cleric who had lost his own father at an early age and had never become a father himself, Basil should have reflected on the irony of his own comment. Modern scholars should see it as exhortation. Just as historians read orations and letters and wills and saints' lives for hints about the authors, so they should be encouraged to investigate autobiographical undertones in theological treatises about Fatherhood and Sonship.[4]

Tombs of Ancestors

Fatherhood and sonship were permanently fused together. In the making of orthodox theology this inescapable connection sometimes raised difficulties. Heterodox Christians who believed that God the Son came into being sometime after God the Father wondered whether God could still be called

"Father" prior to the existence of the Son. One of their leaders was certain, despite the logical bewilderment: "the Father was always the Father."[5]

In everyday life the everlastingness of the relationship between fathers and sons was also a concern. Just as they typically remained together in life, fathers and sons were expected to remain together after death. Although daughters who married were usually buried with their husbands' families, sons were buried with their parents. A tombstone in Pontus commemorated an entire family: "Mother Earth has received three bodies in one tomb, a husband, a wife, and their son." On another tombstone a father stressed that he had prepared a tomb for himself, his wife, their sons, and their grandsons. Families hence tried to retrieve the bodies of male relatives who died outside their homelands. One father in Pontus brought back the bones of his son who had been serving as a legal advisor in Bithynia to be buried with his ancestors in Amaseia. Basil once wrote to a provincial governor to request his assistance for some men from Alexandria who had come to collect a relative's body.[6]

Gregory of Nazianzus acknowledged the lasting connection between parents and sons in commemorative epitaphs he composed for several of his relatives. One was his cousin Euphemius, who had died regrettably young. The "hallowed spot" in which he was buried, with its "spring, streams, stands of trees, and chirping birds," was then renamed after him as "Euphemias" and became a family shrine. Eventually Amphilochius the Elder and his wife joined their son in this tomb, and another son, bishop Amphilochius of Iconium, occasionally visited to pay his respects. The sons in Gregory's family would likewise be buried with their parents, Caesarius sharing a crypt with their mother, Gregory with their father. Like the father in Pontus, his parents had ensured that Caesarius' dust was returned from Bithynia for burial in the family shrine. In his later years Gregory seems to have looked forward to joining his parents and his brother in their tomb. Not only did he compose a series of epitaphs about them, but he also wrote some for himself. These doodling epitaphs indicated again his deep devotion to his parents. In particular, Gregory anticipated rejoining his father. Having already inherited his father's name and his father's episcopal see, he now wanted to share his tomb. "A tombstone covers a distinguished father and a distinguished son, both named Gregory: one stone, two equal luminaries, both clerics. Another tombstone has received the noble Nonna with her renowned son Caesarius." Even after death the parents and their sons would always reside together.[7]

In contrast, after his death Basil remained aloof from his family. Basil died while bishop at Caesarea in Cappadocia, near but still outside his homeland of Pontus. According to Gregory of Nazianzus, the worst consequence for a man who had been killed by bandits "far from his fatherland" was the loneliness of his burial: "the tomb of your ancestors does not hold you." Basil had had a lonely life estranged from his family, and he would have a lonely burial too. Gregory of Nyssa once described the funeral of their sister Macrina. Since Macrina had never married, and since she had been so prominent as an ascetic leader, her family seems to have considered her as the equivalent of another son; so she was to be buried with her parents. Gregory accompanied her funeral procession to the tomb of their parents. When the lid of their tomb was removed, Gregory was distraught at having to view his parents' decomposed bodies and had them covered with a linen cloth. Then he helped place Macrina's body next to their mother's. Since Basil was already deceased, it is significant that Gregory did not mention him. His body was not in the family's tomb.[8]

Instead, Basil had already been buried in another "tomb of ancestors" at Caesarea. In death as in life, Basil resided with his new clerical family at his episcopal see, "the high priest with the priests," and not with his family in Pontus. In his encomium about his brother, Gregory of Nyssa conceded, quite inadvertently, the distance between Basil and his family. When he referred to Basil's tomb, he compared it to the lost grave of Moses: "history says that his tomb has never been found, even to the present day." This was a startling comparison, because if, as was likely, Gregory was delivering this panegyric in Caesarea, he was probably standing next to his brother's tomb. Gregory's sadness hence reflected a family's sentiments. Although he and everyone else knew perfectly well that Basil was buried in Caesarea, from the family's perspective his grave was lost.[9]

Before Macrina's death, she and Gregory of Nyssa had talked one last time about their family. Their conversation had included memories of Basil. Gregory wept. By then, however, memories were all the family still retained of Basil. He may have been thought of as the "common honor of the family," but he had also left the family long ago. At Caesarea Basil had used his own resources to fund a hostel for the poor. This new complex outside his episcopal see was known as "Basilias," Basil's place. In the extended family of Gregory of Nazianzus, a beloved son would give his name to the garden surrounding his family's tomb. In contrast, Basil's final legacy reflected that odd mixture of fierce aloofness and charitable commitment that had

characterized his entire life. After adopting a career that combined estrangement from his own family with service to an ecclesiastical community, it is
not surprising that Basil gave his name to a poorhouse that looked after the
destitute and the ill, strangers and travelers, homeless refugees like himself
who were separated from their families.[10]

Mothers and Daughters

In the early fourth century twenty bishops convened in a council at Caesarea in Cappadocia. At the time the Roman empire was roiled in turmoil as rival emperors fought each other across the Mediterranean world, and the early Christian church in Asia Minor still faced the threat of harsh persecution. But these bishops had issues much more important than civil war or martyrdom to consider, because they had met to talk about women. At the end of their deliberations they issued a series of canons about "certain depravities of women." Married women who committed adultery were to perform penance. Girls who indulged in sex before marriage were to perform penance and could not be called virgins. Women who became prostitutes and had abortions were to perform penance. Women who killed their legitimate children, whether deliberately or unwittingly, were to perform penance. Widows who slipped into a sinful relationship, "prostitution," were to perform penance. Women who became prophetesses and soothsayers were to perform penance. Despite the lack of any precise context, these canons nicely exemplify the essential characteristics of so much of the surviving information about women in ancient society: men talking about women, men worrying about and feeling threatened by women's behavior, men trying to control women's behavior. In these canons, as in many other writings, discussions about gender and sex became displays of power, as men imposed regulations and as they wrote the texts that codified those regulations and explained the rationales behind them.[1]

One prominent manifestation of Christian spirituality was the practice of asceticism. Early Christianity of course did not invent asceticism, and asceticism certainly was not the only means for Christians to express their piety. Ascetic practices might take different forms, ranging along a spectrum of behavior that ran from personal discipline and spiritual meditation to more rigorous expressions of self-denial and overt renunciation such as fasting, poverty, celibacy, a solitary life, or membership in a monastic community, and sometimes to more extreme versions of self-imposed pain and suffering. In Cappadocia moderate asceticism was more common than severe mortification. Basil and Gregory of Nazianzus adopted such a sober ascetic lifestyle at a retreat in the mountains of Pontus. There they studied biblical and ecclesiastical writings, ate and dressed simply, and indulged in some manual labor. At this rustic hideaway they planted a tree and trimmed vines, leveled a bank, and pushed around a wheelbarrow filled with manure: "O earth and sun and fresh air and virtue!" Their languid lifestyle of reading and gardening seems to have been more similar to retirement than to renunciation. The emperor Valens in fact denounced men who abandoned municipal duties to become ascetics as "adherents of idleness." Gregory of Nazianzus once mentioned some relatives who had purchased an estate for a "retreat." In this case too it is not obvious whether these relatives were planning to enjoy a typical aristocratic retirement in the countryside, or whether they intended to adopt a life of serious ascetic renunciation.[2]

The most visible indication of the asceticism of Basil and Gregory of Nazianzus was their decision not to marry. For centuries Christian writers had extolled the virtues of virginity. Even though both men and women were encouraged not to marry, in most cases the targets of these recommendations to virginity were young women. These exhortations hence marked the intersection of concerns about spirituality with issues of gender and hierarchy.

As a result, modern interpretations of early Christian virginity have stressed these supplementary issues often at the expense of the true religious piety. Because the financial stakes were potentially huge, perhaps the church in general supported virginity in order to increase the likelihood of receiving inheritances from unmarried members with no children as heirs. Another possibility is that families encouraged virginity in order to avoid having to fund dowries for daughters. Basil was once dubious of accepting the vows of young girls whom their "parents, brothers, and other relatives" had presented "in order to provide some worldly [advantage] for themselves." The implications for the exercise of power and authority within the ecclesiastical hierarchy were also potentially upsetting. Women might benefit, because virginity or continence during widowhood offered them an opportunity to remain autonomous, or even to acquire semiclerical authority as deaconesses. In contrast, men, and bishops in particular, might benefit, because they were able to regulate deaconesses and impose their patronage over defenseless virgins and widows. Once these modern analyses of virginity and continence begin to highlight issues of empowerment or suppression, they also become discussions of the cultural construction of gender and sex in antiquity. It is not surprising that modern scholarship has often transformed ancient virginity into an aspect of women's studies.[3]

The Cappadocian Fathers have been notable catalysts to these discussions, both because of their own ascetic lifestyles and through their writings.

Basil composed a series of rules that exalted monastic communities, his brother Gregory of Nyssa wrote an important treatise about virginity, and Gregory of Nazianzus composed poems in honor of virginity. The first two chapters in this section investigate other important indicators of their ideas about gender and sex, their relationships with the women in their lives.

Gregory of Nazianzus was emotionally close to his mother but almost completely ignorant about his married sister. In a commemorative oration about his sister, Gregory nevertheless wanted to associate her with great themes of spirituality and asceticism. He soon discovered the difficulty of transcending the sheer banality and normalcy of her life, the nondescript husband, the kids, the arguments over spending, the concerns over appearances. So Gregory instead seems to have used the oration to comment indirectly on his mother and the significance of her life. Since his mother would die very soon after her husband's death, Gregory was always thinking about married women. In his immediate family there was no virgin sister or longstanding widow, and Gregory was an anomaly for not marrying.

In contrast, in the family of Basil and Gregory of Nyssa a virgin sister and a widow were prominent for decades. For many years after her husband's death their mother seems to have controlled the purse strings in the family. The oldest daughter, Macrina, had meanwhile decided not to marry, and she and some of her brothers continued to live with or near their mother. Gregory of Nyssa would eventually write a biography of Macrina that also highlighted his family's achievements during the fourth century. The prominent members of his family were his mother, who was a widow for almost thirty years, his unmarried sister, and his unmarried brothers. A widow and virgins dominated his family, and Gregory himself, to his own apparent regret, was an anomaly for having married. Gregory of Nazianzus thought about his mother and married sister as an unmarried cleric, Gregory of Nyssa about his widowed mother and unmarried sister as a married cleric.

Of necessity the discussions in Chapters 5 and 6 focus on the relationships between sons and mothers and between brothers and sisters. Because the men wrote the texts, it is difficult to complete the triangle of relationships by discussing mothers and daughters. The women remain shadows of either their sons or their brothers.

Chapter 7 is a more speculative discussion of the meaning of virginity. During the fourth century many churchmen composed treatises extolling the virtues of virginity, in particular for women. One possible interpretation of this increased interest in the virginity of women is to connect it with current theological debates. Since these doctrinal arguments often focused on defining the relationship between God the Father and Jesus Christ the Son, they were the theological equivalent of a paternity dispute about the legitimacy of a son. In everyday Greek society, while the maternity of a new child was immediately apparent, paternity was not always so obvious. Basil once compared the inception of an idea to the acknowledgment of a legitimate child. A student "should not conceal [his source] like those worthless women who pass off illegitimate children, but he should sensibly announce the father of his thought." Seclusion represented one strategy to ensure that husbands alone had access to their wives. Perhaps it is not too fanciful to suggest that treatises about virginity, especially women's virginity, were the complements of theological treatises about the doctrines of God the Father and the Son. Among churchmen an obsession with the paternity of the Son corresponded to an emphasis on the purity of women.[4]

Virginity and seclusion also had important implications for ideas about families and for the fates of families. Many of these ascetics, both men and women, continued to live with their parents or siblings, or established a community that included relatives, or joined with others in spiritual relationships that resembled marriages. Even as these makeshift families of ascetics flourished, however, actual families sometimes foundered. In the end, the Cappadocian Fathers choose not to continue their families' lineages. For all their prominence as founders of or participants in ascetic communities, by not having children they had failed to sustain their own families. Their decisions not to marry or not to have children doomed their families to social extinction.

Chapter 5

"Hollow Out a Stone": Nonna and Gorgonia

His mother was always the most important woman in Gregory of Nazianzus' life. Nonna was also a somewhat nebulous presence. Even though she was a powerful influence in shaping her son's career and outlook, Gregory usually talked and wrote about her in passing as he discussed others in his family. Although he delivered funeral orations in honor of his brother, his sister, and his father, there is no extant oration about his mother. If he in fact did not deliver an oration about his mother, then he had passed up an opportunity to talk about heartfelt tenderness and unconditional devotion, his own and hers.

Gregory's relationships with the other members of his immediate family were consistently more strained and detached, clouded with memories of previous indifference, distress, and indignation. He seems not to have had much contact with his sister Gorgonia after she married and moved to her husband's residence. Although he was a fellow student with his younger brother, eventually he had to reprimand Caesarius when the family worried that he had become a prodigal son. Even though he was devoted to his father, Gregory never discarded his resentment that Gregory the Elder had pushed him into the clergy. Gregory certainly loved his father and his siblings, in particular his brother, but none of these relationships within his immediate family seems to have been intimately close. In contrast, when Gregory mentioned his mother, his memories of her affection and concern repeatedly softened and comforted him. Although her expectations for her older son had certainly been no less demanding than those of her husband, Gregory apparently found them more congenial and acceptable. Once, for instance, she had prayed that her two sons would return together from their overseas studies. When Gregory recalled her prayer over ten years later, he still derived "great pleasure" from the memory of having fulfilled her wish for a dual homecoming.[1]

Nonna

Nonna and Gregory the Elder had married most likely during the 320s. Since they had both been born and raised in Cappadocia, their marriage had presumably represented an alliance between two local families. The success of the marriage would seem to have been a challenge from the beginning, however. One complicating factor was a conspicuous discrepancy in ages. Even when men married much later than usual or remarried, they still typically married young women. Gregory the Elder was probably in his forties, perhaps late forties, when he married, while girls usually married when they were in their late teens or early twenties. Nonna was hence considerably younger than her husband, perhaps by twenty or even as much as thirty years. Once they had children, their family of parents and offspring included essentially three generations, the older father, a wife who was young enough to be his daughter, and their children.[2]

Another complicating factor was different religious affiliations. Gregory the Elder had been a member of a local cult of Hypsistarians, while Nonna and her family had already accepted Christianity. As Gregory later phrased it, his mother's devotion to Christianity had been a legacy "from her ancestors." From the beginning of their marriage Nonna was uncompromising in her Christianity. "She never shook hands with a pagan, and she never kissed a pagan woman on the lips, even if the woman was most distinguished in other respects or even a relative." This attempt to transform Nonna's obstinate piety into a virtue was perhaps a veiled admission that she had been unwilling to demonstrate a proper deference to her new mother-in-law and her other in-laws. Since Nonna also began praying for her husband's conversion, Gregory the Elder's decision about religious affiliation became a choice between his Christian wife and his non-Christian mother. If his concern for his elderly mother was anything like his son's later devotion for Nonna, then this was a difficult dilemma. It is not surprising that after he accepted Christianity, he was for a time both estranged from his mother and deprived of his possessions. When Gregory later recalled his father's conversion, he emphasized the alienation: "he left his family and his home, and the reason for his departure was Nonna." With this description Gregory had characterized his father's decision less as a marriage and more as the adoption of an ascetic lifestyle. Since Gregory the Elder had had to disregard his own mother and forego his own inheritance, his marriage really had implied renunciation. By taking a Christian wife he had become an ascetic.[3]

Nonna's impact on her husband's choice of a new religion was a preview of her overall influence in the family. Her husband seems consistently to have yielded to her Christian piety. Already before the birth of Gregory of Nazianzus, and apparently even before her husband's conversion, she had vowed to dedicate her first son to God, "with no anxiety about the future." She tried to push Gregory the Elder toward accepting Christianity through a mixture of frequent "complaints, warnings, and favors," and she readily interpreted one of his dreams as if it implied that he should accept Christianity. "By dripping repeatedly a drop of water is destined to hollow out a stone." The eventual success of her constant fussing earned Nonna a reputation as her husband's "teacher of piety." Gregory in fact credited his mother as the motivation behind her husband's episcopal career: "you made your noble husband first a Christian and then a great bishop."[4]

Gregory the Elder also allowed his wife to administer their possessions. Once he became a bishop, he may not have had the time or the energy to oversee his estates, and in his old age he also suffered from illnesses and infirmities. As the supervisor of the family's wealth Nonna then became the primary instigator of the family's generosity. She was apparently so compulsively generous that Gregory often heard her talk of selling herself and her children into slavery in order to help the poor. This offhand remark obviously lingered a long time in his memory: "for her, not even the Atlantic Ocean was too big to be drained." Nonna's altruistic impulses hence allowed her to step outside the usual roles of a dutiful younger spouse. While still a wife, she had acquired a reputation for generosity that was typically reserved for wealthy men with ambitions or for widows with fortunes.[5]

Nonna's influence on Gregory the Elder was one characteristic that Gregory admired in his mother. Another was her strong emotional attachment for her children, and in particular for Gregory himself. In addition to Gregory the children included a daughter and a younger son. Since daughters typically left their parents' household after marriage, distance might quickly attenuate any emotional closeness between mothers and daughters. Nonna had nevertheless tried to maintain ties with her daughter. Even though Gorgonia had apparently left Cappadocia after her marriage, she continued to acknowledge her parents as the models for her own behavior. Nonna and Gregory the Elder may have visited when their daughter was severely ill, and Nonna, her "aged mother," was certainly in attendance at Gorgonia's deathbed.[6]

Nonna's relationship with Caesarius, the youngest child, was more problematic. After his overseas studies Caesarius had vacillated between his own wish to make a career in the imperial administration and his family's preference that he return to Cappadocia. His brief service under the emperor Julian generated much gossip at Nazianzus about the propriety of a bishop's son's serving at the court of a pagan emperor. Gregory's reactions were most revealing about his attitudes toward their parents, because although he tried to comfort his father about Caesarius' behavior, he did not even inform his mother. Even though he later insisted that his mother had "a man's confidence in a woman's form," at the time he was reluctant to confide in her. His explanation for this hesitation was his apprehension that, because of her "feminine weakness and excessive piety," her grief would be inconsolable. For all his devotion to his mother and his acknowledgment of her influence, at a moment of crisis in the family Gregory had still essentially given in to a stereotype about women as the weaker gender. A few years later Nonna showed her inner strength when she had to cope with Caesarius' death. While Gregory delivered the public eulogy, Nonna seems to have organized the funeral. In order to soothe her sadness she wore bright clothing and treated her son's funeral as a homecoming. She also resumed her role of supervisor of the family's resources by insisting that her son's wealth would be a gift, presumably for the poor.[7]

Despite Nonna's attempts to maintain contact, both Gorgonia and Caesarius had distanced themselves in one way or another from their parents. Gorgonia had moved away from Cappadocia, and Caesarius had initiated an unsuitable career in the imperial administration.

In contrast, Gregory always remained close to his parents, since after his return from his studies at Athens he was reluctant to leave their hometown, and he certainly never considered holding a secular office. Soon after her marriage Nonna had decided that her first son would be a special dedication to God. Before Gregory's birth she had prayed for a son, and she had had a vision that revealed his appearance and his name. The name for her first son was to be "Gregorius," "man of vigilance." Although this name seems to have been common among Christian families in the region, not so coincidentally it was also the name of her husband. This vision was hence additional reinforcement for Nonna's campaign for her husband to convert to Christianity. Gregory the Elder would then be reborn as a Christian, and their first son would be born into a Christian family and named Gregory. After her son's birth Nonna had "purified his hand with the holy books," and she had offered him as a "new Samuel," the Old Testament prophet whom his parents had dedicated to God's service already as a child. This dedication would seem to imply that Nonna had hoped that her first son would become a cleric.[8]

Gregory of course eventually had serious hesitations about serving in the clergy, and his misgivings were most apparent at the moments of his ordination as a priest at Nazianzus and his consecration as a bishop ten years later. These crises also provided Gregory with another opportunity to differentiate his feelings about his parents. In both cases, even though Gregory the Elder was in fact only carrying out Nonna's intentions, Gregory blamed his father for pushing him into the clergy. "My mother's prayer and my father's hand made me a cleric beloved of God." His mother had vowed, but his father had compelled. Gregory hence never criticized his mother for his own misgivings or the misfortunes he thought resulted from his clerical service. All he would remember was her insistence that he fulfill a "mother's desire."[9]

Because of this strong emotional bond, Gregory interpreted some of the important crisis points in his career in relation to his mother's love. Visions of his mother were never far from his personal memories. As a young man when he was sailing from Alexandria to Greece, his ship ran into a heavy storm. Surviving this storm marked a crucial moment in his personal development, since afterward Gregory dedicated himself to God and began to contemplate the necessity of baptism.

Later in his life as he repeatedly meditated upon the trajectory of his life's story, he recorded three versions of this storm. Significantly, in his memories over the years his mother played an increasingly important role. In the period of his depression after his brother's death, Gregory composed an autobiographical poem in which he noted only that this storm, even though it had lasted twenty days, had not been as distressing as the loss of his brother. A few years later in a funeral oration for his father Gregory claimed that his parents had learned of his danger in a vision and had prayed for his safety. He also noted that a boy on the ship had insisted that he had seen Gregory's mother walking on the water as she effortlessly dragged the ship to land. Since this boy was a close acquaintance (perhaps a slave attendant) of Gregory, his vision may have reflected Gregory's own interpretation at the time. Finally, during the interlude of self-reflection after his aborted episcopacy at Constantinople, Gregory composed another autobiographical poem in which he admitted that a passing Phoenician ship had assisted his own ship. Even though in this third version of the storm Gregory did not mention any prayers by his parents, he did note that in his own prayer requesting deliverance he had identified himself as "the offering of his mother's prayer." In this long retrospective poem Gregory was reconsidering the vicissitudes of his life, and especially the significant moments of transition. Even then, years after his parents' deaths, in his memories of this moment of stormy terror and consequent rededication Gregory identified himself with his mother's original vow.[10]

His mother's dedication had become an important memory in the formation of Gregory's narrative of his life, and eventually he was even able to link it with his survival of this storm. Gregory's concern about caring for his elderly parents had likewise been an influential factor in determining his actual behavior. Worries about his parents had made him reluctant to join his friend Basil at his retreat in Pontus. However much he regretted his ordination as a priest at Nazianzus, it at least had given him the opportunity to assist his parents. His consternation over his consecration as bishop for Sasima reflected in part his dismay over the prospect of having to leave his parents. In a later letter to Basil he excused himself from meeting in order to care for his ailing mother. As he aged, Gregory seems increasingly to have appreciated his parents.[11]

In 374 Gregory the Elder died. In his funeral oration for his father Gregory publicly offered himself, yet again, as the provider for his mother. First he recalled a story about his mother. Years earlier during an illness Nonna had had a vision of Gregory as he approached her sickbed with loaves of white bread. She then recovered, and when her son visited the next morning and asked what she needed, she replied that he had already been generous in nourishing her. Gregory obviously found comfort in this story. Precisely at the moment of losing his father Gregory needed to assure himself that his mother had always considered him to be "her most beloved child," and that "not even in a dream was another of us more preferred." With this reassurance he could guarantee his support. In this oration Gregory again compared his parents to the Old Testament patriarch Abraham and his wife Sarah. Now he offered to assume the role of their son Isaac and care for his mother. All he asked in return was "a mother's blessing and prayers," exactly what Nonna had already offered him even before his birth.[12]

Later in 374 Nonna died, apparently while praying in a church. With her death Gregory had lost his entire immediate family of parents and siblings. In the next year he left his hometown to take up a life of contemplative solitude at Seleucia in Isauria, where he lived near the shrine of St. Thecla. Even though Gregory provided no information about his years in Isauria, perhaps it is not amiss to suggest that he had deliberately decided to reside at the shrine of a female saint. St. Thecla had a reputation for her tenderness and affection for the pilgrims who visited her shrine. One pilgrim who had left her family and home spent her first night in the shrine with the saint, who provided comfort by "hugging her in her arms." For Gregory too, St. Thecla may well have become a reminder of his mother's loving embrace.[13]

Memories of his parents remained influential during Gregory's later years. In the will he composed in 381, Gregory was still concerned about the wishes of his parents, "to ignore whose intention I consider disrespectful and disloyal." In the family grave his mother shared a tomb with Caesarius, while Gregory, the first son and his father's namesake, was scheduled eventually to be buried with Gregory the Elder. He would probably have felt more comfortable sharing a tomb with his mother. Not only had resentment and even anger sometimes clouded his relationship with his father, but Gregory once noted that Nonna had in fact preferred him to Caesarius. Throughout his life Gregory's one true love had always been his mother.[14]

Gorgonia

Gregory's immediate family had also included one sister. Even though they were about the same age, Gregory seems barely to have known Gorgonia. Her husband was Alypius, and they had several children. Gorgonia must have married at a typical age when quite young, since she lived long enough to see some grandchildren. She died in 369 or soon thereafter, at the age of forty or a bit older.[15]

In a panegyric Gregory described his sister as the personification of many of the virtues conventionally associated with reputable women. In addition, because she had "loved her husband, her children, and her brothers," he could present her as the paradigm of the ideal to which Christian women should aspire in their roles as wives, mothers, and sisters. Much of this excessive praise was more revealing about the tenuousness of Gregory's relationship with his sister than about his sister's actual life. Because he in fact knew very little about Gorgonia, in many respects he could do little more than idealize his sister. Even the usual rhetorical posturing about the necessity of omitting events in order to conform to the constraints of the genre could not disguise his ignorance.[16]

Gregory mentioned nothing about their early years growing up together in Cappadocia. Perhaps there had been little interaction, since Gregory had soon gone to Caesarea as a student and then traveled and studied overseas until he was almost thirty. If his sister had married at about the age of twenty, then she would have left their parents' household while Gregory was away as a student. Nor, probably, was she in Cappadocia when he returned, since a later tradition claimed that she and her husband, Alypius, had taken up residence in his hometown of Iconium. Since Amphilochius, Gregory's cousin and the son of his mother's brother, later became bishop at Iconium, it is possible that their family already had some connections and relatives there. Gorgonia's marriage, like that between Basil the Elder and Emmelia, represented another alliance between families from neighboring regions.[17]

Yet Gregory probably rarely, if ever, visited his sister. Once women married, they essentially moved from their father's family to their husband's family. In the same way, the sisters of Basil and Gregory of Nyssa seem to have vanished from their brothers' lives after their marriages. The only sister Gregory of Nyssa and his brother Peter did visit was Macrina, who of course never married and continued to live on a family estate. In fact, it is possible that Gregory of Nazianzus had never met Gorgonia's husband. In an epitaph Gregory noted that Alypius had died "not a long time" after his wife, and he himself may not have traveled to his sister's tomb to commemorate her until a year or two after her death. In his panegyric Gregory candidly admitted that all he knew of Gorgonia's husband was . . . that he had been her husband! His visit to deliver this commemorative oration may well have been his first trip to his sister's town of residence.[18]

Gorgonia was hence not central to Gregory's emotional attachments, either while they were children or during the 360s when he was serving as a priest at Nazianzus. In the mid-360s Gregory did have some contact with Alypiana, who was apparently the oldest daughter (and probably oldest child) of Alypius and Gorgonia. Soon after Alypiana married Nicobulus the Elder, Gregory reprimanded the new husband for joking about his wife's small size. He also wrote some letters requesting assistance for Nicobulus, whom he called "my son."[19]

Gregory seems to have become a mentor for his niece and nephew simply because they were living back in Cappadocia. Proximity was a more important motivation for his support than blood ties with his sister. In his letters to and about Nicobulus, Gregory never mentioned that Alypiana was his sister's daughter. Nor did he mention his sister in any of his letters from the 360s. In his funerary oration commemorating his brother, Caesarius, who had died shortly before Gorgonia's death, he never mentioned or even alluded to his sister. In the early 380s, when Gregory elaborated on all the pain in his life, he mentioned only the traumatic deaths of three family members, his brother, his father, and his mother, and of his friend Basil. At the very end of his life when he referred to his "predecessors," he mentioned only "father, mother, brother." As an everlasting indication that Gorgonia was essentially no longer part of the family, the family's tomb was to include only the parents and the two sons. Gorgonia had left the family when she had married.[20]

In his oration Gregory did mention some specific episodes from Gorgonia's married life. One story concerned the severe injuries she once suffered when her mules spooked and overturned her wagon. Even though Gorgonia refused any treatment from a doctor in order to preserve her modesty, she still recovered: "her recuperation was more celebrated than the accident." Another story concerned a grave illness from which Gorgonia only recovered after she had prayed at an altar and removed some of the eucharistic elements. A final story described her final days. As she lay dying, she discussed ideas about the afterlife with her family and friends, and with her final words she recited a Psalm.

These stories provided some texture to an account of his sister's life. Yet Gregory had no firsthand knowledge of these stories, since others had apparently reported them after he arrived to celebrate the anniversary. Gregory admitted to his audience that they already knew about his sister's accident, and that the story had entered oral traditions. "This story is known to everyone, even people far away. The account has spread to everyone and is found on everyone's tongue and in their ears." He also noted that the local bishop had told him the other two stories. This bishop had finally decided to let Gregory divulge the story about the cure Gorgonia had found at the altar. "It is obvious that the story is not boasting because I am now revealing what she kept silent about during her lifetime." This bishop had also leaned over Gorgonia on her deathbed to hear her mumbling the Psalm. Because Gregory told these stories as an outsider rather than a participant, he included little of his own emotional reaction. In his imagination Gorgonia had become essentially a timeless figure with no direct involvement in his own life. In fact, when he mentioned the stories about her accident and her illness, he referred to each account as a "wonder," as if he were recounting the legends and miracle stories associated with a saint's cult. In this case, Gorgonia had performed essentially self-miracles by healing herself. In this panegyric, rather than sharing his own personal experiences and feelings about his sister, Gregory was primarily interpreting others' stories. He too was a bit bedazzled by these wonders.[21]

Gregory's overall interpretation was an odd mixture of fundamentally incongruous attitudes. In one perspective he stressed how Gorgonia had respected, and even embodied, very conventional paradigms of female behavior. Her behavior, such as her silence, self-control, patience, modesty, and discipline, had reflected the traditional female virtues of simplicity, passiveness, and restraint. Gorgonia was an unaffected woman who rejected the use of makeup, lowered her eyes, and rarely laughed; according to Gregory, she had kept herself "within a woman's limits of piety." She had lived up to expectations about subordination and deference. In a society in which a wife addressed her husband as "lord," Gorgonia had acknowledged her husband as her "head" and "master."[22]

In contrast, another perspective that Gregory used in this panegyric seemed to hint that his sister's behavior had also quietly challenged these constraints on typical female behavior. Most notably, Gregory gave Gorgonia credit for promoting Christianity within her family, as well as more widely. After her marriage she had imposed Christianity upon the entire household, and after her own baptism she had taken the initiative in motivating her husband to accept baptism. She had apparently patronized churches and clerics, and among the supporters who attended her deathbed was the local bishop. Gregory was only too pleased to conclude that through fasting and keeping vigils his sister's struggle for salvation had allowed her "feminine nature" to surpass the nature of a man.[23]

These concessions about Gorgonia's more assertive behavior linked Gregory's interpretation in this oration with a larger debate about the implications of the adoption of asceticism. In Pontus one husband had commemorated his wife on her tombstone for her intelligence, character, and good deeds. Christian authors and preachers continued to praise these traditional feminine virtues of submission and obedience that were characteristic of good wives. Gregory himself once eulogized the attributes of a correspondent and exhorted her to pursue the predictable virtues of piety, decorum, justice, and moderation. "The peculiar and proper ornament of a woman is solemnity, firmness, and moderation." But in addition to echoing the usual platitudes, Christian authors were extolling the virtues of asceticism and the rewards for women who remained unmarried. "The unmarried life is more elevated and more divine, even if more laborious and more precarious, while the married life is more humble and more secure." As an indication of this other dimension to his sister's life, Gregory claimed that at the end of her life Gorgonia was looking forward to joining Jesus Christ, "her Beloved and, I might add, her Lover." His sister had been both conventional and radical, the companion of both a husband and a lover. Even though these perspectives fundamentally conflicted, Gregory now wanted Gorgonia to represent both ideals, the appropriately deferential wife and mother, the suitably autonomous and forceful virgin.[24]

Mother and Sister

This ambivalence in Gregory's interpretation also linked his discussion of Gorgonia with his thinking about his mother. Gregory approached his mother in terms of the same contrary impulses. He admired her role as the administrator of the family's resources and her display of masculine qualities, but during the period of Caesarius' unsettling ambitions to serve in the imperial administration he had wanted to protect her feminine weaknesses. As Gregory praised these contrasting images of his sister, he was also trying to reconcile his attitudes about his mother.

Since in fact Gorgonia had been such an unknown to Gregory, he had the opportunity to inscribe her life with other concerns. Another way of reading this oration is to consider it an oblique meditation on his mother, rather than strictly an account of his sister. Nonna in fact often appeared in the oration. After justifying his right to praise his sister Gregory mentioned their parents and described Nonna's influence on her husband. After describing his sister's virtues he claimed that even she had acknowledged that her parents were the sources of her goodness. Nonna had perhaps visited her daughter during her illness, and she was certainly in attendance when Gorgonia lay dying. These direct references aside, Gregory also praised Gorgonia for the same virtues as Nonna, and he modeled aspects of his sister's life on his mother's life. Nonna's insistence for Gregory the Elder to convert was probably the model for her daughter's similar pressure on her husband. Even though Gorgonia had married and moved away, Gregory implied that Nonna had been with her daughter always, from birth to death. Gorgonia's life had been a replay of her mother's life.[25]

In Gregory's writings Nonna was often on the edges, tending to her husband and children, appearing in Gregory's dreams, but never quite coming into focus herself. Gregory had consistently been a bit detached from the other members of his immediate family, his venerable father, his absent sister, his wayward younger brother. Perhaps it was precisely this emotional distance that had made it possible for Gregory to talk about them in panegyrics and analyze their lives. In contrast, Nonna had represented the one true and intense emotional attachment in his life, and his feelings about her would certainly have influenced his ideas about women in general. Yet this close relationship had most likely precluded him from delivering a panegyric directly about his mother. Instead, an oration about a sister whom he barely knew had offered him an opportunity to talk about feminine virtues in general and hence indirectly about a mother whom he dearly loved. In addition to his inability, or reluctance, to resolve his contradictory impulses about married and unmarried women, he never quite untangled his feelings about his mother either. What Gregory could not say directly about his mother, he was able to imply in an oration about his sister.

If the absence of an oration about his mother was significant and not simply a consequence of the haphazard preservation of ancient texts, then the survival of epitaphs might be equally meaningful as a way of measuring his emotional attachments. Gregory's extant collection of epitaphs for members of his family included three for his sister, eleven for his father, and sixteen for his brother. It also included thirty-five for his mother. In his memories Gregory seems to have thought more about his mother than about all the rest of his family. He himself admitted that the number of epitaphs was an indication of their mutual love. "My mother's blood was fervent with love for both of her sons, but especially for [me] who nursed at your breast. Therefore, mother, I have repaid you with so many poems." In the carefully structured format of epitaphs Gregory was finally able to articulate his feelings for his mother.[26]

Chapter 6
Her Mother's Cloak:
Emmelia and Macrina

In the family of Basil and Gregory of Nyssa the most prominent woman was their oldest sister, Macrina. Emmelia, their mother, was certainly also influential, since she was the matriarch of many children and outlived her husband by about thirty years. After her husband's death Emmelia eventually adopted an ascetic life. Once she joined Macrina, however, her daughter took the lead in guiding their community and looking after her mother. Gregory would even credit his sister with having steered Basil away from his arrogant display of his rhetorical prowess. Just as Nonna was thought to have been responsible for her husband's conversion to Christianity and Gorgonia for her husband's baptism, so Macrina had supposedly introduced Basil to his interest in asceticism and become her mother's mentor. Macrina had also looked after some of her younger siblings, including Gregory and Peter, and guided their educations. Already during her mother's lifetime, Macrina had effectively become a substitute parent for some of her siblings. When Gregory summarized Macrina's relationship with Peter, he was perhaps also thinking about her general standing within the family: "she became everything for the young Peter, father, teacher, tutor, mother, and confidant." In this family the oldest daughter had seemingly replaced both parents.[1]

Emmelia

Emmelia had married Basil the Elder probably during the early or mid-320s, about the same time as the marriage of Gregory the Elder and Nonna. Emmelia's marriage represented an alliance between her family from Cappadocia and his family from Pontus. Both families were already Christian, and at Neocaesarea her husband was a noted teacher and advocate. Emmelia had already acquired some familiarity with classical literature, since she later wanted to shield her daughter Macrina from its baneful influence. Emmelia's complaints focused on the indecency of classical literature. In her estimation, tragedies about daring heroines, comedies filled with risqué scandals and liberated feminists, and an epic poem like the *Iliad* that attributed the cause of the Trojan War to the abduction of a beautiful woman were not appropriate reading for her young daughter. "Somehow these outrageously scandalous stories about women would seduce Macrina's delicate and impressionable personality."[2]

Emmelia had good reason to worry about forced abductions and bride theft, since she had grown up under this threat. She had at first decided not to marry. But after the deaths of her parents, her tender beauty made her vulnerable to abduction by one of her suitors. In order to acquire a "guardian for her own life," she married Basil the Elder. Her subsequent move to Pontus was yet another example of the usual practice of a wife's leaving her father's family to join her husband's family. Since she and Basil the Elder had at least nine children, she was probably pregnant or nursing children during most of their marriage. Wet nurses and nannies were also needed to help care for the children. Emmelia did participate in the children's religious education, since she steered Macrina (and probably her other daughters) away from classical literature toward biblical readings and Basil would later acknowledge her influence in the formation of his early ideas about God. When her husband died in the early or mid-340s, she was most likely only about forty years old.[3]

Since women conventionally married considerably younger than men, they were more likely to become widows than were their husbands to become widowers. Mothers were hence closer in age to their children than were fathers, and in addition to caring for their children they might still be caring for their own mothers. Basil once consoled a recent widow who still had to look after both her young daughter and her elderly mother. Widowhood, even for a woman from a prominent family, did not offer an enticing future. Gregory of Nazianzus mentioned several widows who needed help even though they had been married to distinguished husbands. Simplicia's former husband had been "the ornament of our entire homeland," with a reputation as a "defender of orphans." After his death she had had to initiate litigation on behalf of their children, who were now "orphans" themselves. Gregory offered assistance by requesting justice from a provincial governor: "consider the magnitude of her misfortune." Gregory also wrote to two other provincial governors on behalf of another widow, this time his own niece Alypiana, whose husband, Nicobulus the Elder, had died in the mid-380s. Gregory noted that her family had been "distinguished and admired as long as the illustrious Nicobulus was alive." Now, however, because of "misfortunes that have already appeared," "the family is wretched." Although Gregory provided no details about these threats, somehow the imperial treasury seems to have been involved. In another instance Gregory wrote to the metropolitan bishop of Tyana and requested his assistance for some widows who were being "tyrannized and oppressed by the power of that man," although again he was not specific about even the identity of the man who was harassing these widows. In addition to requesting help from provincial governors and bishops, Gregory apparently supported a widow himself, since in his will he made provision for Russiana, "my relative," to receive an annual stipend. Basil likewise interceded on behalf of Julitta, another widow facing financial problems. A lender was apparently pressing for the immediate payment of a debt, and Basil now requested either an extension so that she could sell some property or the cancellation of the interest if she paid the principal.[4]

Financial solvency, threats from magistrates and litigants, and challenges to the administration of their property might well become pressing concerns for widows. Gregory of Nyssa once noted that the problems widows faced included "enemies, insolent servants, and relatives who mock their misfortune or who laugh at their aloneness and look with pleasure and a sharp eye at their devastated household." He concluded that as a result many widows remarried. Emmelia herself was probably too old to be an attractive prospect for another marriage, and she had many young children to look after. Despite these apparent handicaps, she seems to have had few practical worries. After inheriting her husband's properties, she was a wealthy dowager who paid taxes in three provinces. According to Gregory of Nyssa, there was no more distinguished family at the time. Because Emmelia now administered the family's possessions, her children were dependent on her generosity for support. She would have funded Basil's overseas education, and she would presumably have supported her son Naucratius when he abandoned a public career to live in seclusion in Pontus. She certainly supported Basil after he moved to his own ascetic retreat in Pontus.[5]

By raising many children, supporting them, and guiding their religious instruction Emmelia had more than lived up to the traditional idealized image of a proper wife. Once her husband died, however, she seems to have directed increasingly more of her energy into her religious devotion. Sometimes her own piety was overwhelming, even for her children. Emmelia had become a fervent partisan of the cult of the Forty Martyrs. When Gregory of Nyssa was still young, to his dismay his mother once insisted that he participate in a festival for these martyrs at the family's shrine near Ibora. Gregory went begrudgingly and had all his excuses ready: "I was far away, I was still a young man, and I was only a layman." Although he later regretted his insolence, at the time Gregory had complained to his mother about the inconvenient scheduling and her requirement that he attend "for a single service." Emmelia had transformed her sensuality as a wife into a pious spirituality, and her commitment as a mother had now become a rather fanatical devotion to a martyrs' cult. Eventually she decided to adopt a more ascetic lifestyle herself.[6]

This decision followed, and probably was a consequence of, other transitions in her life and family. Her children were beginning to go their own ways. Although Macrina declined to marry after her fiancé's death, Emmelia was able to arrange marriages for her other daughters, who would then have gone to live with their husband's families. Her son Naucratius had meanwhile decided to live as a hunter in the mountains of Pontus. Emmelia had approved of his lifestyle; but Naucratius died a few years later in the mid-350s in an accident. Basil had meanwhile returned from his overseas studies bloated with arrogance over his rhetorical skills. Rather than accepting an invitation to teach at Neocaesarea and return to his family's hometown in Pontus, he taught for a while at Caesarea in Cappadocia, where his brother Gregory of Nyssa may have been one of his students. By the later 350s most of Emmelia's children were no longer living with her. The only children who remained as companions were her oldest child, Macrina, now about thirty or a bit older, and her youngest, Peter, now in his early or mid-teens. About fifty or a bit older herself, Emmelia finally decided to make some changes.[7]

Fifty was an interesting, and dangerous, age. A generation earlier Gregory the Elder had both started a new family and transformed himself into a bishop when he was about fifty. A generation later Gregory of Nazianzus would finally give up on his episcopal service at Constantinople and return to his family's estates in Cappadocia when he was in his early fifties. People seemed to sense they were near the end of their lives; according to an epigram, a man reached old age in his later forties. Even for aristocrats mortality rates increased significantly from their later forties. Basil the Elder had died when he was about fifty, and Basil would die at about the same age and Macrina in her early fifties.[8]

Emmelia now started withdrawing from her everyday concerns. She had already distributed much of the family's possessions among her many children. This distribution represented considerable wealth. Over the years the family's fortune had apparently increased significantly, since Gregory was able to claim that even after this division of property each of the children was better off than their ancestors had been. This wealth most likely consisted primarily of estates and their incomes. Most of the estates were probably concentrated in Pontus and Cappadocia, since Gregory of Nyssa later casually mentioned that he owned an entire village near Ibora, a city near Neocaesarea, and Peter was later living in a house near Neocaesarea. Since Basil would later mention an estate he owned in Galatia, some of these estates were scattered more widely. Once she had divested herself of these properties, Emmelia could contemplate a still more radical reorientation of her life. For this dramatic change her guide would be her oldest daughter.[9]

Macrina

Macrina had been born most likely in the mid- or late 320s. At first she was a perfectly conventional little girl who read her Psalter faithfully, was noted for her skill at working wool, and learned how to bake bread. Like her mother, she too grew up as an attractive young girl, and a crowd of suitors proposed marriage to her parents. Her father, Basil the Elder, arranged an engagement to a distinguished young man who had recently finished his schooling. Since this young man was now able to help Basil the Elder in his legal advocacy, he was most likely already in his twenties. Macrina, however, was still quite young, probably still a young teenager, since their marriage was to be postponed until "she reached maturity." Both the role of the father in arranging the marriage and the age differential of about a decade between groom and bride were quite normal, and it is likely that Macrina had had little say in the selection of her prospective husband. "Roman marriage was clearly perceived as a family affair, not an individual decision based on personal attraction."[10]

Then her fiancé unexpectedly died. Macrina now argued that the engagement arranged by her father had been the equivalent of a marriage, and that she could therefore remain a widow and adopt a life of philosophical solitude: "by nature marriage is a singular event, just as there is one birth and one death." Her parents, however, continued to urge her to marry. Since both of their families had been Christian already for decades, their pressure was perhaps unexpected. Christian writers who promoted the adoption of virginity had often encouraged parents to convince their children, both girls and boys, "to be chaste for Christ." Parents could examine the intentions of their children and they could monitor their behavior, but they were also expected not to hinder those who wished to be virgins. A treatise composed in the early fourth century that promoted the possibility that ascetics could continue to live with their families had suggested that parents should recognize a devotion to virginity, especially by a young girl, precisely in terms of a marriage vow: "do not be eager to stop a daughter who desires to be a virgin, lest you sow some hostility with Christ, the true Bridegroom."[11]

Even though such exhortations were common, Macrina's parents apparently emphasized other priorities. Emmelia may still have had lingering memories about her own vulnerability as a young girl, and Basil the Elder may have been more concerned about establishing a link with another family. Daughters were a currency to circulate between families and establish alliances among men. Rather than respecting his daughter's wishes, Basil the Elder was probably more interested in selecting an apprentice for himself.

Despite her young age, Macrina now objected. Since the story about her engagement that her brother Gregory later included in her biography may well have reflected her own assessment, it is striking that at the time Macrina did not justify her preference for virginity by linking it with biblical teachings, theological doctrines, or a longing to become the bride of Christ. Instead, she argued that she wanted to remain true to the memory of her fiancé. Macrina countered her parents' pressure by insisting that the young man was merely traveling abroad and that "it was inappropriate for her not to safeguard her fidelity to a groom who was off traveling." She furthermore announced that while she waited for his return, she would care for her mother. Her father's death shortly afterward then seems to have removed any additional pressure to marry, and Macrina stayed with Emmelia. In some respects during this period of her daughter's reassessment of her life Emmelia was now reliving her own experiences as a young girl, but with a different outcome. She had once wanted to avoid marriage by adopting an ascetic life, until her parents' deaths left her feeling vulnerable enough to find a husband. Now, in reverse, the death of Basil the Elder would allow Macrina to adopt an ascetic life. Emmelia may well have sympathized with her oldest daughter; both would now remain unmarried.[12]

Interpreting Macrina's decision remains obscure. She herself may not have been clear about her motives. In his retrospective biography of his sister, Gregory of Nyssa would imply that Macrina was only living up to the expectations of her "secret name." Just as Nonna had received a vision about the name of her unborn son, so Emmelia, when she had been pregnant with Macrina, had had a dream that revealed that her first daughter should in secret be called Thecla, named after the young girl who had followed the apostle Paul. According to an apocryphal account, Thecla had abandoned her fiancé in order to be true to Paul's teachings about not marrying. Subsequently Thecla had become a patron saint for virgins, and a treatise about virginity had recommended her example: "follow the footsteps of Thecla, the paradigm you have heard about." Because of the saint's reputation, "Thecla" had become a common name for women in the region. In this case, although Emmelia may have wanted to name her daughter Thecla, Basil the Elder was probably responsible for insisting that his first daughter be named after his mother. He was presumably more intent on preserving the family lineage, while Emmelia was perhaps hoping that her daughter would be able to follow Thecla's example. After her father's death Macrina had the opportunity. The influence of her secret name would have been a preview of her subsequent vocation, and by emphasizing this linkage Gregory, and perhaps Emmelia and Macrina too, could interpret her decision as the fulfillment of the destiny inherent in her hidden name.[13]

For all its attractiveness, however, the difficulty of this interpretation about following a precedent was that it explained too much. Thecla's example could not necessarily be recommended in all respects, because in the process of adopting a strict ascetic life she had forsaken her fiancé and antagonized her mother. For other devout Christian women her life had become both a paradigm of virginity and a recommendation of flight from marriage and family. In contrast, since Macrina herself had rationalized her decision in terms of her undying devotion to her deceased fiancé, she had not followed Thecla's headstrong initiative in renouncing her proposed marriage. At the time she seems to have thought that she had indeed already been married and that she was obligated to remain faithful. In addition, rather than imitating Thecla's radical separation from her family, Macrina seems to have been more concerned about remaining with her mother and her siblings. Thecla had repudiated her marriage and her mother in order to become a virgin; Macrina now remained a virgin in order to be true to her fiancé's memory and to stay with her family. Rather than immediately disappearing into ascetic seclusion or solitude, she assumed responsibility for raising her youngest brother, born shortly before her father's death. If Macrina had married as expected, she would herself probably have had a child about Peter's age. Since Emmelia was preoccupied with administering the family's properties and indulging her pious devotion to saints' cults, Macrina assumed a larger maternal role in the family. Macrina effectively became a mother without having married.

Not only did she remain with her family, but for over a decade, perhaps for fifteen years, she continued to participate in family affairs. In many respects Macrina's decision had highlighted less a refusal to marry and more her intent to stay involved with her parents' family and her own siblings. If she had married, she would have gone off to join her husband's family. Only a decision to remain unmarried allowed her to stay with her mother and assist in raising her siblings. Macrina had forfeited the possibility of a marriage, but still became a nominal mother, a virgin mother; her mother Emmelia now had the opportunity to compensate for a marriage she had apparently never wanted by becoming exceedingly pious after her husband's death. Since Emmelia and Macrina would now raise the same children, the death of Basil the Elder had left them both widows, unmarried women with children.[14]

Macrina and Emmelia eventually retreated into a more solitary residence. During the mid- and later 350s the entire family went through a major transition. The other daughters were on their own, most likely married. After a few years living as a hunter in the mountains Naucratius had died in an accident, and Basil was about to move to his own secluded retreat. Macrina may have been thinking about adopting a more ascetic life for some time, and she had apparently already begun to discipline her behavior. According to Gregory of Nyssa, by demonstrating a stoical control over her own passions Macrina persuaded their mother to restrain her grief over Naucratius' death: "she instructed her mother's soul toward manliness." Gregory also credited his sister with having diverted Basil toward "the goal of philosophy" and "complete poverty."[15]

One possibility is that Macrina had already come under the influence of the teachings of Eustathius of Sebasteia, whose supporters had founded ascetic communities in which they could live true to their ideas about the disapproval of marriage and the rejection of property. But given her involvement in the upbringing of Peter, her mother's affairs, and Gregory of Nyssa's education, it is unlikely that Macrina had already been living in the forests of Pontus since her fiancé's death. She, her brother Basil, and their mother all seem to have gone to their retreats at about the same time, in the mid- or later 350s. For Macrina and Emmelia, Naucratius' death had been one precipitating factor. Previously his pious mother had been "very happy" over her son's "temperance" in his new life, and Macrina had considered him "the dearest of her brothers." His loss now was most distressing for both of them. They were also now free from looking after the other children. Macrina may have decided to remain unmarried in the early or mid-340s, but it was not

until over a decade later that she, and her mother, could retreat to a different life. However much thought and dedication was involved, it was only
changes in their family affairs that finally allowed or compelled them to
adopt a more isolated life.[16]

Macrina and Emmelia settled on a family estate in the highlands of
Pontus, presumably close to the same "remote spot near the Iris River"
where Naucratius had lived. This estate was not far from the town of Ibora,
near which Emmelia had already founded a shrine in honor of the Forty
Martyrs. In a similar fashion another woman would go to live with her children and a large entourage near a shrine dedicated to martyrs. Basil's settlement up in the mountains was close to his mother's retreat. Even though
Basil had adopted his ascetic lifestyle for different reasons, insisted upon
the rugged solitude of his own retreat, and never mentioned his sister when
describing his seclusion, these settlements were somehow linked. Emmelia
was still supporting Basil, and Basil sometimes visited his mother "in the
opposite village." The retreat of Emmelia and Macrina down by the river
included both a community for women and a community for men. Other
virgins lived at the convent, and other men at the monastery. Peter presided
over the monastery, and Gregory of Nyssa sometimes visited. The residence
of Macrina and Emmelia was not far from their hometown of Neocaesarea,
close to a family shrine at Ibora, and virtually a memorial to the memory of
a beloved brother. For all its importance in the history of female asceticism,
their retreat was essentially a family settlement.[17]

In 371 Emmelia died. By then this retreat in Pontus was already no
longer the primary residence for the family members or the central focus of
its interests. The brothers had already scattered, Basil to the clergy and then
the episcopacy at Caesarea, Gregory to Cappadocia where he would soon
become bishop at Nyssa, and Peter perhaps back to Neocaesarea, where he
would later live. Macrina remained, and acquired a reputation as an ascetic,
a philosopher, and a chronicler.[18]

She first of all maintained her commitment to an austere lifestyle. She
shared her meals and lodging with the other virgins equally, and together
they prayed and chanted hymns day and night. Macrina also mortified her
body by sleeping on the ground, where she lay on "a board covered with
sackcloth, with another board supporting her head in place of a pillow." This
self-inflicted punishment reflected an important transition in her image of
her own life. Macrina was sleeping essentially on a cross, every night enact-
ing Jesus' death on her wooden pallet. By now she had transcended her earlier concerns of merely remaining unmarried and caring for her mother,

since by identifying so closely with Jesus' sufferings she also felt compelled to torture and physically abuse her body. In a prayer on her deathbed she argued that God should reward her suffering: "remember me in Your kingdom, because I too have been crucified with You." Not surprisingly, on her necklace she wore an iron cross as well as a hollow ring that contained a fragment of the True Cross.[19]

Macrina also enhanced her reputation for philosophy. In the standard educational curriculum, the study of philosophy had always marked the highest achievement and took years to master. Because of the discipline required, Christians, and in particular the Cappadocian Fathers, had applied the term to an ascetic lifestyle, to monasticism, and more generally to the perfected culmination of a Christian life free from passions. Despite all his own learning in classical philosophy, Gregory nevertheless admired his sister's ascetic achievement: "through philosophy she exalted herself to the highest limit of human virtue." In addition, Gregory seems to have acknowledged that Macrina was in fact familiar with actual philosophical tenets. When he visited her on her deathbed, Macrina had discoursed about the human condition and divine providence, and she had talked about the soul and about life and death. Gregory was truly impressed by this bravura performance: "as if inspired by the power of the Holy Spirit, she explained everything clearly and logically." As a result, Gregory would compose a treatise on the soul and resurrection in the form of a dialogue between himself and his sister. Because he thought that Macrina had demonstrated that she was a philosopher in all senses, in this dialogue his sister was "the teacher," answering questions, raising objections, even silencing him with a wave of her hand.[20]

Even though the other family members had died or left, Macrina continued to be the keeper of the family's memories. She had been named after Macrina the Elder, her paternal grandmother who had told her and her siblings stories about Gregory Thaumaturgus, the patron saint of Neocaesarea, and about her own experiences during the persecutions under the Tetrarchs. On her deathbed Macrina reminisced with Gregory for the last time about their family. She recounted stories about their grandparents, their parents, and even herself. "She retrieved the memories of events from her youth and she narrated everything in sequence, as if in a book." During their conversations Macrina also evaluated members of her family. In the past she had confronted Basil about his arrogance, and he had in turn seemingly ignored her. Now she mourned his death. When Gregory tried to tell her about his own recent misfortunes, Macrina both praised her brother's extensive reputation and belittled him for forgetting their parents' support. Since none of

Macrina's opinions survives directly in her own writings, only these candid assessments remain as indications of her own thinking.[21]

In her solitude Macrina had lived like an ascetic in her community of virgins, had meditated like a philosopher on large theological issues, and had become the guardian of her own family's traditions.

Narrating a Sister's Life

After Macrina's death Gregory himself became the keeper of the family's memories. In the absence of her own writings and of any accounts by other contemporaries, Gregory alone has shaped Macrina's life for subsequent readers in his long epistolary biography and in a letter adding a few more comments.

Unlike Gregory of Nazianzus, who barely knew his sister and had to rely upon platitudes and others' stories to fill out his commemorative oration, Gregory of Nyssa had been deeply attached to his sister and, at least until he became a bishop, involved in her affairs. In his biography he did include some stories that he had heard from others. As he prepared Macrina's body for burial, one of the other virgins at the community mentioned his sister's necklace. Before they covered her body, a deaconess pointed out a small scar on Macrina's side and told the story about the healing of the tumor that left this mark. As Gregory left the funeral, he met a military officer who told him about the cure his daughter had once received at Macrina's settlement. Gregory then concluded his biography of Macrina with "these [stories] from this soldier." But Gregory was also reluctant to test the patience and the credulity of his readers by including any more of these hearsay stories, among them "the unbelievable harvest during the famine" and "the even more surprising accounts about the healings of diseases, the cleansings of demons, and the accurate predictions of future events." Gregory declined to depersonalize his sister with a mere listing of secondhand miracles and wonders.[22]

Instead, he preferred to rely upon his own experiences. "My account is trustworthy not because it is based on listening to others' stories. Because experience was my teacher, my account covers the material accurately without appealing to others' gossip." The warranty of Gregory's account was his personal relationship with Macrina. "The virgin described [in this biography] was a member of my family." Gregory's chronicle of his sister hence became an account of her relationships with himself and others in their family. Even as he composed a biography of his sister, he could not avoid including stories about other family members and even autobiographical stories about himself.[23]

Macrina was in fact a major source of information for this biography, since she had reminisced with her brother about her life and their family. Yet it is also obvious that Gregory has molded these stories, hers and his, to reflect his own assessment of her life. This shaping had started already immediately after Macrina's death when Gregory proposed that it was finally appropriate to cover her body with magnificent garments. Her companions seem to have been startled at this suggestion. Since Macrina herself had consistently dressed in poor clothing, one of the other virgins demurred, suggesting that they needed to learn what Macrina would have preferred, and a deaconess added that Macrina had always been more interested in "a pure life" than "bodily adornment." Gregory persisted, and offered to contribute the garments: "I ordered one of my servants to bring the robe." Since he seems to have brought the robe with him, Gregory had obviously had a particular image of how his sister should appear at her funeral. In death, Macrina would no longer be a long-suffering spinster. When the women were finished with their preparations, Macrina was dressed "like a bride."[24]

In his biography Gregory furthermore connected this image with his version of her final conversation. When he described their final meeting, he claimed that her comments had revealed "that holy and pure love for the unseen Bridegroom that she had nourished secretly in the depths of her soul." As her strength ebbed, "she contemplated the beauty of her Bridegroom and with ever greater haste she hurried to her Beloved." According to Gregory, Macrina had long been thinking about her eventual marriage, and his donation of the bridal trousseau was only an extension of her own longing.[25]

In part Gregory highlighted Macrina's longing in order to make her life correspond with his own theology. In his other writings Gregory stressed the importance of the suppression of physical passions, the attainment of internal tranquillity, the imitation of Christ's life, and the participation of the soul in the divine existence. The models for this disciplined lifestyle were Adam in paradise and the angels in heaven. Both Macrina and her mother, Emmelia, had been successful in achieving this passionless life at their retreat. "Just as souls that are freed from their bodies through death are also freed from the anxieties of this life, so their lives were separated from these anxieties and synchronized for imitation of the life of angels. They had no wrath, no envy, no hatred, no arrogance. Continence was their

[one] pleasure." In his commentary on the passionate relationship between lover and beloved described in the love poems collected in the Song of Songs, Gregory would note that impassability, the tranquillity resulting from a mastery of the passions, was a characteristic of the divine life of angels. With this linkage it was possible for the Song to describe the lover's beloved as both sister and bride, "sister because of her kinship through impassability, bride because of her union with the Logos, the 'Word.'" On her deathbed Macrina's conversation had suggested to Gregory that she had far surpassed human nature, "as if an angel had by divine dispensation crept into a human form." Having concluded that his sister had already achieved the existence of angels, he seems to have decided that at death she should also be presented as the bride of Jesus Christ the Logos.[26]

But in the process of changing Macrina's life into an enactment of his theology about the importance of attaining a state of impassability, Gregory had also transformed the whole meaning of his sister's decision to adopt asceticism. Macrina had certainly told him the stories about the death of her fiancé. In her version she had associated her decision to remain unmarried with her grief, since she was now waiting for her fiancé's return. She had become an ascetic in order to mourn for her fiancé and stay with her mother. Gregory preferred an interpretation that had Macrina looking forward, rather than backward. By having her dressed as a bride and highlighting her longing for her Bridegroom in heaven, he had turned her ascetic life into an anticipation, a preparation for her final marriage with Jesus Christ. On the verge of becoming a bride Macrina had lost her fiancé, and then spent decades mourning his death. On her funeral bier Gregory restored Macrina to her standing as a bride, but this time with the implication that she had spent the previous decades preparing herself for this particular marriage with the heavenly Groom.

The biography of his sister then confirmed this new interpretation of Macrina's asceticism. By the time Gregory wrote this biography, he had himself traveled to the Holy Land and visited some of the shrines associated with the life of Jesus. He was impressed, but not so overwhelmed that he did not prefer to highlight instead the wonders of his home region. Jesus may have lived in Palestine, but his bride had come from Pontus. So Gregory now composed a biography of Macrina that made explicit the inklings inherent in her appearance during her funeral. Gregory concluded this account by stressing that his sister had adopted asceticism in order to remain pure for her beloved Groom in heaven. Devotion to a deceased fiancé was no longer an appropriate explanation for her ascetic life. In the perspective implied by her funeral and clearly articulated in the biography, a bewildered young girl had instead grown up to live and die with the anticipation of becoming the bride of Christ.[27]

Gregory of Nazianzus had known so little about his sister that he could transform his eulogy about her into a meditation about his mother. Although Gregory of Nyssa knew much more about his sister, he too was not reluctant to interpret her life to fit with his own theological teachings. Both men composed the lives of the women in their families in terms of their own preoccupations. Reflections on women were a medium for men to reflect on themselves and their own concerns.[28]

Celebrating a Family

Gregory of Nyssa furthermore had his family's reputation to think about. Even though the local bishop and his clerics participated, Gregory himself, despite his own grief, mindfully staged much of the funeral. "I thought it was possible not to overlook anything appropriate for this funeral." When the wailing of the crowd disrupted the chanting of hymns, Gregory carefully divided the men and women into separate "rhythmic and harmonious" choruses. He himself slowly led the funeral procession to the family tomb. He presided over the uncovering of the tomb, and he and the bishop placed Macrina's body next to Emmelia's remains. He then knelt before the tomb and kissed the dust.[29]

Through this careful choreography Gregory had transformed the funeral of the reclusive Macrina into a public celebration of the entire family. In the past, family members had lived in seclusion on their estate, but now they would reside together in public in the family tomb, itself in a shrine dedicated to the Forty Martyrs. On the estate Macrina could mope about as a forlorn spinster pining for her lost fiancé, but in her tomb she would be remembered as the bride of Christ. The funeral had marked the transition from private asceticism to public commemoration. In his biography Gregory would transform his sister's life in the same way. Macrina had been the historian of the family's traditions, but Gregory now turned her life into a history of the family. The source had become the text, and Gregory would now rewrite it to highlight the entire family rather than only his sister. His sister's life had become another of the family's traditions.

Macrina could become the focus for such a family history only if she were joined with Emmelia, since they had shared in raising the other children and had maintained contact with the other family members. Gregory could not overlook that close association, and in his biography, as in their lives, the two were always linked. When Macrina had suffered from a tumor on her neck that threatened to spread "near her heart," she had been healed after she asked Emmelia to make the sign of the cross over it. The scar that remained was hence both "a memorial of divine intervention" and a reminder of her mother's loving assistance. Only her mother's loving touch had been able to save Macrina's broken heart.[30]

At Macrina's funeral some of the other virgins were still apprehensive about the bright robe that Gregory had provided, and one of them suggested that the robe be covered with "a dark cloak that once belonged to your mother." Mother and daughter were then buried side by side, in accordance with their own request that "the companionship they had had in life not be broken in death." In the end, Macrina was still wrapped in her mother's cloak and embraced within her mother's love. Rather than becoming merely an exemplar of female asceticism, a personification of her brother's theology, and a memorial to her family's prominence, Macrina's life should in addition have become a paradigm of the devotion between a mother and a daughter. From womb to tomb they had remained together. Even death could not interrupt the intimacy of their lives together.[31]

Chapter 7

Was God the Father Married?
Virginity and Social Extinction

In Cappadocia and Pontus many people were living austerely and simply with restricted diets and meager clothing, supporting themselves through manual labor, participating in prayers and celebrating the liturgy. These people were not ascetics or monks. They were simply the majority of the population in the region, struggling to survive in a poor rural economy while also fulfilling some of the expectations of their Christian commitment. Throughout the Roman empire most people were born to poverty and hardship. In contrast, Macrina and Emmelia belonged to a wealthy local family, and for all the simplicity of their ascetic lifestyle they had never had to worry about starving. In fact, during the food shortage in the region during the later 360s Peter was able to supply provisions for the many people who had showed up at their estate "because of its reputation for generosity," and Macrina rescued starving women from the roadways and invited them to join their retreat. Even during their years of austere living their estate had continued to produce a large enough surplus to help feed neighbors.[1]

The characteristic that distinguished religious asceticism from a common life of deprivation and marginal survival was the choice. Because their poverty was involuntary, ordinary people did not receive credit as venerated ascetics. The decision, the vow, the voluntary choice, made the difference. Basil once defined a virgin precisely in terms of her choice and her willingness. "That woman is called a virgin who has willingly attached herself to the Lord, separated herself from marriage, and preferred a life of holiness." Among the women living at Macrina's community was Vetiana, "one of those people noted for their wealth, family, and physical beauty." She was the daughter of a distinguished senator who had served as prefect of Constantinople and prefect of the East, and she had married a general who served on the eastern frontier. Since she was still young when she lost her husband, "she made the great Macrina her guardian and the teacher of her widowhood." Like Macrina herself, her mother, Emmelia, and the other members of their family, Vetiana too had willingly decided to accept a life of seclusion and denial. For these wealthy aristocrats the adoption of an ascetic life was an indulgence.[2]

Choosing an Identity

This emphasis on the vital significance of the voluntary decision has important implications for modern interpretations of Christian asceticism in the ancient world. One concerns the personal motives for the adoption of an ascetic lifestyle. Since the choice was so vital, asceticism should be seen as yet another instrument of self-fashioning, of finding and presenting an identity. Remaining unmarried, becoming a virgin and an ascetic, was for both men and women the deliberate initiation of a long process of self-representation.

Treatises about virginity consistently emphasized the careful discipline and grooming required to undertake and then sustain an ascetic lifestyle of effortless purity. One treatise even encouraged parents to take the lead in helping their daughters protect their chastity by monitoring their conversations with men and their attendance at vigils, assemblies, and funerals. Fathers were also expected to limit the amount of food that their chaste sons were allowed to have "close at hand."[3]

Basil, the bishop of Ancyra during the mid-fourth century, composed another treatise about living as a virgin. His unrelentingly tiresome discussion focused on the interactions between women and men in order to suggest restrictions for female virgins: "a woman's body has acquired an unspeakable power toward a man, and it spontaneously attracts a man's body for joining." Basil then analyzed at length all the temptations inherent in the senses. He even commented on diet and the dangers in specific foods like seeds, vegetables, and herbs. He conceded that a virgin, "the bride of the Lord," could talk with "friends of the Groom," but only under strict supervision. Basil had been educated in medicine and may have been a doctor before he became a cleric, and his medical training showed. His treatise on virginity described more a medical regimen of hygiene and dietetics than an ascetic discipline, and he sometimes seems to have considered women's virginity as a chronic illness requiring quarantine from men rather than as an honored lifestyle. Basil of Ancyra offered advice both to other bishops who were concerned about modulating the behavior of ascetics and to the ascetics and virgins themselves who wanted to discipline their behavior and mold themselves. His and other treatises about virginity and asceticism that appeared during the fourth century were the equivalents of the medical treatises of the famous doctor Galen from the second century. In them medicine had defined "a way of living, a reflective mode of relation to oneself, to one's body, to food, to wakefulness and sleep, to the various activities, and to the environment. Medicine was expected to propose, in the form of regimen, a voluntary and rational structure of conduct." The adoption of virginity or an ascetic lifestyle now offered the same rewards, both a personal sense of self and a mode of public presentation.[4]

Gregory of Nyssa also composed a treatise in praise of virginity. In part he wrote from a sense of regret. In his treatise he mentioned the attractions of marriage, among them the desire for delightful companionship and the opportunity to enjoy a distinguished family, sufficient wealth, and affection. At one time those attractions had impressed Gregory enough that he had apparently married. As a result, as he wrote this treatise he had to concede that he himself could not share in the blessings of being unmarried. He knew firsthand the difficulties of maintaining an ascetic life: "success is not simple." Since the preservation of virginity involved more than the mere denial of sexual stirrings, all strong emotions were threats as dangerous as any sexual lusts. "Anger is adultery, greediness is adultery, envy is adultery, and so are malice, enmity, slander, and hatred." Gregory expected ascetics to walk a fine line, denying themselves the pleasures of eating and drinking but not succumbing to "excessive severity" either. An appropriate comparison was with the decoration of a house. A homeowner wanted the beds and tables to be tidy and orderly so that he could receive guests with confidence. In the same manner ascetics, despite their reclusiveness, were rearranging their lives so that they might present themselves to others.[5]

Like rhetoricians and athletes, ascetics trained in order to present themselves for public scrutiny. Throughout their lives educated men "needed to keep practicing the arts that made them men. Rhetoric was a calisthenics of manhood." Asceticism was a similar calisthenics of Christian spirituality for both men and women. Just as rhetoricians learned the techniques of public speaking, so ascetics had to master "the gymnastics of silence." It is not surprising that Gregory compared his sister Macrina to "a blameless athlete." For all its appropriation of the language of discipline, submission, and obedience, the adoption of an ascetic lifestyle represented an assertion of the self. Ordinary poverty was unfortunate, worthy of pity; voluntary poverty was honorable, deserving of respect. Rather than vanishing into total seclusion, many people embraced asceticism as a way of presenting themselves to others.[6]

Choosing a Gender

A second implication of the significance of the choice to remain unmarried highlights the awareness of other attainable alternatives. For women the options were quite limited. Their traditional roles were within families, first as daughters and sisters, then, after marriage, as wives, mothers, and grandmothers. Even though the legacy of families and the line of succession were transmitted primarily, if not exclusively, through the men, women were necessary for procreation, for supplying the sons. Within their husbands' families the primary functions of wives were reproduction and raising children. Basil once requested assistance on behalf of "a most distinguished woman" who was responsible for some "orphans." This woman had presumably recently become a widow and was now looking after her fatherless children. Significantly, Basil asked for this help primarily in order to "preserve the honor that is owed to the grandfather of these orphans." In Basil's perception, this mother was still looking after the interests of the man in the family, and these orphans now represented the grandfather's hopes for continuing his family's reputation.[7]

Gender determined a woman's role in the household and hence in wider society. When women opted not to become wives or to continue as mothers, they not only rejected their traditional roles. They also renounced their gendered identity as women. After her refusal to marry Macrina had such an odd position that other family members had difficulty describing it and her. Both her mother and her brother searched about for the proper terminology or analogy. The presence of Basil the Elder had defined Emmelia as a wife and mother and Macrina as a daughter. After his death, however, the relationship between Emmelia and Macrina became nebulous, no longer readily categorized as that between parent and child. As an acknowledgment of their closeness, Emmelia noted that she sometimes thought she had never terminated her pregnancy with Macrina, "carrying her inside herself continuously." In her perspective, since she had never in fact given birth, Macrina was not so much her daughter, as simply another manifestation of herself. With regard to Macrina at least, Emmelia had always been a half-virgin, pregnant but not a mother. "Birth" was not an aspect of their relationship. Since they were no longer mother and daughter to each other, their relationship had become ungendered.[8]

In a similar fashion Gregory of Nyssa could barely allow himself to acknowledge Macrina as his sister. In his biography of Macrina he described her as a "sister" only in the context of the activities of Peter, their youngest brother. Peter had been raised by "the oldest of his sisters," he had "always looked to his sister," and he had "worked with his sister and his mother." But Gregory could not bring himself to describe Macrina directly as his own sister. At the beginning of the biography he noted that "the virgin whom I am recalling was not an outsider to my family, but a descendant of the same parents as I." Although Gregory was proud to claim Macrina as a sibling, he also sensed that by remaining a virgin and becoming an ascetic she had given up her feminine gender. Basil of Ancyra had actually encouraged virgins to act like men by presenting a "masculine appearance" and lowering their voices, and he had suggested that through their asceticism they could become "equal to men." Gregory seems to have recognized this transformation in Macrina. "The subject of this narrative is a woman, if indeed she was a 'woman.' I do not know if it is proper to use this name from nature for someone who has surpassed nature." In part Gregory was making a clever connection here between the gender-bending character of Macrina's life and the genre-bending character of this biography. Just as this *Life* had exceeded "the dimensions of a letter," so Macrina had surpassed the boundaries of womanhood. The *Life* mimicked her life. In addition, Gregory seems to have implicitly acknowledged that somehow Macrina had converted herself into a man. Throughout this biography Gregory always seemed to be on the verge of identifying Macrina as his big brother.[9]

Since his sister Gorgonia had fulfilled conventional roles for women by becoming a wife and a mother, Gregory of Nazianzus had had to struggle to associate her life with the virtues of virginity. In contrast, since his sister Macrina had remained unmarried, Gregory of Nyssa had no difficulty in presenting her as a model virgin. But the price he paid for that certainty about her virginity was uncertainty about her gender. Women who voluntarily adopted some sort of sexual asceticism, whether virginity, continence within a marriage, or celibacy as young widows, had hence renounced both their traditional roles within families and their gendered identities as women.[10]

Aristocratic men who adopted sexual asceticism raised some similar concerns about their gendered identities. One example of the assumption of feminine characteristics by men concerns bishops and their sees. Just as the language of marriage was used to describe the relationship between Jesus Christ the Groom and female virgins, so it was also applied to the relationship between bishops and their sees. A see was a bishop's "wife." This analogy of course emphasized both the sacredness and the permanence of the relationship between a bishop and his church. But it nevertheless also presupposed a reversal of the usual expectations about residence. Everyday society emphasized the husband's hometown, while episcopal society highlighted the hometown of the "wife." Rather than the wife moving to join her husband's family, in this case the bishop moved to join his church's congregation.

The departure of a son to become a bishop elsewhere could be disturbing. Gorgonia had left Cappadocia to join her husband, probably in Iconium; so had her cousin Amphilochius, when he became bishop and joined his new "wife," his church at Iconium. Nonna and Gregory the Elder seem not to have been unduly disturbed by their daughter's move to join her husband's family. In contrast, Amphilochius the Elder, Nonna's brother, had been truly dismayed that his son was leaving him to join a new family, his congregation at Iconium. Not only did he think that he was now losing his son's support for his old age. His complaints to his nephew Gregory of Nazianzus also seemed to hint that he thought his son should have married a local bride, that is, that he should have become bishop at Nazianzus. Instead, Amphilochius had left to join his new spouse, his church, in Iconium. In this respect men who became bishops often acted like newly married women.[11]

But they had not lost their manliness. Local aristocratic men had always had a large menu of options for how to live and present themselves. Within their families they were sons and then husbands and fathers, while outside families they could aspire to various public roles. These roles were typically supplements to their roles within families, and not alternatives to them. For centuries men had been able to choose to become local teachers like Basil the Elder, local municipal magistrates like Gregory the Elder before his conversion, noted hunters like Naucratius, imperial magistrates like Caesarius, or soldiers like Nicobulus the Elder. The expansion of Christianity provided yet more alternatives, since they could then enter the clergy or choose to become ascetics and virgins.

A decision to remain unmarried hence had different consequences for women and men. Gender identity is a social construct, arbitrated at the intersection of personal choices and the shared expectations of communities. Because women's traditional roles were defined within families, women who did not become wives and mothers seemed to have lost their gender. Unmarried women might even be classified as men. In contrast, unmarried men did not automatically lose their gendered identity as men. Even though they did not become husbands and fathers, they could still participate in other public roles outside families. Unmarried men could serve as soldiers, municipal magistrates, teachers, or imperial magistrates. They could become clerics and bishops, even if they then sometimes had to move to a new town. Basil remained unmarried, but still taught as a rhetorician, served as a cleric and bishop, interacted with emperors and imperial magistrates, and delivered public sermons. A decision to remain unmarried did not preclude men from the traditional masculine roles acquired through holding secular magistracies or clerical offices. To remove themselves from public life, to lose their gender, they also had to make a conscious decision to adopt seclusion.

Choosing Immortality

The significance of the choice, the conscious decision, should hence influence our interpretation of ascetics' intentions in terms of both their underlying motives and their consideration of other options. Self-representation and gender identity were complementary aspects of the process of coming to terms with virginity. A final implication concerns ascetics' awareness of the practical consequences for themselves and their families.

Classical philosophers had long considered marriage and children as a means of achieving immortality, for the human race in general, for cities that needed new citizens, and for families. Families and their names lived on in the unbroken sequence of successive generations. At weddings orators were expected to praise precisely these hopes for the future by mentioning Zeus' original plan. "Zeus was pleased to create man as nearly immortal by always providing the successive generations of a family to escort the passage of time." "Marriage provides us with immortality." Some Christian authors likewise linked marriage and procreation with immortality. Gregory of Nazianzus once compared marriage and virginity in a long poem. Even though in the end he awarded the prize to virginity, he still praised the rewards of marriage. After Adam and Eve were forced from paradise, "marriage was a bulwark against extinction." Procreation was the key to survival. "Death made mankind transient, children made it steadfast."[12]

Even before the rise of Christianity, however, not everyone had acknowledged these benefits of marriage. In one comprehensive interpretation of dreams, in fact, marriage and death signified each other. Virginity hence seemed to offer another possibility for achieving immortality. Among Christian virgins St. Thecla would become an influential model. The apocryphal account of her life had already presented her weighing of two options to achieve immortality, either through marriage, children, and a future resurrection, or through the adoption of virginity. St. Thecla choose virginity. So did many other Christian ascetics.[13]

Gregory of Nyssa too endorsed virginity, even if with a surprisingly mournful, almost pessimistic attitude about its value. When his family's tomb had been uncovered during Macrina's funeral, he had been embarrassed to glance at his parents' decomposed corpses, "the common shame of human nature." Graves reminded him of the closeness of death. "When men look at the graves of their ancestors, they experience an unlimited sadness that is linked to their lives." Every child was simply more fuel to be consumed by "the power of death." "Physical procreation is a starting point for death rather than life." In Gregory's thinking, the only way to confront the power of death was by stopping the generation of more children. "Corruption begins through birth, and those people who have stopped procreation through their virginity had established within themselves a limit to death." Remaining unmarried was hence a strategy for overcoming death: "virginity is always realized eschatology."[14]

But to save themselves these ascetics doomed their own families. The price for overcoming death was the annulment of their families. Eudoxius was a Cappadocian who became bishop of Constantinople in 360. During his earlier episcopacy at Antioch he had once promoted the doctrine that Jesus Christ was only a creature, created by God. Eudoxius had accepted this formulation that stressed the language of creation because the alternative viewpoint that stressed the language of birth was just too distasteful to think about. As a result, he ridiculed the idea that Jesus Christ was the Son of God the Father. "God was not a 'father,' because he did not have a 'son.' If [there is to be] a son, then it is necessary that there also be a woman, an exchange of vows, conjugal intercourse, verbal flatteries, and finally a small natural organ for procreating." In a classic example of cultural avoidance, Eudoxius declined to accept an answer, because he did not want to contemplate a particular question. In his estimation, the existence of a Father and a Son would have necessarily implied that God had had to marry, and it would have raised the question of whether God had a penis.[15]

Eudoxius' opponents were equally aghast, but primarily at the disrespect implied in even raising the issue. For them, God had simply had a Son while remaining unmarried. Gregory of Nyssa candidly conceded this transcendent paradox, "that virginity is found in a Father who has a Son." As a result, God's behavior was a model simultaneously both for ascetic virgins and for married couples committed to extending their families' legacies by producing heirs. But local aristocrats could not imitate this paradoxical dual outcome. They could choose to have legitimate children by marrying, or they could choose to remain unmarried. Only God could both not marry and have a Son.[16]

For extending families' legacies, sons were more important than daughters. Decisions by daughters to become virgins might place restrictions on the marriage alliances that families could make with other families, but similar decisions by sons were more consequential. "For young males, the potential fathers of noble families, to meditate sexual renunciation was to meditate social extinction." In his extant letters Basil consoled parents only for the deaths of sons or grandsons, and not of daughters. The death of one young son was a burden for the parents, but also a threat to the continuity of the family. This son had been "the heir of a famous household, the prop of the family, the hope of the fatherland, and the offspring of pious parents." After his death, "a great and distinguished family collapsed." Sons were images of their fathers: "when I talked with your most cherished sons, I thought I saw you yourself." In Basil's estimation, daughters seem to have been disposable, while sons were vital for the continuity of families. Without sons, a family was "bereft of heirs."[17]

Despite Basil's recognition of the importance of sons for sustaining family legacies, he and other men choose to remain unmarried. Some families were deeply distraught. Relatives once approached one young man who had entered a monastery in Cappadocia and begged him "to claim his parents' estate and to marry." The Cappadocian Fathers have a name as pregnant with irony as God the Father. Basil, Gregory of Nazianzus, Peter, even Gregory of Nyssa who seems to have regretted his marriage and did not have any children, all choose social extinction for their families.[18]

One way of measuring continuity within families was through the usage of names. Within families names were suggestive, both manifestations of links with the past and expressions of hopes for the future. Gregory of Nazianzus once commented on the potential inherent in the meaning of the name of Basil's mother, Emmelia, "harmony." "She was named for what she was, or she became what she had been named." In Gregory's own family names often memorialized ancestors. In his extended family his cousin Amphilochius, later bishop of Iconium, had been named after his father, Amphilochius (the Elder). Of the children in Gregory's immediate family, his sister, Gorgonia, was named after her maternal grandmother, while he was named after his father. Since Gregory's father had been quite old at the time of his marriage to Nonna, he belonged to an earlier generation.

Gregory's name was hence effectively a simultaneous echo of two generations, grandfather's and father's. This practice of recycling parents' and
grandparents' names continued into subsequent generations. The oldest of
the three daughters of Gorgonia and Alypius was Alypiana, named after
her father. Another daughter was Eugenia, whose name publicized her social
standing of "good birth." A third daughter was Nonna, named after her
maternal grandmother. The oldest son of Alypiana and Nicobulus (the
Elder) was Nicobulus (the Younger). These onomastic tags were bookmarks
in the family's history, each name a reminder of a whole sequence of hom-
onymous ancestors. By reusing these names descendants could ensure that
memories of their ancestors lived on in their own careers and activities.
Because each generation was a reflection and a continuation of previous
generations, the family seemed to remain stable even as family members
died and were replaced. The sequence of ancestors was uniquely linear, while
the family itself, through the replacement of generations, was a repeatable
cycle.[19]

The names of the children in Basil's family were similarly respectful
of the past. Macrina, the first daughter, was named after her paternal grandmother, and Basil, the first son, after his father. Like the first daughter and
the first son in Gregory of Nazianzus' family, Macrina and Basil memorialized their ancestors through their names. The next son was Naucratius,
"ship commander," who defied the prediction of his name to become a
hunter in the mountains. Another son was Gregory (of Nyssa), who most
likely had received his name in memory of Gregory (Thaumaturgus), the
saint with whose cult his father's family had close ties in Pontus. Since an
uncle in Cappadocia was also named Gregory, the name was presumably
common likewise in his mother's family. The youngest son was Peter, whose
name recalled the most prominent of Jesus' original apostles. Peter was "a
very common name for sons of believers." This generation of Basil's family
had had so many sons that their names could honor both their ancestors in
their own family and their spiritual Christian ancestors.[20]

Even as they established links among successive generations, names
were also reminders of traditions and expectations within families. A name
conferred a responsibility. In addition to her public name Macrina had the
secret name of Thecla, after the young girl who had decided to become a
virgin upon hearing the preaching of the apostle Paul. This secret name
defined Macrina's future, since it "previewed her life and indicated that
she would make the same choice as that of her namesake." In the family of
Gregory of Nazianzus the names of the three children were a palimpsest of

different eras and perspectives. Gorgonia's name may have been a legacy within her family, but it also carried overtones of an older link with the frightful Gorgons of Greek mythology: "those who looked at a Gorgon turned into stone." Caesarius had been given an imperial name, reminiscent of the presence of Roman rule in Cappadocia. In fact, perhaps it is possible to speculate that his name had itself contributed to Caesarius' ambition of serving in the imperial administration, as if he too were only trying to live up to the destiny implied by his name. Gregory's name was of course a legacy from his father; but because it had been revealed to his pious mother in a dream, his name furthermore implied a clear Christian association. The names of the three children hence reflected successive phases in Cappadocian society, its acceptance of Greek culture, its incorporation into the Roman empire, and its embrace of Christianity. The names given to this generation of Gregory's family were an epitome in three words of the entire history of Cappadocia during the previous centuries.[21]

Through their names the generation of the Cappadocian Fathers and their siblings had still carefully preserved these ancestral connections. But since the maintenance of these family names required a new generation of sons and daughters, their generation also marked the nominal end of their families. Gregory of Nazianzus' family had some descendants through Gorgonia's daughters and grandchildren. Basil's family apparently had some descendants through his sisters' children. But after their marriages these sisters had effectively joined their husbands' families, and their offspring were the descendants of those other families. None of the sons in these two families had any children, and only one of them, Gregory of Nyssa, had even married. The reluctance among the sons to marry and have children signaled the end to both of these families.

For centuries local aristocratic families had exchanged their daughters in marriages as a form of sociable currency that created social connections and obligations. A marriage was as much an alliance between families as a union between a young man and a young woman. As an indication of these priorities, in a typical wedding oration the panegyrist would praise the distinctions of the families before he mentioned the qualities of the groom and bride. Now, because of these exhortations to virginity and asceticism, churches and monasteries collected more and more of these young people as clerics, monks, and nuns, and removed them from circulation among families. Churches and monasteries also began to accumulate other resources from families, their wealth and estates. The primary heir in Gregory's family was the church he and his father had constructed at Nazianzus. Macrina had turned over her share of her family's possessions to the administration of a cleric. Basil's possessions had most likely gone to the Basilias, his foundation for the ill and poor. In both families the rise of asceticism and a preference for virginity had ended the direct male lineages.[22]

Basil's regulations had helped to institutionalize monasticism in central Asia Minor, and his heirs would include an ecclesiastical foundation rather than his own descendants. Although he and Gregory of Nazianzus had inherited their fathers' names, an institution and not a son inherited Basil's name. The families of both Basil and Gregory ended with their generation. It had been their choice.

Friendship

Gregory of Nyssa was reluctant about marriage in part because of all the unforeseen vacillations. At the moment of his greatest happiness the groom would find himself obsessed by "uncertainty about the future." His new wife might die during childbirth; he himself might die while traveling and leave his wife a hapless widow; they would both age and fade. In the face of this bleak uneasiness, "there is only one escape from these evils: nothing that changes is to be attached to the soul." Gregory was looking for a stability and permanence in his life that would reflect the stability and permanence associated with God's divine existence, and he finally concluded that virginity, remaining unmarried, was the answer. Yet at some point he had disregarded his own misgivings in order to follow the feelings of his heart. His marriage was certainly not the only voluntary relationship in Gregory's life. Like Basil and Gregory of Nazianzus, Gregory of Nyssa had many friends. Men inherited their families and relatives from birth, but they chose their friends. Because friendships were the results of decisions, they were often more revealing about men's selves than were their family relationships.[1]

Just as modern scholars argue about the extent of genuine feelings among family members, so they disagree about the nature of friendship in the ancient world. The traditionally strong emphasis in classical studies on political and diplomatic history has often subtly influenced readings of personal relationships by interpreting them in terms of pragmatic obligations and calculated cooperation. In this perspective, friendships were primarily instrumental. In contrast, the more recent emphasis on sentimentality within the ancient family has influenced interpretations of relationships outside the family too. In this perspective, friendships were primarily emotional. Chapter 8 discusses these contrasting interpretations in terms of the letters of Basil and Gregory of Nazianzus. Even as they followed the conventions of epistolography, Basil and Gregory used letters as vehicles for expressing their feelings. For them, the protocol of letters enhanced, rather than repressed, emotional contacts. Since letters and friendships were often virtually synonymous, in a similar fashion the conventions and obligations of friendships assisted, rather than precluded, expressions of true affection

and generosity. Form and feeling, obligations and emotions, were supportive rather than contradictory.

Chapter 9 discusses Basil's and Gregory's friends. Men defined themselves in their friendships. Not only did friendships mark choices, acts of
will; these relationships were also public, as men revealed their decisions to
their community, their family, and their other friends. Every friendship was
another aspect of self-representation, as men fashioned and then presented
their relationships in public. Examining their relationships with friends
provides an opportunity to evaluate Basil's and Gregory's notions of themselves. For all the similarities between their backgrounds and educations,
they behaved and responded quite differently when interacting with others.

Chapter 10 examines their mutual friendship. Although for decades
each was the other's best friend, these differences in the ways they corresponded with their other friends might have raised doubts about the success of their friendship. Sustaining a friendship was inherently difficult. The
important apprehension when evaluating ancient friendships is not the
friction between obligations and emotions, but the tension between permanence and change. Friendships presupposed consistency in values, character,
beliefs, and devotion. Friendships were supposed to be stable enough to
become the foundation of men's essential identities. Over the decades, however, both Gregory and Basil would change in response to new situations
and unforeseen opportunities. Not surprisingly, their own friendship eventually collapsed. While Basil was seemingly indifferent, Gregory agonized
over the end of their friendship for years, even after Basil's death. Late in his
life, Gregory was still trying to reassure himself that, despite the end of their
friendship, he had always been true and loyal. As he thought about his
friendship with Basil, he was searching for his own consistent self, trying
to find a trajectory of permanence and stability that would give meaning
to his entire life.

Chapter 8

"Your Soul in Your Letter": The Emotional Life of Letters

Letters, and especially collections of letters, are valuable historical sources. The surviving literary legacy of the Cappadocian Fathers includes over six hundred letters, over half of which were composed by Basil and most of the remainder by Gregory of Nazianzus. These letters provide the most detailed accounts of events in their adult careers, primarily during the 370s for Basil and the 370s and 380s for Gregory. A series of letters could become the equivalent of an ongoing journal or a memoir, as Basil himself admitted to one of his steady correspondents: "nothing prevents my letters from being a diary of my life." Because of this more intimate setting, letters, especially private letters, would seem to have offered Basil and Gregory opportunities for personal introspection and confidential confession that were not available in public sermons and abstract theological treatises.[1]

Gregory also used another literary genre for recording his inner feelings and deepest thoughts. Throughout his adult life, and in particular during his last decade, he evaluated his life in autobiographical poems. "In my writings I have followed another path too by recording a bit of my calamities in verses." The composition of poems presupposed great respect for all the constraints of the genre, among them the demands of various meters, the requirements of appropriate vocabulary, and the expectations about different dialects. In the ancient world there were similar requirements about the composition of letters. Gregory once explained the protocol of epistolography to a grandnephew. The three necessary characteristics of good letters were concision, clarity, and charm. The length of letters had to match the significance of the subject matter; their presentation was to be conversational rather than oratorical, comprehensible by both the learned and the uneducated; and their style was to be modest, with only a few gnomic proverbs, witticisms, and literary tropes. Even private letters were expected to follow the rules.[2]

Formalities and Feelings

These constraints seem to cast one shadow over the usefulness of these letters for historical analysis, since they suggest that authors were concerned more about protocol than candor, more about form than substance and emotion. A related handicap is a consequence of how authors interpreted and applied these requirements. Often the letters of Basil and Gregory were both flamboyantly prolix and maddeningly oblique. Some letters seem to contain nothing but platitudes written according to "the rule of friendship." Basil and Gregory rarely mentioned the names or offices or titles of their correspondents, and they often only hinted at the events or issues they went on to ponder. Other letters that discussed more substantial issues were still often hedged in conventional flattery, paralyzing politeness, commonplace sentiments, distracting references to classical literature and biblical texts, baffling circumlocutions, and artificial analogies. In one letter Basil acknowledged his verbosity: "you see how I am going around in a circle, hesitant and reluctant to reveal the reason why I am composing these words." Rather than simply saying how pleased he was to receive a letter, Basil turned his happiness into a metaphor that was so elaborate as to become disingenuous: "like water sprinkled in the mouths of race horses who furiously pant at high noon as they inhale dust in the middle of the track, so [welcome] was your letter." Rather then writing because of whim or impulse, Gregory claimed that he needed to wait for "another pretext for a letter," and that the initiative came from outside himself: "if it is necessary to tell the truth, you supplied this pretext through your respect and your invitation."[3]

What the letters give with one hand they have apparently taken with the other. Many of the letters were very formal, sometimes almost formulaic school exercises. As a result, they seem trivial, repetitive, even inadequate. Basil himself once complained that letters were "lifeless." His preference was for face-to-face conversations, when he could "explain the particulars clearly in person and elaborate them in detail." Even correspondence between friends of long standing lacked the spontaneity and self-disclosure that seem to guarantee authentic relationships. Their friendships appeared somehow always to have been at the beginning, just getting started, in the making. Their letters were tentative, like repeated letters of introduction between men who had in fact known each other for years. Both fulsome compliments and unexpected reticence seem to have sucked the possibility of true feelings and candid insights out of the letters. In this sense, the protocol of letters seems to pose an additional obstacle for historians inter-ested in the emotional attachments between correspondents.[4]

Even more problematic than this dismissive characterization of the let-ters is a common deduction about the nature of the relationships between correspondents. It is all too easy to make the relationships resemble the letters, and to characterize friendships too as rigid and formal. The letters seem only to chart political alliances and networks of support and to derive from one-dimensional friendships based entirely on mutual interests. Such friendships seem to have been merely manipulative, instrumental, or utili-tarian, in which ulterior motives and secret schemes had taken priority over genuine sentiments and deep feelings. The more precisely modern historians dissect the political implications of these letters, the more the expressions of sympathy, the affirmations of loyalty and friendliness, and the concern about correspondents' health and family can appear to have been calculat-ing and insincere. The dominant characteristic of these letters, and therefore of the relationships between correspondents, becomes affectation rather than affection.[5]

One method for sidestepping these restrictions is to insist that the cor-respondents were truly sincere in their affections. Genuine emotions could accompany requests and favors despite the formalities and protocol. Another approach opens up still more opportunities. Rather than highlighting a dis-tinction, even a tension, between form and feeling, it is possible to identify the two. "There was no sincerity without form and no form without sincer-ity." The protocol of the exchange of letters replicated the expectations of the friendships that it supported in two important ways. Protocol served to overcome some of the stubborn barriers that interrupted friendships, and it acted as a means for facilitating rather than inhibiting intimacy and emo-tional connections.[6]

Two obstacles to sustaining a friendship were geographical distance and temporal interludes. Because transportation was slow, communication was equally slow and unreliable. The hopefulness in letters that friends might visit was evenly matched by the listing of excuses of why they could not travel and visit. When men did decide to visit, they were at the mercy of the weather and terrain. Usually they visited each other on special occa-sions, such as at the festivals of saints or ecclesiastical councils, or they met in passing while on their way elsewhere. Even during the benign seasons the highlands of Cappadocia and eastern Asia Minor made travel over land difficult. When men could not travel themselves, they relied upon couriers to carry their letters. Although Basil and Gregory usually praised their couriers, they could not always find men going in the right directions, and unreliable couriers were a nuisance. The end result was that often friends exchanged only a few letters a year, and met less often. Absence and delay were the normal state of affairs.

Their letters enabled them to transcend these handicaps. "I exchange letters on every occasion," Basil noted with a hint of scolding to a correspondent who had neglected to write to him. Letters shortened the distances between friends. "Friendship unites what is separated." "We who are widely separated by an interval of space are joined together through our discourse in letters." Letters were men's "shadows," the only form of conversation available for those who were separated. A letter was a better representation of a man than any painting could be. "I saw your soul in your letter," Basil wrote to one correspondent. Letters also made the intervening time intervals vanish. The Cappadocian Fathers had much time on their hands, especially during the winter. Blanketed by snow sometimes for months on end, hidden in their homes like hibernating animals, all they could do was talk. "Flowers blossom in spring, ears of corn bloom in summer, apples ripen in autumn; the fruit of winter is conversation." Men therefore had to be careful in their letters not to write anything amiss or anything too suggestive, since their correspondents would likely brood upon it for weeks, "fantasizing during the months when leaves fall." But despite a lapse of weeks or months, the give and take of letters pretended to be immediate and prompt. Men resumed correspondence without missing a beat, always assuming that their friends were still interested and concerned: "after a long interval I address you whom I prefer over anyone else." When men met again after long separations, they needed polite salutations to revive their friendship. "Did you have a good trip? Where did you come from? Why? Did you come on your own initiative, or is there some reason for your visit?" Letters likewise lubricated a friendship. The awkwardness of reacquaintance dissolved in the recitation of the proper formulas.[7]

An exchange of letters maintained a sense of emotional intimacy over space and time. Reciprocity was an important component of friendships, and in an exchange of correspondence the significant feature was not necessarily the content of the letters, as rather simply the exchange. "The gift that is offered to you in a letter is the letter itself." Men did not need to state their feelings explicitly, because the letters were themselves tokens of affection and interest. Gregory once thanked one of his correspondents for the "testimonials of love" he had sent. Along with the letters men often sent small gifts, such as herbs, dried fruit, or candles. Like these apparently trivial gifts, the letters carried an emotional significance that far exceeded the value of the information they communicated. Correspondents hence sometimes complained about the length of the letters they received, not necessarily because they wanted to know more, but because they wanted to feel more loved and more prized. Even a few words, like a few herbs, were as precious as gold. More words were better. Basil admitted that before reading a letter, he looked at its length in order to estimate how much love he could expect: "I love this letter as much as it surpasses the [usual] size." Rather than simply conveying feelings, the letters were the physical representations of the sentiments.[8]

Many of the letters also contained requests. Patronage was an important duty of local aristocrats, and they often represented or introduced people to others, both long-standing friends and new friends such as imperial magistrates. The exercise of patronage was important for asserting hierarchies of influence, because by requesting and granting favors men verified their relative standing and influence. The exercise of patronage also reaffirmed friendships among peers. Friendships had to be seen to exist, and an exchange of favors was a visible indication of mutual affection. Exchanging favors and letters was simultaneously an exchange of feelings. Gregory once decided the best way of indicating his loyalty to the bishop who had replaced him at Constantinople was by sending a letter and making a request. "In order to give a demonstration of our confidence in each other, I am sending this request to you, and may you enthusiastically agree with me."[9]

Favors and letters were indications of openness and candor, a form of self-disclosure. Men made themselves vulnerable when they sent letters and submitted requests, since there was no guarantee that the recipient would reply with a letter or agree to the request. When Basil once wanted to learn about the doctrinal preferences of some clerics in Lycia, he suggested that the investigation be conducted at first "without any letters." A blind letter of inquiry would have been too intimate. Once Basil was sure of their orthodoxy, then he proposed sending a letter with an invitation to meet. Because a letter exposed the sender to the mercies of the recipient, a reply or a favor was an expression of warmth and devotion. Gregory asked one correspondent to open his heart by admitting a young man into his confidence, and he argued that this willingness would be "a reminder of our friendship." Letters were claims on correspondents' affections. "This is my first letter and my first request," Gregory wrote to one man; "all the more reason for you to grant my request."[10]

By establishing mutual obligations an exchange of letters maintained a sense of equality and complementarity. A friend may have had claims on another's generosity and he may have expected a return for his own benefactions, but he could neither request nor bestow favors with those expectations. "Our friendship is pure and guileless, because of our similar habits and similar pleasures." Friends were usually social and cultural equals, or at least pretended to be peers, but at any given moment their friendship was unequal and uneven, because one partner, having received a letter, was always expected to reply: a letter was a "whip" that compelled him to write in return. Receiving a letter put a man in second place, sending one, in first place. A common complaint in the letters was therefore about laziness or tardiness, since even in an intermittent correspondence hesitation might be a sign of failing interest or indifference: "if this letter is brief, it is nevertheless longer than silence." Silence was ominous. "If you have any regard for our friendship, it will become apparent in the letters you send." "From my letters know that I am your friend; from your silence, I know that you dislike me. Write; be a friend to your friends." Because a man could not allow a friendship to lapse while he still owed a letter, the obligations of replying by letter could effectively preserve friendships despite the miles and the months. Even as a letter satisfied the necessity of replying, it was an inducement for a response. A true friendship consisted of writing and receiving letters continuously.[11]

Friendship and an exchange of letters blended into each other. Reciprocity between friends, the expression of emotions, the giving of favors, the fulfillment of obligations: letters not only provided opportunities to perform these expectations of friendship, they also materialized them. Five hundred years later one reader thought he could still detect "Basil's personal disposition from his letters." Letters and requests were a form of self-disclosure, as tender as loving endearments, as intimate as a kiss. Letters were a friendship. Gregory once succinctly exemplified this identification when he sent a book to a correspondent as a "remembrance of friendship." It was no coincidence that the gift he choose was the *Letters* of Aristotle. As recompense all he expected was letters from his correspondent. The essence of their friendship was letters, old *Letters* and their own.[12]

Letters and Friendships

Discovering emotional commitments in, rather than behind or next to, the protocol of letters has significant implications for interpreting friendship in the ancient world. The protocol of letters merged with the protocol of friendships, and employing such formalities was first of all an indication of high regard for friendships. "In denying friendship formal bonds our society seems to undervalue love, not value it. . . . In all societies but our own, ceremonial trappings add to the meaning of friendship, they do not demonstrate its weakness." Friendship presupposed such formality and rituals that Gregory once referred to it as a tyranny: "how you tyrannize us with friendship!" Gregory was probably chuckling as he wrote that opening sentence. Because rules and expectations made friendships predictable and comfortable, they allowed men to be candid and affectionate.[13]

Another consequence was more disconcerting. Even as protocol minimized some handicaps to maintaining friendships, it accented others. One was self-consciousness. Protocol allowed and even encouraged men to discuss almost anything candidly, but only as long as they did so correctly. Men hesitated to write even as they knew that they must; in one letter Basil tried to decide between reluctance and necessity. Concern over appearances displaced reticence over subject matter.[14]

A second difficulty was rigidity. Because letters were so identified with friendship, they made it difficult to distinguish a category of lesser acquaintances. In their letters the Cappadocian Fathers sometimes complained about various people they had encountered. Yet when they sent letters to those same people, they were consistently laudatory and flattering. Letters compelled men to compartmentalize, almost dichotomize their feelings. They could be critical about people when writing to others, but they were reluctant to criticize when writing directly to the same people. In one letter Gregory began by complaining about an episcopal election, but then suddenly stopped. "I will certainly not accuse your Piety. . . . I do not wish to annoy you at length, lest I appear to be burdensome right at the beginning of our friendship." In another letter Gregory gently reminded his correspondent of the limits of complaining. "It is necessary that those who offer friendly criticism do so without exceeding the boundaries of friendship."[15]

These concerns about self-consciousness and rigidity made letters sometimes difficult to interpret, even by recipients, since the slightest impropriety could be misconstrued. Bishop Eusebius of Caesarea once took offense to a letter in which Gregory had suggested how he might mend his relationship with Basil. Gregory had to explain that he had written that letter not "insolently," but "spiritually and philosophically." Since formalities and emotions merged together, the demands of protocol did not eliminate affection in friendships. But they did sometimes make it difficult to understand and interpret those feelings. Without the easy give and take of face-to-face encounters, only tight rules could preserve friendships over time and over the miles; but those same high expectations magnified the smallest of misstatements. Proprieties facilitated the expression of feelings and maintained friendships; improprieties, even merely perceived improprieties, could ruin them. Letters, carefully constructed and repeatedly exchanged, were the only guarantees of intimacy and closeness. "If you have any care for my friendship," Gregory once informed a correspondent, "it will be evident from your letters."[16]

Basil, Gregory, and their friends wrote and exchanged letters constantly, and the surviving letters no doubt represent only a small portion of their total correspondence. The protocol of letter writing, both the conventions of the letters themselves and the expectations of maintaining an exchange of letters, provided a means for them to share not just information and ideas, but also their feelings and emotions. Since letters created and sustained friendships, those friendships too presupposed an etiquette of behavior and feelings. Intimacy was a consequence of predictability and reliability, and a true friendship was supposed to be stable enough to be the enduring core of a man's identity and sense of self.

The greatest challenge to preserving a friendship was hence not the absence of emotions or the lack of intimacy, but alteration and innovation. With this sort of static and rigid perspective on friendship, the surprise is that particular friendships endured, rather than that they might fall apart. Growing up, maturing, making and admitting to mistakes, reacting to unexpected successes or misfortunes, seizing opportunities: all the usual vicissitudes of a normal life might threaten the stability and durability of a friendship.

Chapter 9
Best of Friends:
The Friends of Basil and
Gregory of Nazianzus

Basil and Gregory of Nazianzus were the best of friends. They had known each other probably since they were teenagers, when they met while studying together at Caesarea in Cappadocia. Basil had moved to Caesarea most likely from his hometown of Neocaesarea in Pontus, and Gregory from his hometown of Nazianzus. This friendship between the son of a grammarian and the son of a bishop flourished for decades, in part on the foundation of their mutual interests in classical culture and Christianity. Yet this friendship combined two men with very different perspectives on relationships and their potential for personal involvement. Those fundamental differences were also apparent in their friendships with others, including some friends they had in common.

Basil's Friends

In his later years Basil still had other friends from his youth. He once wrote to a provincial governor on behalf of an acquaintance. Basil had essentially inherited this friend "from our parents in the past." As a result, because their families had been friends, this man was "no different than a brother." Basil also interceded on behalf of another man with whom he had been a friend "from my early boyhood." In this case Basil was requesting this favor from a magistrate who was also a long-standing friend, since Basil had met him "at almost that same time."[1]

Other long-standing friends had been fellow students. Basil once complimented a man whom he had admired "ever since school lessons." Since he mentioned that he had known this man "since boyhood," perhaps they had studied together with Basil's father in Pontus. Basil wrote to another schoolmate with whom he had "in my youth" shared "one home, a single hearth, and the same teacher." Basil may have shared lodgings with this friend when they were students together at Caesarea. During their years as students at Athens, Basil and Gregory had befriended some "very chaste and unaggressive" comrades. Gregory later wrote a poem in honor of Hellenius, a long-standing friend whom he had met through Basil. Hellenius and Basil had presumably also been friends for a long time, and in the early 370s Hellenius delivered some letters to Basil. Hellenius was a native of Armenia. Armenians had been among the students taught by Basil's father, and some of them had gone on to study at Athens while Basil was there. So Basil had known Hellenius perhaps since they had been students together in Pontus, or perhaps since they had studied together in Athens.[2]

Some of Basil's friends were hence men he had known for decades, almost all of his life. Basil himself insisted upon his true feelings for these men. When introducing one he explained that their abiding fraternal affection was due "not to mere habit, but to a very precise disposition of friendship that cannot be surpassed." This longwinded and rather sterile description of their friendship suggests that Basil was protesting too much. Since schoolmates were also rivals, it would be difficult for them to become affectionate friends. At Athens some of Basil's acquaintances from his schooldays in Pontus had even tried to embarrass and intimidate him with aggressive questioning. According to Gregory of Nazianzus, although these fellow students had claimed to be friends, their true motivation had been envy at Basil's reputation.[3]

As a result, perhaps it is not surprising that in later years Basil's relationships with these boyhood chums and schoolmates appeared mechanical and stiffly formal. Admittedly, only one or two letters survive to characterize each friendship, but those letters consistently put the friendships into a context of perfunctory patronage. Usually Basil was making a request on behalf of an old friend, or he was making the request to a boyhood friend. The exchange of letters seemed to have generated its own emotional momentum. These men were still now friends because of the requests and the letters, and not necessarily because of some lingering youthful attachments. In fact, Basil at first thought that one old friend deserved to suffer for having slighted the provincial governor. Even though an exchange of letters implied the existence of affections, Basil no longer seemed to have any for these old friends. In only one case did he become nostalgic and wish "to return to our youth again in our memories." The protocol of letters may have been a vehicle for emotions, but with these old friends Basil seems to have let it substitute for his lack of feelings.[4]

The most prominent of these boyhood friends was Sophronius. Since Basil noted that they had shared "an intimacy from boyhood," and since Sophronius was a native of Cappadocia, perhaps they had been students together at Caesarea. During Basil's priesthood Sophronius was serving as a clerk in the imperial administration, and during Basil's episcopacy he served as a high-ranking magistrate at the emperor Valens' court. Of Basil's boyhood friends Sophronius had had probably the most impressive career in the imperial administration. Basil corresponded with Sophronius apparently quite often, but always very properly, even when writing about people and issues that affected both of them deeply. When he mentioned the problems facing their mutual friend Gregory of Nazianzus or the disastrous consequences of the division of their fatherland of Cappadocia, he still addressed Sophronius as "your Excellence," "your Perfection," "your Magnanimity," and "your Dignity." Basil commonly used such abstract titles when addressing imperial magistrates, but with Sophronius, a fellow Cappadocian and a boyhood friend, they left an impression of excessive distance and remoteness. Basil likewise appealed to Sophronius' affection for Gregory, his concern for his hometown of Caesarea, or his sympathy for the petitioner, but he rarely mentioned any personal connection with himself. At most he occasionally thanked Sophronius for the "great favor" that he also would receive from the magistrate's generosity.[5]

Only once did Basil explicitly discuss their friendship. During the mid-370s the imperial court of Valens resided at Antioch. Basil once wrote to complain that lobbyists had misled Sophronius: "flattery infects a friendship and destroys it." In his estimation, Sophronius should have remembered the weight of their long-standing friendship. "From my early youth to my current old age I have loved many, but I know that I preferred no one else than your Perfection for a friendship." Basil was of course worried about his reputation at the court of a hostile emperor like Valens, and in this case the issue was precisely his own loyalty to Sophronius. He therefore insisted that he had "never sinned against friendship." Only when he was trying to defend his own innocence before Sophronius did Basil appeal directly to their boyhood friendship.[6]

Despite this one cry of true concern Basil was always punctiliously correct and rather prim with Sophronius. In fact, even when he noted that he preferred no other's friendship, he still referred to Sophronius in the abstract, as "your Perfection." Basil's insistence upon propriety hence emerges even when he recalled his friendship with a man who, he claimed, had always been his most valued friend.

This aloof detachment was apparent also in other friendships. Before he became bishop of Caesarea, Basil's closest relationships had been with his mentor Eustathius, bishop of Sebasteia, and, of course, with Gregory of Nazianzus. Significantly, both relationships curdled during the first years of his episcopacy. During his episcopacy Basil's closest friendships were with three other bishops. Eusebius of Samosata had already become another mentor, Meletius of Antioch was a fellow metropolitan bishop who was also confronting the emperor Valens, and Amphilochius of Iconium became a protégé. None lived in Cappadocia. During his episcopacy Basil's closest relationships were with bishops he met in person only infrequently. With some of his boyhood friends Basil had used the formalities of letters to disguise, even substitute for, his lack of emotional involvement. With these three bishops the protocol of letters made possible alliances that he could not count on achieving through face-to-face meetings.

Eusebius of Samosata and Basil had begun to correspond during the later 360s. Eusebius had traveled to Caesarea to support Basil's consecration as bishop in 370, and Basil had repaid the visit by traveling to Samosata two years later. Basil confided in Eusebius about his grief over his mother's death and about his concern over the schemes of his brother Gregory of Nyssa. Eusebius was in fact apparently the only person with whom Basil now discussed his feelings about members of his family. Basil also consulted with Eusebius on various ecclesiastical issues, such as their plans for securing the support of bishops in the West and for resolving theological disputes with bishops in eastern Asia Minor. Their friendship had hence progressed from a lopsided mentorship between an experienced bishop and an ambitious priest, through the adoption of Eusebius as a substitute father, to a working relationship between two prominent bishops. The only challenge to this friendship was a disagreement over the means of ensuring doctrinal orthodoxy. Eusebius had hoped to reconcile Basil with bishop Eustathius of Sebasteia, while Basil remained suspicious of Eustathius' motives. In his reply Basil noted that he had once broken off contact with another bishop, even though his colleague had "so many claims to a friendship with me." This comparison implied that Basil would do the same with Eustathius, and perhaps even, if necessary, with Eusebius too. At the end of his letter Basil suggested that his friend should stop writing him about the possibility of a reconciliation.[7]

In 374 Eusebius was forced into exile in Thrace. Although Basil struggled to maintain contact, he now filled his correspondence with excuses for his inability to write or send letters. Even if he could no longer consult with Eusebius, he continued to champion him. In a letter to bishop Peter of Alexandria he defended the orthodoxy of both Eusebius and bishop Meletius of Antioch. Initially Basil had enlisted Meletius' support for his attempts to coordinate links with the bishop of Alexandria and bishops in the West. In a letter to bishops in Italy and Gaul, the first three eastern bishops to sign were Meletius, Eusebius, and Basil. In 372 Meletius too had had to go into exile. Despite his banishment, Meletius remained an influential contact for Basil's ecclesiastical plans. Meletius was a native of the province of Armenia Secunda, and he had retreated to his family's estate in the province of Armenia Prima. With these connections Basil hoped that Meletius, even in exile, could now help improve his relations with other churchmen in eastern Asia Minor. Basil's letters to Meletius and his references to him in other letters were consistently laudatory, but also straightforward and direct. Even though he sometimes referred to Meletius as "the man of God," he avoided the adulation that he used with Eusebius of Samosata. This was a professional friendship, an alliance between two bishops who seemed to consider each other a peer and a mutual supporter in their disputes both with the imperial court and with other bishops.[8]

One component of Basil's strategy for extending his influence in the region was the recruitment of sympathetic bishops. Basil and Amphilochius met for the first time apparently after Basil had become bishop. They were introduced through a friend of Amphilochius who had abandoned a career in public affairs and gone to live in a poorhouse near Caesarea. There this young man had met Basil, who so impressed him with his comments about the virtues of a life of poverty that he hoped Amphilochius could meet the great bishop too. Amphilochius had previously been a legal advocate and an orator. When they did meet, he listened to Basil explain Christian philosophy. Soon thereafter Basil recommended Amphilochius to become the new bishop of Iconium.[9]

Since Iconium had recently become the capital of the new province of Lycaonia, Amphilochius was now a metropolitan bishop like Basil. Yet even though Amphilochius was an episcopal peer, he seems always to have thought of Basil as his mentor and teacher. The foundation of their relationship was an interest in biblical questions and ecclesiastical issues. When Basil complimented Amphilochius upon his selection as bishop, he encouraged him to improve his preaching and impose order on his churches. To help with ecclesiastical discipline, Basil offered advice, perhaps based on his own experiences, on dealing with a subordinate bishop. When Basil suggested that Amphilochius should visit, he linked the invitations with the celebration of festivals in honor of martyrs at Caesarea. Basil furthermore relied upon him to help keep in touch with churchmen in nearby regions to the south and west, such as Isauria, Lycia, and possibly Pisidia. In return, Amphilochius flattered Basil by sending him many questions about theological doctrines, biblical exegesis, and church discipline. In all of these questions Basil appreciated most that Amphilochius was interested in learning, and not in trying to put him on the spot.[10]

Basil became an ecclesiastical patron and a spiritual adviser for Amphilochius. Given Basil's austere personality and his tendency toward manipulation, this relationship could easily have remained simply a formal mentorship and a partnership of expediency. The surprise is that it clearly developed into a intimate, almost sweet, friendship. Basil occasionally mentioned the difficulties over his brother's see of Nyssa. Even though he did not detail his concerns about his brother as directly as he did to Eusebius of Samosata, he did begin to share his anxieties with Amphilochius. He also shared his deepening depression over his failing health and his declining influence in the face of opposition from rival churchmen. As compensation he confessed that he looked forward to hearing Amphilochius' advice. A letter from Amphilochius was "a token of the voice that is sweetest and the hand that is most beloved of all to me." Basil found his myriad questions most stimulating, and eventually he dedicated his treatise on the Holy Spirit to "brother Amphilochius, beloved and most precious of all my guides." Since Basil was always a bit prickly about his reputation, Amphilochius had clearly worked at this relationship. In particular, Basil now admired Amphilochius' "stateliness and discretion."[11]

By the mid-370s Basil was running out of friends and ecclesiastical supporters. Meletius of Antioch was already in exile, Gregory of Nazianzus was preparing to retreat into solitude, and his brother Gregory of Nyssa would soon be banished. In 374 Basil lost two important mentors, Gregory the Elder, who died at Nazianzus, and Eusebius of Samosata, who was sent into exile. Not so coincidentally, in 374 he began to expand his friendship with Amphilochius. Not only did he rely increasingly more upon Amphilochius' assistance and advice; he also conceptualized this friendship in more intimate terms. One invitation for Amphilochius to visit was a true plea from his heart. "From the perspective of a father's heart, every opportunity to hug a beloved son is welcome." Basil now adopted a paternal perspective, and, exceptionally for him, he even sentimentalized the relationship.[12]

Gregory of Nazianzus' Friends

Despite their own friendship, and despite their overlapping interests in Cappadocia, their surviving letters suggest that Basil and Gregory of Nazianzus did not share many friends.

Gregory mentioned only a few friends from his boyhood days. One was Philagrius, who had once been a student with Caesarius, Gregory's brother, at Alexandria. Gregory and Caesarius had studied together in Cappadocia, and Gregory had visited his brother, and probably Philagrius too, in Egypt. Philagrius eventually returned to Cappadocia. After Caesarius' sudden death he and Gregory had consoled each other by remembering their studies together and the teachers they had shared. They also occasionally met in order to discuss classical literature and biblical texts. In 383, about thirty or perhaps even almost forty years after they had first studied together, Gregory was grateful that Philagrius, his friend, would still listen to his explanation of why he had ceased to serve as acting bishop at Nazianzus. Another long-standing friend was Hellenius, whom Gregory had met through Basil, most likely while they were all students at Athens. Gregory renewed their friendship during the early 370s, when Hellenius was serving as an imperial tax assessor at Nazianzus. As he requested concessions for local monks, Gregory effusively praised Hellenius' "fiery prowess" at rhetoric and his "great reputation."[13]

Another friend, perhaps a boyhood friend from Cappadocia, was Eustochius. Gregory and Eustochius had certainly been students together at Athens, and thirty years later their friendship still revolved around classical culture. Gregory once suggested that Eustochius should grant a favor "for the sake of culture and Athens," and he reminded him that they had shared "common fathers of eloquence." One of those teachers they may have shared at Athens was the sophist Himerius. Since Himerius had often used allusions to Greek mythology and classical literature in his own orations, his students may have absorbed his interests. In his letters to Eustochius, Gregory included citations from and allusions to classical poets, and he mentioned both the orator Demosthenes and Alexander the Great.[14]

Eustochius had returned to Cappadocia to become a rhetorician at Caesarea. In the early 380s Gregory was advising one of his grandnephews about higher education. Since this young man had gone to study with Stagirius, another teacher in Caesarea, Eustochius was miffed at Gregory. In reply, Gregory defended himself for having introduced his grandnephew to Stagirius. Eustochius seems to have complained that Gregory's behavior had been "neither that of a friend nor that of a gentleman." This accusation cut deeply, and Gregory insisted that he had not forgotten "Athens, your friendship, or your companionship." The image of Athens was still the essence of their relationship, since there they had studied classical literature and developed their friendship. Even though Eustochius was annoyed that this young man was studying with another teacher, Gregory insisted that he himself had nevertheless acted "like a friend."[15]

Familiarity with classical culture allowed Gregory to maintain some boyhood friends and to establish friendships with rhetoricians and teachers in Cappadocia. In these friendships Gregory seems consistently to have preferred to share references to classical literature rather than to biblical writings. Even though he admitted that Philagrius had an excellent education in "matters of the divine," and even though they had once met to discuss the meaning of a Psalm, Gregory still preferred to cite verses from Homer, argue about Plato's views on death and Aristotle's on happiness, and send his friend a copy of Demosthenes' orations. The essence of Gregory's friendships with Philagrius and other boyhood chums was their mutual delight in classical literature.[16]

The friends whom Gregory shared with Basil included Sophronius, Gregory of Nyssa, and Amphilochius. With these friends too Gregory preferred relationships based upon enjoying a common interest in classical culture.

During the later 360s Gregory asked Sophronius for assistance several times. They had probably been friends for a long time, since Sophronius had perhaps been a schoolmate in Cappadocia and he had been a friend of Gregory's brother, Caesarius. Even though Sophronius was successfully advancing in the imperial administration, Gregory reminded him that "goodness remained the same among friends." In his requests Gregory often appealed to their common homeland or to their mutual friendship. In his estimation, the basis of their friendship was, predictably, classical culture. When Gregory requested assistance for a young upcoming student, he mentioned the importance of culture for a magistrate like Sophronius, since "eloquence provides a eulogy for your virtues." As recompense for his support, Gregory once offered "my most beautiful possession, culture." During the 370s when Sophronius was serving at the court of the emperor Valens in Antioch, they may have lost contact. Although Basil continued to correspond with Sophronius, Gregory apparently did not. Instead, he renewed his friendship with Sophronius later, most likely at Constantinople. Gregory served briefly as bishop at the capital in 381. Sophronius had apparently retired there after his service at court, since he became prefect of Constantinople at about the same time. Their revived friendship was close enough that after Gregory returned to Cappadocia, he complained that he had been separated from Sophronius' friendship.[17]

Gregory became a friend of Gregory of Nyssa with Basil again acting as broker. Their friendship too emphasized their common interest in classical literature. Even when Gregory of Nazianzus once chided his friend for his ambition of becoming a rhetorician, he did so in a letter that was marinated in allusions to classical texts. During the 370s Gregory of Nazianzus sometimes commiserated with his friend. Then they also shared the misfortune of having been swept up in the highhanded schemes of Basil. In 372 Gregory of Nyssa visited his friend soon after Basil had compelled Gregory of Nazianzus to accept an unwanted consecration as bishop of Sasima. Gregory of Nazianzus was not sure how to interpret this visit. At the beginning of his oration he discussed the characteristics of a "true friend," and seemed to wonder whether Gregory of Nyssa qualified. Since Gregory of Nyssa "shared my name and my soul," they should have been natural comrades. In addition, since Basil had recently consecrated Gregory of Nyssa as a bishop, Gregory of Nazianzus might have hoped that he had come to console him as a fellow victim of Basil's ambition. But Gregory of Nazianzus also described Basil and Gregory of Nyssa as Moses and Aaron, famous brothers from the Old Testament, and then wondered whether his friend had come merely as Basil's mouthpiece to encourage him to take up his new episcopacy. In that case Gregory of Nazianzus shrugged off his friend and his visit as too late, "the pilot after the storm, the remedy after the scar has formed." In his bitterness he could not decide whether Gregory of Nyssa was now embarrassed at Basil's "tyranny" or annoyed at Gregory of Nazianzus' recalcitrance. "Which of your brothers do you censure?"[18]

Gregory of Nazianzus remained in contact with Gregory of Nyssa. In 375 they exchanged letters about recent disputes with "heretics." Gregory of Nyssa compared them to snakes who had crawled out of their dens at springtime; Gregory of Nazianzus thought they would only hiss a bit before retreating. Presumably this exchange referred to the confrontations between Basil and the vicar Demosthenes, which led to the exile of Gregory of Nyssa. Gregory of Nazianzus himself then retreated into solitude in Isauria. After

Basil's death Gregory of Nazianzus sent a letter of condolence in which he comforted himself with having inherited the companionship of Gregory of Nyssa. In subsequent letters he encouraged his friend after a difficult journey, and he consoled him for the loss of a companion.[19]

The friendship between the two had long revolved around their awkward relationships with Basil and the tribulations they felt they had experienced because of Basil's schemes. After Basil's death each had finally found an independent identity, Gregory of Nyssa by assuming a role of ecclesiastical leadership in the region, Gregory of Nazianzus by serving as bishop at Constantinople. Gregory of Nazianzus could now also look back with equanimity at a moment when he had resented Basil and doubted Gregory of Nyssa's friendship. In 383 as he introduced the new bishop of Nazianzus, he explained to Gregory of Nyssa that the selection of this bishop was not uncanonical. Eleven years earlier Gregory of Nazianzus had complained to Gregory of Nyssa about his consecration as bishop of Sasima. Now he noted that even though he had recently been acting as bishop of Nazianzus, in fact the see was open for a new bishop, because he had been "pledged" to Sasima. This concession marked perhaps the only time Gregory of Nazianzus was actually eager to identify himself as the bishop of Sasima. Gregory of Nyssa was most likely the only one of his friends who could appreciate the irony.[20]

Amphilochius was Gregory's cousin, and also another of his friends. Their friendship was a legacy of sorts, derived "from their fathers." During the 360s they too shared a relationship in which familiarity with classical culture was an important component. The first extant letter from Gregory opened with a quotation from the classical poet Pindar. As a student of the famous rhetorician Libanius, Amphilochius had himself become a noted orator, and years later his teacher still remembered how his young protégé had been able "to make old men jump to their feet." Once Amphilochius started a career as an advocate, Gregory occasionally approached him with petitions. In another letter containing a request for assistance he explained the nature of friendship by citing some lines from another ancient poet. When Gregory later appealed for support on Amphilochius' behalf, he described him as a philosopher. After Amphilochius returned to live in Cappadocia in the early 370s, Gregory sent him short notes that were stuffed with citations from and allusions to classical literature. In his estimation, Amphilochius had become that rarest of friends, a comrade whose learning was both Christian and "Greek." Once Basil had represented that combination of Christianity and classical culture; now Amphilochius had become Gregory's cultural soulmate.[21]

During this period when Gregory was coping with the agony of his unwanted consecration as bishop of Sasima, his friendship with Amphilochius still provided an opportunity for playfulness and joking. Their relationship changed dramatically, however, after Amphilochius became a bishop with Basil's support and devoted himself to ecclesiastical affairs. Gregory was dismayed enough to suggest that the same "mutual friends" who had once "tyrannized" him into becoming a bishop had done the same to his cousin. In part Gregory was upset because Basil had now convinced Amphilochius to do what Gregory had never been willing to do, give up caring for his elderly father in order to become a bishop. Since Amphilochius then moved to Iconium, Gregory was furthermore upset at having seemingly lost "my only good advisor." Although they apparently remained in contact through letters, they may not have seen each other again until 381, when Gregory served briefly as bishop of Constantinople and Amphilochius attended the ecumenical council there.[22]

After that council Gregory returned to Cappadocia. He was at least flexible enough to recognize that he could no longer share his love of classical culture with Amphilochius. Spiritual and ecclesiastical concerns would define their friendship, and Gregory now filled his letters with allusions to biblical verses. According to Gregory of Nyssa, Amphilochius had even become an "imitator of the great Paul," the apostle Paul who was the original founder of the Christian church at Iconium. Gregory of Nazianzus acknowledged that his cousin had become an influential churchman, and he complimented him for his mediation of ecclesiastical disputes. Since he could no longer present himself as Amphilochius' comrade in classical culture, he defined their friendship in different terms. Legend claimed that one of the apostle Paul's converts at Iconium had been the virgin Thecla. Since Gregory had lived for several years at a shrine of St. Thecla in Isauria, he associated himself with the saint in claiming credit for his cousin's success as a churchman. "Along with St. Thecla I directed Amphilochius to God, Amphilochius who is the booming messenger of truth and my glory."[23]

This claim nevertheless hinted at a bit of nostalgia too. In an epigram Gregory had once described himself in the same way, as the "booming messenger of truth." Significantly, he had continued by characterizing himself as "the young prince of both kinds of knowledge," that is, of both classical literature and biblical wisdom. Now, as he thought about his cousin, Gregory may not have said so explicitly, but he knew that Amphilochius too had once been such a "young prince." Even as he took pride in Amphilochius' ecclesiastical prominence and reluctantly conceded that he and his cousin were to be only spiritual soulmates, Gregory wanted to savor one small memory of their earlier mutual delight in classical culture.[24]

Comparing Friendships

It is risky to generalize about the friendships of Basil and Gregory of Nazianzus. Their letters are of course by far the richest sources of information about their friends and their friendships. Although hundreds of their letters survive, much is clearly missing from the extant collections. Both Basil and Gregory were involved in putting together initial collections of their letters. Gregory compiled a collection for a grandnephew that included "as many of my letters as possible." Basil may have published some of his own important letters, and his brothers Gregory of Nyssa and Peter of Sebasteia later probably initiated a collection. Even with their own involvement and the participation of family members, there were always so many obstacles to the survival of ancient texts that their collections could easily have ended up resembling the collection of the extant letters of Gregory of Nyssa, which has only about thirty letters and includes correspondents who cannot be identified with certainty. Gregory of Nyssa corresponded with Gregory of Nazianzus, Amphilochius of Iconium, Meletius of Antioch, and the sophist Libanius, to mention only some of the most celebrated of his friends. But without an extensive corpus of letters to provide texture to his relationships, he is consistently overlooked in modern discussions of friendship in late antiquity.[25]

For modern historians the omissions in these collections of letters are sometimes heartbreaking. Even though Basil and Gregory themselves later corresponded with some young acquaintances, the extant collections include no letters from their own boyhoods or young adulthoods. Both Basil and Gregory were already about thirty years old when they appeared in their earliest extant letters. In their letters both referred to other acquaintances for whom no letters survive, and there were many prominent men in the region, imperial magistrates, churchmen, and local notables, with whom it is most unlikely that they did not exchange letters. An even more obvious omission is the absence of letters of reply from their correspondents (except when they wrote to each other). As a result, they often seem to have been shadow-boxing, talking to themselves, and by default their friendships resemble monologues rather than dialogues.

Despite these difficulties, it is possible to suggest some comparisons. In particular, their relationships with their mutual friends highlight some of the differences between their attitudes about friendship. Basil was consistently quite proper and matter-of-fact with his correspondents, sometimes even distant, remote, almost emotionless. For him the protocol of letters seemed to overlap, and hence sometimes to hide, his own inflexible sternness and emotional constipation. Basil consistently addressed Sophronius with the generic abstractions that turned magistrates into the personifications of various virtues. He was always a bit hesitant about the abilities of his brother Gregory of Nyssa, and he sometimes chided him for his meddling in ecclesiastical affairs. The one exception to this characteristic aloofness was Amphilochius, whom Basil increasingly cast in the role of a beloved and dutiful son.

In contrast, Gregory of Nazianzus seemed to try to establish more of an intimacy and emotional connection with his correspondents. Although he praised Sophronius' merits, he rarely addressed him as a personified virtue. His description of Sophronius as his "foremost friend, an authentic friend" seemed more sincere than Basil's similar assertion, since Gregory made this claim in the context of introducing Sophronius to a petitioner and not in the context of trying to save his own reputation. Gregory took Gregory of Nyssa seriously as a churchman, and he was playful in his joking letters to Amphilochius. In fact, Gregory's personal relationship with these three men only diminished once they became more involved with Basil and his zealous ecclesiastical affairs during the 370s. Once these men became to interact more with the dour Basil, Gregory seemed to withdraw from contact. Only after Basil's death did Gregory revive his own relationships with these friends.[26]

A second contrast focuses on traditions and literary preferences. Basil related to his friends primarily through biblical allusions and ecclesiastical concerns. He reminded Sophronius that even though he was an imperial magistrate, he could distribute favors only "with God." He interacted with Gregory of Nyssa and Amphilochius primarily as fellow churchmen. Although Gregory of Nazianzus did not ignore biblical references, he also used many more references to classical culture and ancient Greek literature. The best example of this contrast is the influence of Gregory and Basil on the transformation of Amphilochius from his career as a rhetorician to his tenure as a bishop. During the 360s and early 370s Amphilochius had shared with Gregory a mutual delight in allusions to classical literature. Once he became a bishop, however, he asked Basil questions exclusively about biblical exegesis and ecclesiastical discipline. By then Gregory was no longer in orbit around Basil. As Amphilochius became an increasingly important participant in Basil's implacable world of ecclesiastical politics, he and Gregory seemed to slip away from each other. Amphilochius had converted from Gregory's playful enjoyment of classical culture to Basil's stern ascetic and biblical outlook. Even when Gregory and Amphilochius renewed their friendship in the early 380s, they never again shared a mutual enthusiasm for classical culture.[27]

A final contrast highlights the implications of the geographical scope of their correspondence. While bishop of Caesarea, Basil seemed to want to attach Cappadocia primarily to regions to the east. He had links with Pontus through his family, and with both the Armenian provinces and the kingdom of Armenia through ecclesiastical connections. One of his important early mentors had been Eustathius, bishop of Sebasteia. Another important friend was Meletius, the bishop of Antioch who in fact spent most of the 370s in exile in the Armenian provinces. The two cities toward which Basil looked for ecclesiastical guidance and leadership were Antioch and Alexandria. He hence corresponded extensively with bishops and clerics at and in the vicinity of Antioch, and with bishops such as Eusebius of Samosata along the middle Euphrates River. He appealed directly to Athanasius, the distinguished bishop of Alexandria, in particular for assistance in resolving disputes at Antioch: "what might be more critical for the churches throughout the world than the church at Antioch?" Sometimes he also hoped for the support of bishops in the West, including the bishop of Rome. In contrast, Constantinople barely existed in Basil's thinking. His ecclesiastical world consisted primarily of eastern Asia Minor, Armenia, Syria, Palestine, and Egypt. This tall quadrangle, stretching from the Black Sea south through the eastern Mediterranean to the Nile River, reflected essentially a Near Eastern perspective on the church, almost a pre-Roman perspective that emphasized the prominence of Caesarea, Antioch, and Alexandria.[28]

Gregory had a different perspective. Many of Basil's correspondents in the eastern regions barely registered in his letters or his activities. Basil once noted that he and Gregory had had conversations with Eustathius of Sebasteia at their retreat in Pontus during the later 350s, but Gregory never mentioned Eustathius in his writings. Gregory knew of Eusebius of Samosata through his father, and he sent a letter to Eusebius in the name of Gregory the Elder inviting him to attend Basil's consecration as bishop. During this visit Gregory did not meet Eusebius, and an illness again prevented him from a meeting as Eusebius traveled through Cappadocia on his way to exile in 374. Gregory may have thought that Eusebius would be an effective patron on his behalf before God, but he did not go out of his way to meet him. Gregory apparently never met Meletius of Antioch until Meletius came to Constantinople while Gregory was leading the Nicene community there. In fact, Gregory had few if any contacts at Antioch. When he later did ask for assistance in uniting the factions at Antioch, he wrote to his friend Sophronius at Constantinople. Because he blamed Alexandria for being the source of the Arian heresy, he criticized it as "a vain city filled with all evils, a kettle boiling without reason."[29]

With few contacts and limited interest in Antioch and Alexandria, Gregory's personal and ecclesiastical viewpoint instead looked west to Constantinople, and his brief service as bishop there only confirmed that outlook. Unlike Basil, Gregory acknowledged the importance of the new capital both in the Roman empire and in eastern Christianity, and he now adopted essentially a Greek perspective that linked Cappadocia with Constantinople and the old Greek cultural world of the Aegean. Gregory's perspective also seemed to look to the future, when Asia Minor would join with the classical Greek world to become the heartland of the Byzantine empire. Basil looked east to the past, Gregory west to the future. Mount Argaeus was the highest mountain in Cappadocia, and from its peak climbers claimed to be able to see both the Black Sea and the Mediterranean Sea. If Basil and Gregory had ever mounted to its summit, they would have stood back to back, Basil looking toward the Near East, Gregory toward Constantinople.[30]

In some respects these contrasting outlooks reflected simply different times. Basil was bishop during the 370s, when a heterodox Arian bishop presided at Constantinople and Valens' imperial court was at Antioch. As a result, he would naturally turn his back on the nominal capital and look east and south. In contrast, Gregory's service at Constantinople during the late 370s and early 380s coincided with the early years of the reign of Theodosius in the eastern empire. During the first years of his reign Theodosius resided in northern Greece or at Constantinople, and he was a supporter of orthodox Nicene Christianity. As a result, Gregory and other likeminded bishops would naturally look to his court and Constantinople.

Yet these different outlooks were also the predictable consequences of much earlier developments in the lives of Gregory and Basil. As a young man Gregory had traveled through the eastern Mediterranean world to Palestine and Egypt. The goal of his travels had been his further studies in classical culture, and the culmination of his trip had been his years of study at Athens. In contrast, Basil traveled through the eastern Mediterranean world after his studies at Athens. His trip represented virtually a rejection of his education in classical culture, since he had visited Syria, Palestine, Mesopotamia, and Egypt in order to observe and meet ascetics. After his trip to the Near East, Gregory always preferred to associate himself instead with the classical culture of the old Greek world. After his trip Basil wanted to reject that classical culture and promote a strict ascetic lifestyle.[31]

For both of their perspectives, an image of Athens was essential. Gregory thought of Athens as the culmination of his aspirations, a place where he had been happy studying classical culture and which he regretted leaving. Basil was only too relieved to leave Athens and abandon its associations with pagan culture. Athens marked a fulfillment to Gregory's longing for immersion in classical culture, but a catalyst for Basil's search for an ascetic lifestyle. Athens was also the place where their friendship had sprouted and flourished. But since their reactions to Athens already crystallized such fundamental differences between the two, it is difficult to imagine how their contemporaries could have considered them to have been exemplars of best friends.

Chapter 10

Worst of Friends:
The Friendship of Basil and
Gregory of Nazianzus

Basil and Gregory of Nazianzus were the worst of friends. Even though they had known each other since their days as teenaged students in Caesarea and remained associated with each other well into their middle-aged years, their personalities never quite meshed. Basil was domineering and sometimes a curmudgeon, Gregory passive, conciliatory, and usually the obliging sidekick. Basil repeatedly took the lead in their relationship, dominating their coterie of students at Athens, pressuring Gregory to visit and stay with him at his retreat in Pontus, assuming that Gregory would patch up his fissure with bishop Eusebius of Caesarea, expecting him to support his own candidacy for the episcopacy of Caesarea, convincing Gregory's father to join in consecrating him as bishop of Sasima. This friendship continued for decades, and repeatedly Gregory seems to have been content to be subordinate. When he intervened in the conflict between Basil and bishop Eusebius, Gregory described himself as "insignificant and more inclined to reconciliation." Once Basil received the proper respect, Gregory conceded, then he too would cooperate, "just as shadows follow bodies."[1]

In the early 370s their friendship essentially collapsed. Its demise was a wrenching experience for Gregory that motivated him toward further personal scrutiny that went on for years. Because his relationship with Basil had been so intertwined with his attraction to classical culture, his attitude about ecclesiastical service, and his devotion to his parents, all his feelings were suddenly adrift. Other people nevertheless continued to think of Basil and Gregory as friends, and in later Byzantine society their friendship would be idealized as a paradigm friendship. Their friendship had clearly had many dimensions. To observers it had appeared worthy of imitation; for the two participants it had been both exhilarating and abrasive. On the surface their relationship seemed to have been a classic example of a perfect friendship, but in its intimate details it was a friendship that went sour and should never have become a model for subsequent friendships. Significantly, it would be Gregory's own writings, even as they detailed the pain in the relationship, that contributed to the formation of this image of an ideal friendship.

Becoming Friends

Gregory and Basil had first met probably at Caesarea, where they were both students. Since Gregory later politely begged off describing Basil's student days at Caesarea, they may at the time have been only passing acquaintances. Although they then both planned to continue their educations at Athens, they went separately, Gregory after first traveling to Palestine and Egypt, Basil by way of Constantinople. Their initial encounters at Athens set the tone for their friendship. Gregory later admitted that he had been impressed by Basil's "steadiness of character and the maturity of his eloquence." As a result, he somehow convinced the other students not to subject Basil to the usual raucous hazing of newly arrived students. Also at Athens were other students who had known Basil from their days together as schoolboys in Pontus. When they began to resent Basil's reputation, they tried to provoke him in a hostile interrogation. For the sake of a good argument Gregory initially supported them, before switching to defend Basil as he routed his opponents. As a consequence, Gregory seems to have replaced these former friends as Basil's confidant. These incidents were a preview of their subsequent relationship. Basil always seemed to be more venerable and more mature than his peers, and Gregory cast himself as his squire to protect him from criticism. Basil's success and aloofness made others resent him, and Gregory, even if as here sometimes reluctantly, consistently defended him.[2]

Gregory reveled in his studies at Athens. Initially Basil seems to have been uncertain, and Gregory now took the initiative in cheering him up. This reassurance previewed another common pattern in their friendship: once Gregory had encouraged and supported his friend, Basil went his own way, often without consulting Gregory. Eventually Basil asserted himself, and in a circle consisting of themselves and some sober-minded fellow students, he became the acknowledged leader. Gregory was truly pleased that their friendship grew too, and eventually he described the two of them as a "distinguished pair."[3]

Yet in his retrospective account Gregory also left the impression that throughout his stay in Athens Basil had been bored, or distracted by other interests. In contrast to Gregory's evident delight, Basil thought that Athens represented an "empty happiness." Basil was the first to leave, after studying at Athens for about five years, and he would soon insist that he had been glad to go: "I departed from Athens despising everything there." Gregory stayed. Although he would later claim that he had remained at Athens only a short time before "longing" compelled him to rejoin his friend, in fact he had stayed, perhaps even as a teacher, for another three or four years. The discrepancy in their friendship had become clearly apparent for the first time. At Athens Gregory had been able to enjoy both his immersion in classical culture and his friendship with Basil. Once Basil left, he had to choose between culture or friendship. Even though later in life he was reluctant to admit it, at the time he had chosen Athens, "the source of culture."[4]

Gregory seems to have hoped that after his return to Cappadocia he and Basil would be able to recreate their life at Athens. Basil had meanwhile come under the influence of Eustathius of Sebasteia and his ideas about asceticism. He had furthermore traveled throughout the eastern Mediterranean in order to meet and observe other ascetics. In the later 350s Basil now wanted to cultivate a similar ascetic lifestyle. He also wanted Gregory to join him. At Athens both had apparently already decided to adopt an ascetic life. The problem was to agree upon a spot where they could live together.[5]

Gregory proposed they live half of the time in a district near Nazianzus so that he could look after his elderly parents. Basil complained that that district had cold winters and too much mud, and he rather haughtily rejected the suggestion. Instead, he left for Pontus, where he established himself on a family estate on a mountainside. From his new retreat he began to question Gregory's commitment: "with reluctance I have abandoned those empty hopes that I once had about you." Gregory refused to be drawn by his friend's scoffing, and instead asked for more details of Basil's lifestyle. In a letter that was an anticipation of his later monastic guidelines Basil described some of his key principles. The most important was "separation from the world." Only this sort of total withdrawal could cleanse men of distractions, among them their concerns about marriage, children, wife, and household. In this list of distractions Basil had at least had the good grace not to include caring for parents, which was Gregory's primary concern. This description of a disciplined daily regimen was now attractive enough that Gregory went to join Basil.[6]

Basil and Gregory had different goals for this retreat. Basil wanted to establish a new life of asceticism and renunciation. His mentor Eustathius of Sebasteia visited and expounded his ideas in long conversations. Basil also emphasized the study of the Bible: "the most helpful path to the discovery of [a man's] duty is the scrutiny of the inspired Scriptures." Gregory had gone to Pontus hoping to recreate their experiences at Athens. He seemed to think that since Basil had been dissatisfied at Athens, perhaps he would be happy enough at his own retreat that they could revive both their friendship and their study of classical texts. In a jaunty letter Gregory set out his three objectives: "smile, fill up with learning, and enjoy our friendship."[7]

Basil's austere ascetic outlook with its emphasis on biblical studies and Gregory's lighthearted perspective with its focus on classical culture were inevitably incompatible. The one joint literary production from their time together in Pontus was the *Philocalia*, an anthology of extracts from the writings of Origen. Since Origen had a reputation for having incorporated Greek philosophy into his theological interpretations and biblical exegesis, perhaps their interest in his writings represented a compromise between their different objectives. If another souvenir of their stay was any indication, Gregory may well have done most of the work on this anthology. The other testimonial of their fellowship was a plane tree that Gregory described as "a memorial of my diligence at your retreat." While Gregory had planted the tree, Basil had only watered it.[8]

Differing notions of literary studies defined one possible contention between the two. Another was ideas about their friendship. In order to care for his parents Gregory had first suggested that they divide their time between Pontus and a district near Nazianzus. An additional reason for this suggestion that they commute between Basil's estate and Gregory's hometown was to maintain "equal honor in their friendship." Gregory was always sensitive about the balance in their relationship. At Athens they had been peers as students. But now that Basil was redefining their relationship in terms of an ascetic lifestyle, Gregory seemed to be trying to catch up. He did not know much about this new lifestyle, and his heart did not seem to be in it.[9]

Gregory tried to preserve the jollity, and hence the evenness, in their relationship by occasionally twitting Basil's obsessions. Basil had compared the setting of his retreat to an ideal of beauty from Greek mythology, Calypso's island; Gregory thought it resembled a biblical image of despair, the barren desert in which Moses and the Israelites had been lost for years. Basil had complained about the mud near Nazianzus; Gregory noted that the loaves of bread they were eating in Pontus had the consistency of slime. Basil had seemingly not been sympathetic to Gregory's concern for his parents; Gregory slyly noted that Basil was surviving on his estate only through the good graces of "that famous nourisher of the poor . . . your mother!" To one correspondent Gregory would explain that friends of long standing were entitled to joke with each other even about important subjects. But with Basil, Gregory admitted that he could not be sure whether his friend was teasing or being serious. In fact, in the outline of his daily regimen Basil had specifically excluded any use of jesting in conversation. In his estimation, merriment was not part of an ascetic life: "according to the narrative of the Gospels, the Lord never laughed." Gregory was dismayed, although in one of those heartfelt outbursts that make him such an appealing personality, he admitted that he wanted their togetherness to continue: "I would rather breathe you than the air." Basil's sternness now threatened again to upset the balance, the nonchalant give-and-take, in their friendship. So Gregory returned to Nazianzus to care for his parents.[10]

Gregory's father, the bishop of Nazianzus, then ordained him a priest. Since with this ordination Gregory had jumped past Basil in the ecclesiastical hierarchy, his promotion at first threatened to upend their relationship. As if to indicate that their equality was still intact, Gregory's immediate reaction was to flee to Basil's retreat in Pontus for a few months. Eventually this ordination seemed to even out and strengthen their friendship. In the spring of 362 Gregory returned to Nazianzus to take up his new clerical duties. Later that year Basil became a priest at Caesarea.

Soon after his ordination Basil wrote to Gregory, apparently to explain and justify his own promotion. During his period of self-reflection before assuming his own priesthood Gregory had examined membership in the clergy and become critical of men who thought of clerical offices in terms of authority rather than service. Since Basil had become a priest only after he had failed in his candidacy for the episcopacy at Caesarea, in his letter he was perhaps trying to shield himself from any suspicion of opportunism. Gregory seems to have accepted Basil's explanation. As before at Athens when he had tried to cheer up his friend upon his arrival, so Gregory now again offered encouragement to the new priest. In his estimation, they had both been compelled to become priests, even though they both would have preferred the lowly life of philosophical asceticism. Gregory could then have extended his role as adviser. Since he had become a priest first, he again had the opportunity to take the lead in their friendship. But he once more declined. Unlike Basil, who after being the first to commit to asceticism had then scoffed at his friend's hesitation, Gregory was now consoling rather than critical. He was as much committed to their friendship as to their new clerical service: "what have you done that is not praiseworthy?"[11]

Basil did not share Gregory's acceptance of their clerical offices, however, and he increasingly went his own way without conferring with his friend. Gregory had warned Basil that as priests they now faced opposition from heretics. In fact, Basil was already involved in theological debates, and he was working on his refutation of the heterodox teachings of Eunomius. While composing this treatise Basil apparently did not consult with Gregory, and they seem to have drifted apart. In a letter to Gregory probably from this period Basil complained that his friend's letters were too short. Basil's theological obsessions were one reason for their separation; another was clerical service. Even though he had at first considered the priesthood to be an unwanted burden, Gregory now helped his father at Nazianzus. In contrast, Basil seems to have thought that his priesthood was inadequate consolation for his failure to become bishop. He had a falling out with Eusebius, the new bishop of Caesarea, and out of pique he simply returned to sulk at his retreat in Pontus for a few years. Basil's own exalted estimation of himself and his standing now seemed to have exposed him as one of those clerics who would put their own ambitions before their duty and service.[12]

Eventually Gregory took the initiative in reconciling Basil. Bishop Eusebius had invited Gregory to attend councils, but not Basil. Gregory was flattered, even as he recognized the implicit threat to his friendship with Basil. By "honoring me and dishonoring him" Eusebius' favoritism might have upset the harmony in their relationship. Eusebius also seems to have suggested that Gregory may have misjudged his friend and their friendship. Gregory was indignant: "I do not doubt my decision about him." He furthermore turned the blame back on Eusebius by claiming that he had insulted Basil, and he forcefully suggested that Eusebius should show some respect to his own priest. Eusebius was predictably annoyed at this advice and accused Gregory of belittling him in return. Gregory then offered to help convince Basil to return and assist his bishop, especially since the presence of the emperor Valens and his court in Cappadocia in 365 presented a potential challenge to churchmen in Cappadocia. In a letter to Basil he noted that Eusebius was now demonstrating his "conciliation and friendship," and that Basil should announce his good sense by taking the initiative in approaching Eusebius. Gregory also offered to help his friend. "If it seems appropriate for me to join you, to stay with you, and to travel with you, I will not refuse." So Basil now returned.[13]

Gregory had consistently worked at maintaining his friendship with Basil. For all his deference and humility, he had soothed Basil at Athens, encouraged him after becoming a priest, and now helped to reconcile him with his bishop. His goal had always been to preserve the evenness, the balance, the equality in their friendship, as fellow students, fellow priests, and helpers for their bishops. In return, Basil seems increasingly to have taken Gregory's support for granted. Since Basil now effectively appropriated leadership of the church at Caesarea, he could begin to view Gregory as another of his subordinates. Basil's rather haughty treatment of Gregory became apparent when bishop Eusebius died in 370 and the episcopacy at Caesarea became vacant.

Becoming Bishops

Although Basil was an obvious and a strong candidate to become bishop, his selection was not without opposition. Immediately before a conclave of bishops was scheduled to meet to select a successor, Basil invited Gregory to visit. Since a few years earlier Gregory had volunteered to join his friend when he returned to Caesarea, Basil may now have thought that the offer was still outstanding. In order to ensure Gregory's acquiescence, Basil feigned a serious illness, as if he wanted only to whisper a final farewell to his friend. Gregory started his journey, but soon halted and returned. Once he had observed the other bishops hurrying to the city, he realized that Basil wanted him in Caesarea simply to bolster his chances.[14]

Gregory was resentful. Piety, not influence or popularity, was supposed to be the determining factor in selecting a new bishop. Even more upsetting was the recognition that Basil had been thinking only about himself. "I was surprised that you did not think that the same [office] was appropriate for you and for me. We shared culture and a life, and from the beginning God harmonized everything." As usual, Gregory was concerned about maintaining the balance in their friendship. This time, however, his concern about Basil's subterfuge had also become a doubt about his friend's loyalty and consideration. Eusebius' suggestion of a few years earlier that Gregory should reconsider his friendship with Basil, seems to have lingered in the back of his mind. When they next met, "I will have more complaints, more severe complaints."[15]

Gregory the Elder, Gregory's father and the long-serving bishop of Nazianzus, then indicated his support for the selection of Basil in one letter directly to the clergy, monks, magistrates, council members, and people of Caesarea, and in another to the bishops who were meeting. He also invited bishop Eusebius of Samosata to visit and support Basil, and eventually he himself traveled to Caesarea to participate in Basil's consecration. Although Gregory had composed these letters in his father's name, he still kept his distance. He did not accompany his father to Caesarea, even though it meant missing the opportunity to meet Eusebius. Gregory now admitted to Eusebius that Caesarea had a worthy bishop. But Basil's promotion had again brought Gregory's ambivalent feelings to the surface. Even as he congratulated his friend upon becoming bishop, he expressed his misgivings. Two concerns had kept him from visiting. He had first of all wanted to protect Basil from himself, because if too many of Basil's supporters gathered, his critics might rightly accuse him of "tasteless ambition." In addition, Gregory had wanted to protect himself from Basil, because only by keeping his distance could he preserve his own resolve and his own reputation. A few years before he had offered to help Basil at Caesarea. Now he rescinded that offer for good. "I will not run to you; do not personally ask this of me."[16]

Basil found this skepticism incomprehensible. Years earlier he had similarly been annoyed that Gregory had hesitated to join his ascetic retreat in Pontus. Once there, Gregory had spent some of his time gardening in a vineyard, pretending to be a vintager. In his reply to Gregory's congratulations, Basil now tainted the memory of that earlier idyllic interlude. He angrily accused Gregory of treating him like "a bunch of small grapes," grapes so tiny that they were typically left for gleaners. To soften the brittleness in their friendship, Gregory responded with witty banter. He conceded that although he may have insufficiently applauded Basil, so had everyone else: only Basil's own eloquence could adequately praise Basil. He used flattering puns, referring to Basil as the *basileion*, the "fortress" of culture. As in the past, Gregory again tried to preserve the equality in their friendship by using witticisms and jests.[17]

In this case, however, the humor was a bit forced. Praising Basil for his expertise in classical culture was a distinctly odd compliment to use at the moment when he had just become a bishop, and Gregory seems to have preferred to conjure up their past intimacy rather than confront the present situation directly. Even in his jokes he could sense that their relationship had changed irrevocably. Having become the metropolitan bishop for Cappadocia, Basil would always be his superior in the local ecclesiastical hierarchy.

Gregory could also perceive that Basil was now not merely his metropolitan. Caesarea was "the mother for virtually all the churches." Once it received a new bishop, it had put aside its widow's weeds. Since Basil had taken the church at Caesarea as his bride, his new standing as a paternal figure throughout the region would also distort his relationship with his friend. Gregory's ultimate response was a cry of desperation and a memory of a better time. "O culture and Athens and virtues and literary efforts!" At Athens they had been a pair. Their shared interest in classical culture and then their common service as priests had maintained the evenness in their friendship, and it had been possible for Gregory to tease his friend with droll puns and jokes. But now that Basil had become a metropolitan bishop and an ecclesiastical father figure, his promotion had capsized that balance, with seemingly no possibility of righting it.[18]

Basil, typically, was rather obtuse about the implications of his promotion for his friendship with Gregory. He seems to have thought that friends such as Gregory were expected not only to assist his ambitions, but also to be ambitious themselves. His instant solution to the uneasiness that had appeared in their friendship was to raise Gregory's rank by offering him the possibility of becoming a bishop. Then Gregory declined the offer. Two years later, however, he did not have the same opportunity of rejection.[19]

In 372 Basil had Gregory consecrated as a bishop essentially against his will. The emperor Valens' decision to divide Cappadocia into two provinces had the potential to diminish Basil's episcopal authority in the region. Not only would there be a new rival metropolitan bishop in Cappadocia, but he would lose his jurisdiction over the suffragan bishops in the cities transferred to the other province. Despite his earlier dismay at the time of Basil's consecration, Gregory now again offered to help. He extended this offer with his usual self-effacement and quiet flattery of his friend. "If you wish, I will join you and perhaps share some advice. But you need an advisor only if the sea needs water!" Basil seems to have interpreted this offer literally. In spring he traveled to Nazianzus, where he and Gregory the Elder consecrated Gregory as bishop of Sasima, a dusty little village in the no-man's land between the two new provinces. This consecration was apparently part of Basil's plan to enhance his metropolitan authority by consecrating more loyal bishops. Gregory was distraught enough to resort to a characteristic response, fleeing to seclusion in the mountains. This time he ran away not to join Basil, but to escape him.[20]

With this consecration Basil's actions had more than upset the balance in their friendship. Friends could be candid together, but each also had to be careful to evaluate in advance the feasibility and propriety of any requests. Basil had miscalculated Gregory's intentions, and he had then ignored Gregory's own explicit preferences. In Gregory's perspective, an episcopacy at Sasima had been entirely "your idea." At the moment of his "suffering," his consecration, Gregory had stated flatly that he would not participate in any of Basil's schemes against the new metropolitan bishop. "Before all else, give me seclusion."[21]

Basil compounded Gregory's anguish with a few pointed insults. Not content with badmouthing Gregory by saying he was "stupid," "unworthy of life," and "lazy," he also suggested that Gregory was "neither a man of culture nor a friend." For decades, classical culture had been the defining characteristic of their friendship, and Basil now claimed that Gregory had betrayed both by failing to support him. These accusations that he was neither a proper gentleman nor a true friend cut deeply, and Gregory's usual gentle banter turned caustic. For years he had been both a defender of Basil's arrogant behavior and the target of Basil's complaints for not supporting all his plans. "I am weary from being criticized for your behavior." Gregory was now so disillusioned from this betrayal that he doubted his own capacity for friendship. "From your friendship I learned only this one lesson, not to trust friends." In Gregory's estimation, Basil's actions had ruined his trust in friendship.[22]

"Do Not Insult Me"

This dissension was perhaps only to be expected. Not only were their personalities different, and not only had their interests and careers developed differently. All along Basil and Gregory had represented different notions of friendship. At Athens they had both had the leisure and the inclination to indulge in an effortless relationship of shared interests and shared activities. But once Basil became more involved in ecclesiastical affairs, he gave priority to the spiritual love found within Christian communities. Personal friendships seem to have become but one, lesser aspect of this spiritual kinship, and for the sake of the needs of the community they could even be shoved aside. Basil's emphasis on a unity achieved through spiritual love reduced the importance of personal friendships and sometimes judged them to be superfluous. To one correspondent he explained that a "friendship of this world" was inferior because it required direct face-to-face contact, while those familiar with "spiritual love" could achieve a "spiritual joining" simply through "the community of faith." Gregory was not the only friend to be dismayed at this aloof haughtiness. When another correspondent once complained about the "arrogance" that Basil displayed after acquiring power, he explicitly linked that accusation with another, "forgetting friends."[23]

In contrast, Gregory was reluctant to allow the abstract demands of ecclesiastical communities to interfere with his personal friendships, and especially with his friendship with Basil. That friendship was meant to remain pure, disinterested, and untainted by private plots and ecclesiastical feuds. Gregory's friendships were commonly sentimental and emotional, while Basil's tended to become instrumental and formal. In his concern over ecclesiastical affairs Basil seemed to think that no request was unreasonable, even a request of someone like Gregory who wanted no part of such schemes. Gregory in contrast was so respectful of both Basil and their friendship that he would never have put his friend in such a dilemma.[24]

Gregory never served as bishop at Sasima, and instead assisted his father as adjunct bishop at Nazianzus. He and Basil remained cordial, but also a bit cool and remote. Gregory soon reported to Basil on a visit from the new metropolitan bishop of Tyana. He and his father had resisted the suggestion that they switch their loyalties, and Gregory had declined an invitation to a council. When he did agree to act as a mediator, Basil responded with annoyance and implied that Gregory was hobnobbing with his rival.[25]

Gregory did not back down. He acknowledged that Basil too was a metropolitan bishop, but he also chided him for talking down, in particular to him and his father. Gregory the Elder may have been only a "micropolitan," a smalltown bishop, but he had supported Basil's selection as bishop. Gregory himself may now have been "a bishop without a city," but he was older than Basil. This age difference had perhaps gnawed at Gregory ever since the beginning of their friendship. In his relationship with Basil, not only was he a bit older, but he had been the first to arrive at Athens and the first to become a priest. Yet he had never used his seniority to vaunt himself over Basil. In contrast, when Basil had been the first to adopt an ascetic lifestyle and now the first to become a bishop, he had interpreted his priority as superiority over Gregory. Since Basil's promotion and subsequent behavior had effectively ruined the equality in their friendship, now Gregory was no longer reluctant to mention age explicitly as another distorting factor in their relationship, although this time one in his favor. "Do not insult me."[26]

In another letter Gregory reported on a conversation about Basil's theology at a banquet where some guests were discussing doctrines. Gregory noted that he had defended Basil's teachings about the Trinity by clarifying the differences in their statements about the Holy Spirit. He explained that he could openly proclaim the divinity of the Holy Spirit because he was such an obscure preacher, while Basil had to be more circumspect because he was so prominent. In addition to serving as a straightforward report about ecclesiastical affairs and doctrinal concerns, this letter also indicated the lingering conflict in Gregory's thinking about his friendship with Basil.

Gregory was still unsure whether Basil's recent uppity actions should cancel out decades of friendship. At the beginning of this report he had again hinted at the possibility of restoring their friendship by seeming to reply to one of Basil's earlier accusations that he was unworthy to live. "If there is any advantage to living for me, it is your friendship and your company."[27]

Whether by design or through simple oversight, Basil did not pick up on this overture. In his reply he implied that by reporting the comments of an opponent Gregory himself was offering some veiled criticism of Basil's theology. Since Basil had not liked the message, he was annoyed at the messenger. His letter was stiff with protocol, the politeness hardly hiding the vexation. Basil insisted that because he had put "love for you" before "every distress," he would accept this news "as was proper." He also slipped in an evaluation of his past behavior that shifted any blame from himself. "I pray to holy God that for my remaining days and hours I will persist in the same disposition toward you as in the past, when I knew of nothing in which I had failed in my duty, whether small or great." Basil then waved off his critics and claimed he had no time to reply. Gregory understood perfectly well the perfunctory tone of this letter: "you hide the face of your distress under respect, as if under a mask." Gregory anguished compulsively, while Basil blithely moved forward. Any remorse Basil may have felt about their friendship he seems to have kept hidden. Only once did he even hint at any sorrow, when he suggested that Gregory should be governing a church that was "equal to his talent." Even then he concluded Gregory should learn to be the kind of bishop who conferred honor on a see, rather than taking honor from it.[28]

These polite exchanges were all that remained in their relationship. Although Basil complained that they no longer visited, any talk about living together had become hollow: "we do not meet together." He also suggested that if they were to live together "for most of the year," it would be possible both to revive their "old agreements" and still perform "our current obligations to the churches." In his reply Gregory indicated that he would be ready to join Basil. But when Basil did summon him, Gregory politely refused. Years earlier he had at first been reluctant to join Basil in Pontus because of his concern for his parents, but then had eventually given in. Now, however, Gregory's attitude had changed. At about this same time he complimented one of his cousins for having first cared for his dying mother before joining a community of ascetics. Gregory likewise now preferred to stay at Nazianzus to care for his ailing mother. This time his parents took priority, and he stayed away from Basil.[29]

In 374 Gregory's aged father died. Even though Nazianzus was no longer in his ecclesiastical province, Basil attended the funeral for Gregory the Elder. At this funeral Gregory delivered a panegyric in which he reviewed some of the highlights of his father's life and episcopal career. Since Gregory the Elder's career had eventually intersected with both Basil's and Gregory's episcopal careers, Gregory also had the opportunity to begin to review and evaluate his own relationship with Basil.

In some respects Gregory the Elder's career had previewed Basil's career. Both, for instance, had confronted emperors, Gregory the Elder against Julian in 362, Basil against Valens almost ten years later. There were also important, but subtle, differences. Gregory the Elder had become bishop late in life, "after waiting for a little while." His selection had not been marred by any of "today's self-satisfaction and disorder," and his promotion had followed "the law of spiritual sequence." Later in his oration Gregory seemed to provide a pointed contrast to his father's selection as bishop when he noted that dissension had plagued Basil's selection as bishop at Caesarea. Gregory also stressed the smallness of his father's see. Despite the insignificance of Nazianzus, Gregory the Elder had nevertheless been both content and influential as a "micropolitan" bishop. Throughout the oration Gregory constantly praised his father's many virtues. In particular, he noted his father's lack of guile, his capacity for forgetting transgressions, and his total immunity to anger: "he kept no grudges against those who offended him." Gregory was perhaps aiming these comments about his father in Basil's direction. Gregory the Elder had been a model bishop, unassuming and humble. His life had furthermore provided a model for a true friendship, with no resentments, no anger, and no duplicity.[30]

Toward the end of his oration Gregory slipped in a brief comment about the participation of both his father and Basil in his own episcopal consecration. "I reproach both of you for one event. You seized me and delivered me to this burdensome and treacherous marketplace of souls under the guise of the noble name of the clergy. As a result, I have experienced misfortunes, and more are expected." This unwanted consecration was clearly still a sore point for Gregory, although he was also at the time unwilling to elaborate and simply continued to discuss more of his father's virtues. Even though he seems to have reconciled himself to his father's "paternal and spiritual tyranny," he was still unsure about his feelings toward Basil. When he mentioned Basil's selection as bishop of Caesarea, he praised him as "my companion and colleague, the partner of my soul, and, if I may speak with more boldness, my comrade in life and in culture." With this description

Gregory again seemed to be arguing with himself about their friendship, uncertain whether he should again offer to help, wondering how to react to Basil's presence. In fact, he was not even sure why Basil had come to this funeral. At the beginning of his oration he had mentioned three possible motives: to reassure the congregation, to honor Gregory the Elder, or to observe him. To imagine that Basil had come to console him seemed almost wishful thinking.[31]

Abandoning a Friendship

This funeral was perhaps the last time Basil and Gregory saw each other. At the end of his funeral oration Gregory mentioned his mother and vowed to look after her. After his mother died later in the year Gregory stayed on as acting bishop of Nazianzus, until in 375 he left for a secluded retreat in Isauria. His departure itself marked another step in his reevaluation of his friendship with Basil, in two respects.

As metropolitan bishop Basil had inherited the standing of a common father in the region. In a later retrospective evaluation Gregory explicitly noted how that new paternal image had intruded in his consecration as bishop of Sasima. In Gregory's estimation, it may have been appropriate for Gregory the Elder to insist that his son become a bishop, but Basil was also behaving as if he were "another father for me, and a much more burdensome one." "It is necessary to endure that man [Gregory the Elder], even when he behaves like a tyrant. But there is no need [to endure] this one [Basil] for the sake of a relationship that bestows damage rather than deliverance from misfortunes." Even though Gregory had recently lost his own father, he was not about to accept Basil as a replacement and become his dutiful filial subordinate. His cousin Amphilochius of Iconium could play that role. In fact, in a letter to Amphilochius, Basil would eventually allude to his bafflement about Gregory's "sudden" departure: "the reason is still now unknown." By the time Basil found out, Gregory had been gone for a year. He had apparently never even informed Basil about his departure.[32]

In addition to rejecting Basil's paternal authority Gregory also revealed his own ideas about a proper place for a retreat. Basil had previously insisted that they go north to the wilds of Pontus. Now that he could make his own choice, Gregory went south to the shrine of St. Thecla just outside Seleucia. Around the shrine were many monastic retreats where he might have stayed. The shrine also included a church, gardens, a bath house, and, significantly, a library. Seleucia itself was a big city, the capital of the province of Isauria and therefore the equivalent of Caesarea in Cappadocia. It was known for being "marvelous and very charming," with a temperate climate. It also was home to many rhetoricians, and had a reputation for "the eloquence of the Muses." St. Thecla herself was thought to appreciate the presence of teachers and orators: the saint was "a friend of culture and a friend of the Muses, and she always took pleasure in the orators who praised her with their eloquence."[33]

Gregory's idea of an appropriate location for a retreat was an artists' colony near the sunny Mediterranean coast, not a rustic lodge in the overcast mountains. Rather than a life of ascetic hardship, Gregory wanted to find a life of philosophical retirement. For centuries Greek and Roman notables had been accustomed to take breaks from public affairs by adopting a life of leisured retirement and devoting themselves to the study of classical texts. Gregory went to Isauria hoping to immerse himself in classical culture and recreate his experiences at Athens.[34]

Whatever Basil may have thought about the end of their friendship is lost. Since he was a correspondent of the bishop of Seleucia, he may have heard occasionally about Gregory's life there. Shortly before his death he may have restored enough communication with Gregory to encourage him to assume leadership of the orthodox Nicene community at Constantinople. But Basil also had a bottomless capacity for reticence about people from his own past who reminded him of painful experiences or of influences he later discounted. In his extant writings he never mentioned his father, his sister Macrina, or his teachers at Athens. During the 360s he had feuded over theological doctrines with Eunomius, a fellow Cappadocian; thereafter he barely alluded to him. His friendship with Gregory too was now cooped up in his unspoken memories, never to be dusted off for subsequent restoration.[35]

In contrast, Gregory could not give up thinking about their friendship. He and Eunomius became inverted reflections of each other, each pondering his treatment by Basil. In his exile Eunomius would silently sulk for over a decade about his enmity with Basil. Gregory likewise would brood on his friendship with Basil. His earlier commitment to this friendship had become morosely tragic, almost ineffably pathetic in its compulsion to try to revive the relationship. In a later account Gregory would state pointblank that he had been an "afterthought" in Basil's schemes. Already at the time he had likewise known that he had become superfluous. Soon after his consecration as bishop he had compared himself to the scaffolding that was dismantled and discarded once the bricks in a vault could support themselves.

He had been "a bone thrown into a pack of dogs." A relationship between friends was supposed to presuppose reciprocity, equality, and complementarity, but Gregory seems to have thought that his friendship with Basil was peculiarly one-sided, uneven, and incompatible. Despite this realization, he could not contemplate a divorce and seemingly kept on hoping for a reconciliation.[36]

Two considerations made it difficult for Gregory to abandon this friendship. One was the common stress on the intimate association between friendship and personal identity. A man inherited his parents and siblings from birth, but he chose his friends. The choice, an act of will, distinguished friends from relatives. Throughout his relationship with Basil, Gregory had repeatedly emphasized his choice. When bishop Eusebius of Caesarea had suggested that he reconsider his friendship with Basil, Gregory considered it an insult. "From the beginning I chose him as the companion of my life, my culture, and my most lofty philosophy, and now I hold on to him." Even after his painful consecration he still highlighted the importance of his choice, this time in a letter to Basil. "From the beginning I chose you as the guide for my life and my teacher of doctrines, and now I [still] choose you."[37]

This choice was furthermore supposed to fit into a notion of the human personality as somehow static, unchanging, permanent. Gregory did not change with each new friend that he chose, but merely exposed to both himself and the public a bit more of his essential personality. The choice of a friend was a moment of self-discovery, as a man found out more about himself, and a moment of self-revelation, as others found out more about him. Once true friends had chosen each other, their friendship was to be immutable and undeviating, immune to the fickleness of the mundane world.

Such a view of friendship and identity was of course too rigid to maintain over a long time. To identify self with another was to invite uncertainty and eventual confrontation. Circumstances changed for both partners; more important, such a linkage gave each partner too much influence on the other's sense of self. The slightest deviation or misstep by one partner in a friendship could endanger the other's identity. Neither could grow or mature or change without threatening the other's serenity and confidence. Gregory may have concluded that Basil had misbehaved in their friendship, but if he were to admit that his choice of Basil had been outright wrong, it would cast doubt on his own judgment. Gregory, and others, would then have reason to distrust the consistency of his own personality and the stability of his own identity.

A second, related inhibition was the close connection between Gregory's devotion to classical culture and his friendship with Basil. As his uneasiness with Basil grew, Gregory had sometimes tried to invoke a better time and an ideal relationship by mentioning one word: Athens. For young men obsessed with studying classical culture Athens was legendary, almost a fantasy; one young man had claimed that in order to see the haze of Athens he would even spurn marriage with a goddess! But for Gregory Athens would always represent not one but two related obsessions, both his friendship with Basil and his immersion in classical culture. In a later epitaph for Basil he would invoke both concerns: "O culture, o common home of friendship, o beloved Athens!"[38]

At Athens Gregory and Basil had studied rhetoric, philosophy, and other aspects of classical culture. A higher education in these subjects involved more than mere learning, however. These young students were grooming themselves, "educating a man's character" by adopting standards of expected behavior and public deportment. Young men assimilated with the books they read and studied. One teacher was lauded as "a living library and a walking repository of the Muses." To a sophist in Cappadocia Gregory offered some advice about education. "Since I am addressing an educated, cultured man, it is enough to say this. Be worthy of yourself and of the books with which you live. These books contain many life stories, many characteristic habits, many pleasures and successes, and, of course, many misfortunes and failures." Decorum, propriety, indifference to favor, control of anger and grief: educated men were expected to have so internalized these norms as to become the embodiments of them. In a similar fashion men merged with the friends they had chosen. In his later accounts Gregory emphasized precisely that coalescence by stressing that he and Basil had shared one soul in two bodies. "We lived in one another and with one another." For Gregory, the idea of Athens conjured up that simultaneous merging with culture and with a friend.[39]

Like the exchange of letters, both culture and friendship had rules. Rhetoric and eloquence implied the use of correct grammar, proper vocabulary, exact pronunciation, and disciplined control over voice, breathing, and posture. Mistakes resulted in mockery and embarrassment. One sophist from Cappadocia had been criticized at Athens for his heavy accent, "confusing the sounds of letters, shortening the long syllables, and lengthening the short syllables." Friendships also had rules, implicit expectations about equality and reciprocity, and any disregard of that protocol led to complaints or even the end of a relationship. This combination of his commitment to classical culture with his commitment to Basil now made it difficult to Gregory to end their relationship. Because he had linked the two commitments, a failure to live up to expectations in one could lead to questions about the other. A similar linkage connected the protocol of exchanging letters with the expectations of friendship. Men sustained friendships by continuing to exchange letters, while a hiatus in correspondence might lead to the end of a friendship. A break in the connection between friendship and culture might have similar dire consequences for Gregory. His friendship with Basil had become another aspect of his commitment to classical culture. Admitting a mistake in this friendship would have challenged the correctness of his devotion to culture, and perhaps even raised suspicions about his basic competence in rhetoric. It would have been as embarrassing as mispronouncing a word.[40]

"Always the Same Person"

Basil had less difficulty breaking up with Gregory, because he had never accepted the same connection of their friendship with classical culture. In all of his extant letters he mentioned Athens only twice, once to underline his pleasure at leaving and once merely to offer an illustrative example from ancient history. When he eventually provided a short survey of the development of his commitment to asceticism, he pointedly dismissed his youthful studies as vanity and futility. Long ago he had abandoned Athens and what it represented, and he had wanted to redefine his relationship with Gregory in terms of ascetic and ecclesiastical concerns. Appeals to "Athens" had no significance for him. At the banquet that Gregory reported on to Basil some of the guests had associated the two simply by saying "Athens": "they mentioned our friendship, Athens, and our harmony and agreement in everything." For Gregory, this passing comment had momentarily revived the possibility that their friendship might not be over, and he seems to have reported this loose talk to Basil in the hope that it might renew his feelings too. Basil's stiff reply had ended that hope.[41]

Even though Basil may have been insensitive and even careless in his friendship with Gregory, he too had one relationship that he found difficult to abandon. Soon after his return to Cappadocia from his studies at Athens he had chosen Eustathius as his guide for his increasing interest in an ascetic lifestyle. He had remained attached to Eustathius for almost the next two decades, during his retirement in Pontus, during his tenure as a priest, after

his consecration as bishop of Caesarea. At the very beginning of his episcopacy he had appreciated Eustathius' assistance. Then some of Eustathius'
supporters encouraged Basil's opponents at Caesarea who were murmuring
that their bishop's "proclamation of the ascetic life" was only a "pretense of
temperance," adopted merely to acquire support. This whispering about
Basil's asceticism was a serious threat. Just as Gregory had associated his
friendship with Basil with their mutual commitment to classical culture, so
Basil had associated his friendship with Eustathius with their mutual devotion to asceticism. To challenge one was to threaten the other.[42]

Basil's reactions now mixed his overt need for reassurance with latent
suspicion of his mentor. His first response was to hope that Eustathius' "love
for me would remain constant." His next reaction was to begin to wonder
about his friend's doctrinal orthodoxy, in particular regarding his theology
of the Holy Spirit. Other bishops in eastern Asia Minor had already become
suspicious of Eustathius' theology, and their suspicions carried over to Basil.
On his way to see these other bishops in 373 Basil stopped off to visit Eustathius, who reassured him of his orthodoxy. But when these other bishops
complained that Eustathius had subsequently recanted, Basil became indignant. He was reluctant to think that Eustathius would tip over so easily: "I
base my conjecture on the man's essential goodness." Basil could sense that
conceding a flaw in his friend's theology would threaten his own conviction
of the rightness of his commitment to asceticism.[43]

Although Eustathius then signed a declaration of his orthodox theology, Basil pressed him for explicit confirmation of his theology of the Holy
Spirit. This time Eustathius' response was to attack Basil's own orthodoxy by
dredging up his earlier association with Apollinarius, the bishop of Laodicea
in Syria whose doctrines about Christology were under attack. Basil then
lowered his opinion of Eustathius' theology still further by describing him
as a "true disciple" of the detested heresiarch Arius. By now their relationship had deteriorated into reciprocating denunciations. Yet Basil was also
struggling to understand the collapse of their friendship. He was furthermore worried that his authority would be undermined if others began to
doubt the stability of his convictions. One correspondent was in fact openly
concerned about the effect of this failed friendship on Basil's true self: "he
has now become someone else."[44]

A few years later when Basil finally wrote a long defense against Eustathius, he started by claiming he had been silent for three years. After these
years of introspection the explanation he had finally reached was a demonstration of consistency in his own life and thinking. In pursuing his

devotion to an ascetic life he had occasionally met people who he thought were his companions, but who had in fact accepted secret teachings. In contrast, Basil maintained that he himself had never deviated in his theology. "I never held opinions about God that wandered about, nor did I unlearn them later after changing my mind." In responding to accusations he repeatedly insisted that he had held the same doctrines, "from boyhood" no less. By insisting on the consistency of his theology, Basil was prepared to refute accusations that he had introduced "innovations" into his theology of the Holy Spirit. He furthermore claimed that his opponents had been fickle in their own thinking, "similar to clouds that are wafted about on changes in the breeze." "They adjust the words of the creed according to circumstances, adapting it this way and that to fit with current misfortunes."[45]

With this perspective Basil could finally abandon his friendship with Eustathius with a clear conscience. Eustathius and his supporters had repeatedly changed their thinking, while he had remained doggedly loyal to an ascetic life and his orthodox doctrines. "Always the same person, through God's grace I have never been affected by changes in events." Even as he dismissed this long-standing friendship, Basil insisted upon the stable core of his own identity.[46]

Autobiography and Friendship

Gregory could not fall back on a similar unswerving commitment to asceticism or on an insistence about an undeviating continuity of theological pronouncements. Instead, he now adopted the different approach of rewriting his life. By precluding any possibility of reconciliation, Basil's death meant that their relationship would always be unfinished, forever pending. Now the only future for the friendship was to reconsider the past. The stability that Basil insisted upon in his theology, Gregory would find in his own history.

After his aborted tenure as bishop of Constantinople Gregory returned to Cappadocia, where one of his primary activities became the contemplation of his own past. His concern was not to write a plain autobiography, nor to provide moral instruction from his own triumphs and mistakes. He wrote primarily to reassure himself that his life had followed a single consistent pattern. The end of his friendship with Basil had been unsettling enough that he had eventually banished himself from Cappadocia. His recent experiences in the capital had again raised the question of apparent disjunctions, and after he returned to his homeland he needed to find for himself an unwavering, constant trajectory in his life. Gregory now examined his friendship with Basil through the media of a self-reflective poem, a collection of his letters, and a lengthy oration.

Gregory had already used long autobiographical poems to analyze his feelings, one over a decade earlier after his brother's death when he was feeling alone, another immediately after his departure from his episcopacy at Constantinople. In the first poem he had mentioned in passing his earlier studies at Athens, "the pride of Greece," and in the more recent poem he may have alluded obliquely to Basil as the sponsor who had originally encouraged him to go to the capital. In neither poem had he mentioned or discussed Basil directly. In fact, even if the allusion about a sponsor had referred to Basil, Gregory had not wanted to talk about him: "who he was, I cannot say."[47]

Gregory completed yet another long autobiographical poem apparently in 382, within a year after his return to Nazianzus. In this self-reflective poem Gregory was still smarting from his experiences at the capital. Throughout his life he had been reluctant to serve as a cleric and become a bishop. At Constantinople he had finally agreed to become bishop, but he had then been run out of town. These misfortunes had challenged his sense of a consistent self, and back at his hometown Gregory was now trying to locate his recent experiences in a stable pattern for his life. This time he also took the opportunity to evaluate his friendship with Basil.

At the beginning of this poem Gregory introduced himself as "a man utterly without falsehood who has suffered much in many twists and turns." This introduction already defined the two themes that Gregory would emphasize in this poem, that he had remained true to himself and others, and that others were responsible for any apparent rifts in his life. The early influences on his life were predictable. One was his parents: "I had the best exemplars at home." The other was books, editions of classical Greek authors: "a fervid passion for books possessed me." In this retrospective account Gregory had kept culture as one of the defining characteristics of his life, but he now linked it with his parents' love. He also emphasized the importance of classical culture in his life long before he went to Athens and before he met Basil. After visiting other schools in the eastern Mediterranean Gregory finally did go to Greece: "then, Athens and culture." There he was associated with Basil, "the great prize of our generation," and there they were joined together as companions. "We were a pair, celebrated throughout Greece." Although Gregory claimed that they now shared "one soul," he also stressed that the bond that had held them together had been not culture, but "God and our longing for higher concerns." Gregory then skipped any mention of his stay with Basil in Pontus. Instead, his primary concern after he returned to Cappadocia was looking after his elderly parents. Only when his father tried to "tyrannize" Gregory by having him become a priest did he finally join Basil in Pontus. He then returned to assist his father and later to deal with the grief over the death of his brother Caesarius.[48]

So far in this account Basil had been only a character actor with walk-on roles as Gregory's companion at Athens and his confidant back in Cappadocia. Then Gregory confronted the episode of his consecration as a bishop. A decade after this fiasco he still clearly criticized and blamed Basil for his behavior. His description of Basil was a parody of his description of himself at the beginning of the poem. "In other respects Basil was utterly without falsehood, but toward me he was false." To understand his consecration Gregory had to explain the change in Basil's attitude. "What happened to you? Why did you abandon me so suddenly?" With these rhetorical questions Gregory effectively discounted any possibility of blame on his part and transferred the explanation for the breakdown of their friendship to Basil's duplicity. Basil had changed, while he had behaved properly. "Pontus, the city of Caesarea, and all our common friends know how I deferred to my friend." Even though Basil may have thought he had acted according to the expectations of friendship, in Gregory's later perspective "a law of friendship that honors friends in this way ought to disappear from life." The relationship that had developed at Athens was now broken. "Athens, our common pursuit of culture, the one mind in two [bodies], the marvel of Greece: everything was shattered and thrown to the ground." In this retrospective account Gregory had compressed his friendship with Basil to make it seem less significant, and he had blamed Basil entirely for its ending. One quarter of the way through his poem, Gregory never mentioned Basil again.[49]

Gregory's father now came to the rescue. As in his funeral oration for his father, Gregory was not hesitant to criticize his father's participation in his consecration: "my father was the second to kick me." But since his father then asked his son to help him at Nazianzus, Gregory was able to continue caring for his parents. By stressing his return to his parents Gregory was again able to downplay the significance of his relationship with Basil. In this perspective his friendship with Basil had been only an interlude, a temporary interruption in comparison to his long-standing devotion to his parents.[50]

Gregory then moved on to the next great discomfiting episode in his life, his service at Constantinople. This time he made clear immediately that he was again not to blame. "This account is an indictment against my enemies and a testimony for my friends of the injustices I suffered, even though I did no injustices." At the capital one of Gregory's opponents had been Maximus, who had even intrigued to become bishop. In his retrospective account Gregory found in Maximus some of the same characteristics he had attributed to Basil. Maximus was a charlatan, an impostor who had tried to charm Gregory with his interest in classical philosophy. Even though Gregory eventually acquired the support of the emperor Theodosius, he was still upset that he had been duped again. His ideal was for everyone to be completely transparent, to have "the same character, either exempt from evil or soaked in evil." But Maximus had turned out to be "another Proteus," the illusive shape-shifter of Greek mythology. Gregory's experiences with Maximus at the capital had helped him analyze his earlier relationship with Basil. With regard to both his friendship with Basil and his dealings with Maximus, he could now claim that he had remained the same, while his friend or his opponent had shifted and changed.[51]

In this retrospective poem Gregory had found one strategy for dealing with the end of his earlier friendship with Basil. He had first of all transferred the blame to Basil and concluded that his friend had betrayed him. Since he insisted that his interest in classical culture had appeared already very early in his youth, he had separated it from his friendship with Basil. He highlighted the roles of his parents, who had been the most important influences in his earlier life and to whom he had constantly returned. His father, despite his involvement in his consecration, had nevertheless rescued him from having to leave his family. By associating parents, culture, and friendship, and by making Basil responsible for the failure of their friendship, Gregory had been able to find a consistent pattern in his life. He had always been loyal to classical culture, friends, and parents, and while others may have been duplicitous, he had "overcome everything that changes." "To tell one's story . . . becomes an affirmation of power, even when the story contains emphatic defeats . . . or evidence of limitation or revelations of folly." The explanation Gregory offered in this retrospective poem conferred confidence and satisfaction, because the consistency of viewpoint in this version of the story of his life had become a demonstration of the stability of his identity throughout his life.[52]

Panegyric and Friendship

In this autobiographical poem Gregory paid a price for his narrative consistency, since he had had to shift the blame for the end of their friendship to Basil. However readily he would do so in rewriting his life's story, it was more difficult to reprove his friend in his heart.

Another opportunity to ponder the friendship came from his grand-nephew Nicobulus. Late in his life Gregory put together a collection of letters to help Nicobulus learn how to write proper letters. In this anthology he included a selection first of Basil's letters to him, then of his own letters to Basil, and finally of many others of his letters. In the process he must have reread these old letters and thought about their meaning. When he then shared some of his reactions with his grandnephew, it is notable how his thoughts drifted back and forth between the letters and their friendship. "I always honored the great Basil before myself, even though he thought the opposite more correct." Although this sentiment explained Gregory's decision to give priority to Basil's letters in his collection, it also seems to have reflected his lingering feelings about his friend. "I hope that we have been joined together in all respects, and at the same time I offer an example to others of restraint and deference." Even as Gregory explained the inclusion of both of their letters and the placement of his second, he seemed again to be recalling aspects of his actual friendship with Basil, their merger, his subordination. Letters had been at the core of their friendship. Back then the exchange of letters had been an important means for sustaining their friendship over the decades. Rereading the letters now in his final years brought back old memories and old emotions, and left Gregory feeling nostalgic and forgiving.[53]

After his return to Cappadocia Gregory was invited to deliver a panegyric apparently on an annual anniversary commemorating the day of Basil's death, most likely at Caesarea. These sorts of public orations tended to be highly stylized and excessively laudatory, typically composed in careful accordance with the rules of the genre of panegyric. Although the second part of Gregory's oration corresponded more or less to those expectations, the first half was surprisingly intimate and confessional. Gregory had obviously decided to use this oration as yet another opportunity to think again about his friendship with Basil. The distinctive oddity is that he then chose to share those private feelings at a public occasion. In this panegyric, or at least in the version he eventually published, Gregory exposed personal details about both Basil and himself in their relationship.[54]

Gregory began this oration with the typical platitudes and the usual compliments about Basil's ancestors, parents, and early education. "The oration is a pleasurable experience and simultaneously an exhortation to virtue." He mentioned his friendship with Basil, but only in passing and primarily to establish his credentials. Once he reached the point in Basil's life when his friend had gone to Athens, however, Gregory inserted himself directly into the narrative. "At this point in the oration I wish to include some of my affairs." The specific topic he wanted to discuss was the origin and development of "our friendship, or rather our mutual spirit and mutual nature." The recollection of the progress of their friendship was a tingling memory that Gregory described in terms of "the spark of our merging," "the conspicuous and lofty blaze of our friendship," "the mutual and continuous enhancement of our warming desire." In a public commemorative oration this was surprising language, since this vocabulary of heat and burning was more commonly used of private erotic passion. In this case it was not so much the relationship that had been on fire, as rather Gregory's current memories and the accompanying feelings. Since he was here describing their years of study together, he was recalling not just their mutual devotion, but also his pleasure in having been at Athens.[55]

Then Basil left. As Gregory recalled Basil's departure, he seemed to consider his abandonment the turning point in their friendship, perhaps even the beginning of the end of their friendship. Gregory accepted some liability, since he had wanted to stay. But he again placed most of the blame on Basil. "I will accuse that divine and impregnable soul." Gregory also claimed that he had nevertheless been faithful to their friendship. "I was betrayed by Basil, who was persuaded to abandon me who was not abandoning him." This outburst was again surprising, and not simply because it was so embarrassingly candid. In a eulogy an accusation was entirely out of place. A panegyrist was expected to praise the subject of his oration, not indict him. As Gregory recounted his memories, however, he was unable to control his anguish. Their tenure at Athens had represented an exceptionally happy period, and Basil's departure had irrevocably ended it. "It was similar to the splitting of one body into two. Both halves died."[56]

Even though Gregory continued with the account of their interactions, their close interconnectedness had disappeared, both from their lives then and from the narrative in the panegyric. Gregory hinted that he had visited Basil in exile in Pontus when his friend was feuding with bishop Eusebius of Caesarea, he noted that Basil had finally returned at his suggestion, and he mentioned their contact after Basil had become bishop. But he also was rather reticent about the two contentious episcopal consecrations that had in fact upset their relationship. Gregory did not mention his role in the selection of Basil as bishop. Nor did he explicitly mention his own consecration as a bishop. When he described Basil's attempt to consecrate more bishops, he praised the scheme overall before noting his own bitterness over being treated as a mere accessory. Gregory explained Basil's behavior this time by again suggesting that his friend had changed and become unfaithful. "This is the one aspect I cannot praise, his innovation toward me and his disloyalty. The passage of time has not dulled the pain."[57]

His distress over Basil's premature departure from Athens and his anguish over Basil's insistence that he become a bishop marked the two moments when Gregory had had most reason to doubt their friendship. In this oration he explicitly linked the two by noting the consequences. That initial separation had been the cause of "all the uncertainty and discomfort in my life." His participation in Basil's later scheme was likewise the cause of "all the uncertainty and confusion in my life." These were the two times when Basil had tried to divert Gregory, first away from Athens and devotion to classical culture, then into ecclesiastical politics. Any wobbles in the trajectory of Gregory's life had hence been due to Basil's unfaithfulness.[58]

Athens and Jerusalem

When collecting their earlier letters Gregory had been forgiving toward Basil. In his long autobiographical poem he had been more critical by blaming Basil for his own misfortunes. Since Gregory seems to have completed that poem shortly after he delivered this panegyric, the same preference for censure had apparently influenced him in both the poem and the oration.

In fact, the interpretation in this oration was more subtle and nuanced, because Gregory was able to surpass the mere assignment of blame in order to invent yet another strategy for understanding his relationship with Basil. Since his self-reflective poem had been about his own life, he could indulge his own despair and look for scapegoats. Then he had come to terms with his friendship with Basil by acquiring control over the narrative of his own life. But this panegyric was meant to be a celebration of Basil's life. Even though in the oration he still blamed Basil for his apparent innovation and disloyalty, he also supplied another, more sympathetic perspective in which Basil's behavior had itself been unwavering and stable. This time he would come to terms with their friendship by acquiring control over the narrative of Basil's life. Just as Gregory had looked for a consistent trajectory in his own life, so he now found a consistent pattern in Basil's life, which was his devotion to his service as a bishop.[59]

In the first part of his oration Gregory had followed an approximate chronological narrative into the early years of Basil's episcopacy. But once he mentioned Basil's plan to consecrate more bishops, he stopped talking about events in Basil's career. Rather than continuing with a sequential narrative of highlights from Basil's episcopacy, in the remainder of the oration he instead catalogued his many virtues, among them self-control, celibacy, generosity, and eloquence. He also compared Basil to a long list of biblical heroes and argued that he had surpassed them all. This emphasis on Basil's overall excellence turned him into a generic paradigm of the exemplary bishop. Because Basil had merely become what he was always destined to be, the first part of Gregory's oration should be read less as an historical survey, and more as a preview of the later revelation of these virtues. In his panegyric Gregory emphasized that Basil had always shown these episcopal qualities. Already as a young man Basil had seemed to be "a priest for the Christians, even before his priesthood." During his priesthood he assumed "the power in the church" by effectively sharing episcopal authority. When he eventually became bishop, he had received the office "from God, by divine favor." In Gregory's estimation, throughout his life Basil had been behaving like a bishop, and his actions had always been aimed toward "the increase of the church."[60]

Having outlined this consistent pattern in Basil's life, Gregory had almost no choice but to concede an acceptable rationale for Basil's imperious actions in disregarding their friendship. "Basil's ideas surpassed human affairs, and before he died he had removed himself from this world's concerns. He did everything for the sake of the Spirit. Although he knew how to respect a friendship, he dishonored it only at the moment when it was necessary to honor God more, and when it was necessary that hopes [for the future] took priority over broken [obligations]." With this discovery of a consistent pattern in Basil's life Gregory could offer a defense even for Basil's apparent arrogance. "What his critics call vanity was, I think, firmness, steadfastness, and stability of character." Even though Gregory still thought that Basil had been disloyal in their friendship, he could also acknowledge that Basil's behavior had at least been consistent. While he had always identified their friendship with a commitment to classical culture, Basil had associated it with the needs of episcopal service and the extension of the ecclesiastical community.[61]

By complaining that Basil had changed, Gregory was probably correct in implying that his friend had modified his notion of friendship after their early years as students together, but to come to terms with Basil's innovation he had to project his friend's new ideas all the way back to those early years. From the beginning Basil had been consistent in his behavior and thinking. But so had Gregory himself. By the time Gregory delivered this panegyric he was able to epitomize their contrasting commitments in iconic images. Two cities now represented their long-standing but differing notions of friendship. Gregory had linked their friendship with classical culture, Basil with ecclesiastical affairs. Gregory was a "lover of Athens"; Basil was "metropolitan of the heavenly Jerusalem."[62]

In retrospect Gregory had found different strategies for coming to terms with his relationship with Basil. While rereading their letters he had been conciliatory. While writing an autobiographical poem he had been more bitter and recriminatory. Since the subject of that poem was his own life, he had been ready to transfer blame for his misfortunes to others, including Basil. Gregory also composed that poem with his experiences at Constantinople fresh on his mind, and the duplicity he had seen there in others, in particular in his rival Maximus, probably influenced his thinking about Basil's behavior. This bitterness still infected his perspective in his panegyric about Basil. But since the subject of that oration was Basil's life, he was more willing to consider the possibility that Basil too had been following a consistent pattern in his behavior.

By then Gregory had in addition recovered a sense of equality in their relationship. Basil's promotion as metropolitan bishop had completely upset the evenness in their friendship. Even Gregory's subsequent promotion to become a bishop would not have restored the balance, since his proposed see of Sasima was a nondescript village. But by the time Gregory delivered this panegyric, he had in fact surpassed Basil in the ecclesiastical hierarchy. However briefly, he had served as bishop of Constantinople. At the end of this panegyric he felt confident enough to address Basil directly and describe himself as "a comrade and a man with the same rank." Once Gregory had regained his balance, he could be generous again.[63]

Lost Love

Classical Greek literature had offered several paradigms of a model friendship. Probably the most celebrated was the affection between Achilles and Patroclus, as memorialized in Homer's *Iliad*. In his panegyric about Basil, Gregory would mention two other remarkable friendships from ancient mythology, the alliance between Orestes and Pylades, two cousins who had joined together to avenge the murder of Agamemnon, Orestes' father, and the bond between the twin sons of Molione. In biblical traditions the most common paradigm of friendship was the relationship between David and Jonathan. Romans had lauded the model friendship between Scipio Aemilianus and Laelius. During the fourth century even some educated Greeks knew about this Roman model, and the emperor Julian used it to characterize one of his own relationships: "Scipio loved Laelius and was loved by him in return." To these Greek, biblical, and Roman paradigms of ideal friendships Byzantine readers now added Basil and Gregory. "I am in the habit of mentioning Basil and Gregory," noted Severus, bishop of Antioch in the early sixth century, "and having their names constantly upon my tongue." A tenth-century encyclopedia identified each simply as a bishop and the friend of the other.[64]

Gregory himself had contributed to the transformation of his companionship with Basil into an exemplary friendship through the format of his panegyric about his friend. Because he would combine the self-analysis in the first half of his panegyric with praise for Basil's episcopacy in the second half, the entire panegyric seemed to be an extended treatise of model-formation, and a model friendship was matched to a model bishop. Gregory's attempt to comprehend and soothe his own hurt was read instead as a prescriptive model of an ideal friendship, a celebration rather than a lament. Most people, not only later Byzantine readers but even Gregory's own contemporaries, presumably just did not know about the pain in the relationship. At the banquet Gregory attended the conversation had focused on him and Basil: "everyone was talking about our friendship." Even though this banquet was held about a year after Gregory's bungled consecration as bishop, people still naturally paired him with Basil.[65]

In his later years Gregory often thought about Basil. These were painful memories. "How can I remember these events without crying?" In the autumn of his life Gregory was now indulging in sentimental nostalgia as he recalled his first love and consoled his broken heart. He reread tattered letters, he teared up, he was both bitterly reproachful and generously forgiving, and at night he still dreamed about Basil. Eventually he seems to have come to terms with this lost love. He accepted an interpretation of his own life that highlighted his abiding loyalty to their friendship, and he found a perspective on Basil's life that allowed him to admire Basil's episcopacy while not overlooking his friend's faithlessness. For a while the trajectories of their lives had overlapped, before going off to separate destinies.[66]

Yet for all his skill and insight at reinterpreting this breakup, Gregory never lost hope for reviving their friendship. In addition to an autobiographical poem, a collection of letters, and a panegyric he used yet another literary genre to reflect on their relationship when he composed a series of epitaphs for Basil. Back at the beginning of their friendship Gregory had identified himself with Basil when they had merged their selves, "two bodies, one soul." In one of these epitaphs, despite all the hard feelings of the intervening years, he again merged with his friend by writing from Basil's perspective. In this epitaph he had Basil identify himself as "a friend of Gregory, whom I loved with my heart." Gregory had now put into Basil's mouth the words of devotion and love he had always wanted to hear in person.[67]

In this case, however, he was optimistic rather than mournful. As schoolmates at Athens they had been true friends, united in their singular devotion to classical culture. Then family obligations and ecclesiastical politics had intruded and corroded their friendship. Since they had never adequately resolved their estrangement, Gregory now hoped that they would eventually enjoy "a friendship in heaven." Gregory never stopped imagining that it might be possible to recreate the atmosphere of Athens, and hence their friendship too. Perhaps heaven would be like Athens.[68]

Epilogue:
A Fourth Cappadocian Father

The Cappadocian Fathers always appear as a trio, two brothers and their mutual friend, each a bishop and an important theologian. Their significance as churchmen has become their distinguishing characteristic. In that theological and ecclesiastical context, however, there could well have been a fourth Cappadocian Father.

One candidate was Amphilochius, a cousin of Gregory of Nazianzus. Amphilochius had been educated in classical culture and started a career as an advocate and orator. Then he moved on to become bishop of Iconium. As a theologian he composed a treatise about the Holy Spirit, and as a church leader he attended the ecumenical council at Constantinople in 381 and presided at a council that condemned some mendicant Christians. These were impressive accomplishments. At the end of the fourth century the biblical scholar Jerome, in one of his compulsive rankings of churchmen, reviewed his predecessors and peers in terms of their erudition in both classical and biblical texts. When he listed Cappadocians, he included Amphilochius with Basil and Gregory of Nazianzus, but did not mention Gregory of Nyssa. Amphilochius was poised to become one of the top three Cappadocian Fathers. Yet despite his reputation, Amphilochius was not an original or influential enough of a thinker to be classified among the great Cappadocian theologians. At another council even he conceded that he was only borrowing from the authority of Basil's writings.[1]

Another candidate might have been Eunomius, a contemporary from Cappadocia who did become an important theologian in his own right. He too was a native of Cappadocia who studied classical philosophy, and he eventually became a bishop at Cyzicus. His theology was influential for a time, before becoming the object of others' scorn. He lost his opportunity to be remembered as a Church Father once Basil and Gregory of Nyssa decided to confront his doctrines and deface his life. Eunomius was a casualty of the search for a Christian doctrine of God during the fourth century.

Yet another candidate might have been Julian. Julian had grown up on an imperial estate in Cappadocia, where he had studied classical culture and Christian texts. Then he had gone off to listen to the lectures of famous teachers at cities in the old Greek world, including Athens. To that point the trajectory of his life had closely mirrored the early careers of Basil and Gregory of Nazianzus. Once Julian became emperor, however, he tried to associate classical literature exclusively with the paganism he was by now openly promoting. Gregory of Nazianzus was deeply dismayed at this betrayal. Yet, with his own passion for classical culture, Gregory in fact had more in common with his opponent Julian than with his friend Basil, who had simply downplayed the significance of classical culture. Julian represented alternatives that the Cappadocian Fathers either rejected outright or struggled with all their lives. Julian was the Cappadocian Father who got away.

A junior episcopal colleague, a theological rival, an educated but pagan emperor: modern discussions of these three possible additions to the usual trio of Cappadocian Fathers often only reinforce their roles as churchmen. Since Amphilochius was a theological protégé, Eunomius an influential contemporary theologian, and Julian a lapsed Christian, it is all too easy to discuss them as yet other contributors to the making of the Cappadocian Fathers as ecclesiastical leaders.

Yet these particular relationships also highlight some of the other roles of the Cappadocian Fathers. The two other volumes in my trio of books about late Roman Cappadocia discuss aspects of their interactions with Roman rule, Greek culture, and Christian society. *Kingdom of Snow* focuses on the nature and effect of Roman rule in Cappadocia and the disputes over the fate of classical Greek culture in an increasingly Christian society. One of the main characters in that book is, of course, Julian, who would return to Cappadocia as an emperor in order to confront his own upbringing as a Christian. *Becoming Christian* emphasizes the impact of Christianity on Greek society in Cappadocia. The Cappadocian Fathers had to figure out how to rewrite history to correspond with their new Christian lifestyle, how to communicate with ordinary believers who were not familiar with classical culture, and how to define themselves as Christian bishops. One of the minor characters in that book is Amphilochius, who was the recipient of Basil's letters about enforcing the new Christian morality. One of the main characters is, of course, Eunomius, who was a rival not just to the theology of the Cappadocian Fathers, but to their local prestige too.

This book has stressed the roles of the Cappadocian Fathers as family men and friends. Modern scholarship on friendship in the ancient world and on Roman families has flourished in recent years, and the lives of the Cappadocian Fathers can serve as models of the current state of scholarship and for future research. In this context too there might have been a fourth distinguished Cappadocian. Macrina, the sister of Basil and Gregory of Nyssa, became an exemplar of ascetic spirituality and was noted for her familiarity with classical philosophy and Christian doctrines. Asceticism, philosophy, and theology were attributes that Gregory of Nyssa greatly admired, especially when he was so uncertain about the significance of family relationships, both in his own marriage and with his siblings. As a result, Gregory tended to transform consideration of family into discussion of theology. The one aspect of family Gregory and other theologians were willing to discuss openly was the relationship between God the Father and God the Son. In contrast, despite a few exceptions, such as Gregory of Nazianzus in his autobiographical musings and his funeral orations, they often seemed reluctant to talk about their own families. In his biography of Macrina, Gregory of Nyssa even declined to describe her as his sister.[2]

In accordance with his prejudices, modern scholars have defined the field of patristics largely in terms of theology, asceticism, spirituality, and ecclesiastical affairs, not family relationships or friendships. Such a narrow perspective has regretably often excluded discussion of the significance of gender identity. In contrast, a discussion of families of necessity raises the issue of gender. Gregory wanted to avoid that obligation, and he preferred not to think of Macrina in the context of a family as his sister. Instead, she had to be unmarried, an ascetic and a virgin. Most importantly, she had to be presented as learned, a theologian and a philosopher. Theology was masculine, involving a Father and a Son. Gregory's distorted representation of his sister has hence made her eligible for inclusion among the great Cappadocian theologians. By highlighting her theological prowess and spiritual leadership, Gregory thought of Macrina in terms of some of the Christian ideals of manliness. Modern scholars have again followed his lead. To become the fourth Cappadocian, Macrina has had to be imagined as a theologian in her own right, a potential Cappadocian Father rather than a possible Cappadocian Mother.

Abbreviations

ACW	Ancient Christian Writers (Westminster).
Becoming Christian	R. Van Dam, *Becoming Christian: The Conversion of Roman Cappadocia* (University of Pennsylvania Press, forthcoming).
Budé	Collection des Universités de France publiée sous le patronage de l'Association Guillaume Budé (Paris).
CChr.	Corpus christianorum (Turnhout).
CPG	*Clavis patrum graecorum.* CChr. (Turnhout). Vols. 1–5, ed. M. Geerard (1974–1987); Supplementum, ed. M. Geerard and J. Noret (1998).
CSEL	Corpus scriptorum ecclesiasticorum latinorum (Vienna).
FC	The Fathers of the Church (Washington, D.C.).
GCS	Die griechischen christlichen Schriftsteller der ersten Jahrhunderte (Berlin).
GNO	Gregorii Nysseni opera (Leiden).
IGR	*Inscriptiones graecae ad res romanas pertinentes.* Vols. 1, 3–4, ed. R. Cagnat et al. (Paris, 1906–1927).
Kingdom of Snow	R. Van Dam, *Kingdom of Snow: Roman Rule and Greek Culture in Cappadocia* (University of Pennsylvania Press, 2002).
LCL	Loeb Classical Library (Cambridge, Mass. and London).
NPNF	A Select Library of Nicene and Post-Nicene Fathers of the Christian Church (reprint, Grand Rapids, Mich.).
PG	*Patrologia graeca* (Paris).
PLRE	*The Prosopography of the Later Roman Empire* (Cambridge). Vol. 1, *A.D. 260–395,* ed. A. H. M. Jones, J. R. Martindale, and J. Morris (1971). Vol. 2, *A.D. 395–527,* ed. J. R. Martindale (1980).
SChr.	Sources chrétiennes (Paris).
Studia Pontica 3.1	*Studia Pontica III: Recueil des inscriptions grecques et latines du Pont et de l'Arménie,* Fascicule 1, ed. J. G. C. Anderson, F. Cumont, and H. Grégoire (Brussels, 1910).
Teubner	Bibliotheca scriptorum graecorum et romanorum Teubneriana (Leipzig and Stuttgart).
TTH	Translated Texts for Historians (Liverpool).

In the notes, B = Basil of Caesarea, GNaz = Gregory of Nazianzus, and GNys = Gregory of Nyssa.

Notes

Introduction

1. GNaz, *Carm.* II.1.12.48, with *Becoming Christian*, Chapter 10, for Gregory's autobiographies.

2. Theodosius: Paulinus of Nola, *Ep.* 28.6.

3. Lake: Vitruvius, *De architectura* 8.3.9, on the effects of bitumen.

4. Melania the Elder: Palladius, *Historia Lausiaca* 55.3.

5. G. W. Bowersock, P. Brown, and O. Grabar (eds.), *Late Antiquity: A Guide to the Postclassical World* (Cambridge, Mass., 1999).

6. Tome Neuvième, "Qui contient les vies de Saint Basile, de Saint Grégoire de Nazianze, de Saint Grégoire de Nysse, & de Saint Amphiloque"; this ninth volume of Tillemont's *Mémoires* was published posthumously in 1703. For the lingering influence of his conclusions, see Van Dam (1996) 17–18. The appreciations of Tillemont came from no less of a critic than Edward Gibbon: see Gibbon (1897–1902) 3:48n.126, mule, (1984) 151, accuracy.

7. For unhelpful suspicion of "ever new contrivances and vogue approaches" when applied to patristic texts, see Spira (1984) 5.

8. Students: Zachariah Scholasticus, *Vita Severi Antiocheni*, tr. Kugener (1903) 37–38, 48, 53–54, 80.

Fathers and Sons Introduction

1. On blanket conclusions, note the recommendation of Saller (1994) xi, on "the need to distinguish between the normative order of Roman culture and the diffused experiences and individual choices of daily social life."

2. Affection in Roman families: Dixon (1991), (1992) 30, "A strong sentimental ideal of family feeling developed in Roman society." For a realistic assessment of the strains and pressures in the relationships between Roman parents and children, see Bradley (1991) 125–49. On Augustine's family, see Shaw (1987a) and Clark (1999) 9–21. Quotation from Bradley (1991) 177, referring to the advantages of investigating Cicero's letters; note also Bradley (2000), who uses data derived from a work of fiction to compensate for "Roman family case-histories, which are never more than partially or episodically known even in the best examples such as that of Cicero's family" (282).

3. On life expectancy in the Roman world, see Parkin (1992) 67–107, and Saller (1994) 12–25. Gentleness of Gregory the Elder: GNaz, *Orat.* 7.3.

4. For a notable exception to the deficiency of discussions about brothers, see Bannon (1997).

Chapter 1. Basil and Basil the Elder

1. Anonymous accusations: Pliny the Younger, *Ep.* 10.96–97. Wife: Tertullian, *Ad Scapulam* 3.4. Earthquakes: Cyprian, *Ep.* 75.10, a letter from Firmilianus, bishop of Caesarea, to Cyprian, bishop of Carthage, about a persecution in 235; for discussion, see Barnes (1971) 269–70, and Clarke (1984–1989) 4:250–51, 263–65. Gregory Thaumaturgus: GNys, *Vita Gregorii Thaumaturgii, PG* 46.944A–948D, referring most likely to the edict of the emperor Decius, perhaps to the emperor Valerian; for Decius' insistence on universal sacrifice, see Rives (1999).

2. GNys, *Vita Macrinae* 2, persecutions, 20, displeasure. GNaz, *Orat.* 43.5, "living martyrs," Maximinus, 6–8, seven years, mountains. GNys, *Vita Macrinae* 2, also noted that Emmelia, Basil's mother, had been "orphaned" before her marriage. Eusebius, *HE* 8.12.1, 6, tortures in Cappadocia and Pontus, 9.7.12, Maximinus' letter, with the excellent discussion of this letter in Mitchell (1988). Diocletian reigned until 305, and Galerius until 311. Upon hearing about Galerius' death Maximinus extended his control to include Asia Minor: see Barnes (1982) 66–67, for Maximinus in Asia Minor, and Mitchell (1982), for the impact of his persecutions in Galatia. The emperor Licinius defeated Maximinus in 313.

3. Macrina's recitation: GNys, *Vita Macrinae* 20, with Alexandre (1984) 33–38, for Gregory's ideas on martyrdom and his family, and Helleman (2001), on Macrina's association of martyrdom and asceticism. Tombstones: *Studia Pontica* 3.1:101, no. 83 = Merkelbach and Stauber (2001) 355, no. 11/03/05, memories; *Studia Pontica* 3.1:106, no. 91 = Merkelbach and Stauber (2001) 361, no. 11/05/01, parents. Breathing tombstones: GNaz, *Orat.* 43.5. For Macrina the Elder, see also Chapter 6.

4. Mythological ancestors: GNaz, *Orat.* 43.3, with *Becoming Christian*, Chapter 3, on the significance of Basil's ancestry. Family tomb: GNys, *Encomium in XL martyres* 2, *PG* 46.784B, with *Becoming Christian*, Chapter 7, on the Forty Martyrs.

5. Tragedy: B, *Ep.* 136.

6. Wisdom of old age: GNaz, *Orat.* 43.23.

7. GNys, *Vita Macrinae* 21, mentioning Basil the Elder's education, reputation in courts, and fame as an orator; for Basil the Elder's age, see Chapter 6, on the date of birth of Macrina the Younger, his oldest child. Kopecek (1973), and Karayannopoulos (1981) 379–83, argue that the family had curial rank, in preference to Treucker (1961) 7–16, arguing that the family had senatorial rank; the suggestion of Fedwick (1979) 38n.4, that Basil's family were landowners who "had no part in the contemporary political life," endorsed by Treucker (1981) 409n.18, may be correct about service in the imperial administration, but all substantial landowners were involved in cities. But note that Basil and his brothers never seem to have worried about having to serve as municipal magistrates or members of a municipal council. For a comparable career, note the Gallic aristocrat Ausonius, a slightly younger contemporary of Basil the Elder, who also started out as a grammarian and an advocate: see Kaster (1988) 102–6, 124–25, 247–49.

8. GNaz, *Orat.* 43.12, teacher of virtue, 17, students from Armenia. Although the orator Themistius mentioned that he had once studied rhetoric "on the very edge of Pontus near the Phasis [River]" (*Orat.* 27.332d–333a), the proposal of Vanderspoel (1995) 34–35, that Themistius had been a student of Basil the Elder at Neocaesarea is improbable. Aubineau (1966) 36, and Fedwick (1981) 5, suggest that Basil was born in ca. 329. Basil called both Cappadocia and Pontus his homeland. But since his father had made his career in Pontus, it is more likely that Basil was born there and not in Caesarea; for the debate, see Maraval (1971) 38n.2.

9. My blood: GNaz, *Ep.* 174.4.

10. B, *Ep.* 37, a petition on behalf of "my foster brother, the son of the woman who nourished me"; *Ep.* 137, a letter on behalf of "my most revered mother Palladia." The foster brother eventually became a priest: B, *Ep.* 36. Young child: B, *Ep.* 102; this new bishop at Satala was Poemenius: B, *Ep.* 122. Macrina the Elder: B, *Ep.* 204.6; also *Ep.* 223.3. Note that Macrina, the oldest child in the family, and even Peter, the last child, also had wet nurses: GNys, *Vita Macrinae* 3, 12. On wet nurses, see Rousselle (1988) 51–58, and Bradley (1991) 29: "in all cases nursing implies a general disruption of contact between parent and child, and it seems plausible that physical distancing was matched by emotional distancing."

11. B, *Ep.* 37, payments; *Ep.* 223.3, mother's influence. For his parent's possible involvement in his early upbringing, note B, *De iudicio Dei = Prologus* 7.1: "From the beginning I was educated by Christian parents, and immediately after birth I learned the sacred writings from them"; but these "parents" may have been only relatives.

12. GNaz, *Ep.* 190.4, charlatan; *Ep.* 192.3, words. Orator and advocate: Philostratus, *Vitae sophistarum* 525. Aetius at Anazarbus: Philostorgius, *HE* 3.15, with Kaster (1988) 5–6, 376. Because Basil the Elder was not explicitly identified as a grammarian, the prosopographical catalogue in Kaster (1988) does not include him; but like a grammarian he seems to have taught boys in their preteens and early teens, before they typically went on to study with a rhetorician. To avoid conceding that Basil the Elder was a grammarian Bernardi (1992) 140n.2, suggests, without any evidence, that he could have been the head of a school that offered teaching in grammar. For the usual interaction between family and education, see Kaster (1988) 11: "entry into the grammarian's school was the first step beyond the confines of the family."

13. Grammar: GNaz, *Carm.* II.2.4.63–64. Quotations about guardian from Kaster (1988) 17–18. Beatings: B, *Hom.* 12.5.

14. Friendly rivalry: GNys, *Ep.* 11.3–5. Beating of Hypatius: Callinicus, *Vita Hypatii* 1.7, with Bartelink (1971) 17–19, for the chronology. Education of Aedesius: Eunapius, *Vitae sophistarum* 461, with Penella (1990) 63–65. GNaz, *Carm.* II.2.3.14–15, good family, 137–42, hospitality, 198–215, poet and wedding, 297–304, disobedient sons, 333–36, pride. Note that Gregory composed and addressed this poem to Vitalianus in the guise of Petrus; for the possibility that Vitalianus had once slighted Gregory himself, see McLynn (1998). This Vitalianus should probably be identified with the Vitalianus who received GNaz, *Ep.* 75: see Hauser-Meury (1960) 179–80, "Vitalianus I" and "Vitalianus II," and Gallay (1964–1967) 1:93n.1.

According to the edition in *PG* 37.316–17, the recipient of GNaz, *Ep.* 193–94, was named Procopius; both Hauser-Meury (1960) 149, "Procopius I," and *PLRE* 1:744,

"Procopius 7," identify this Procopius with the Procopius who received GNaz, *Ep.* 90, 128. In his newer editions, however, Gallay (1964–1967) 1:111, 129, (1969) XXIV, 77, corrects the heading to GNaz, *Ep.* 90 and identifies the addressee of that letter as a man named Anysius. Gallay (1964–1967) 2:84–85, (1969) XXXIV, 140, also corrects the heading to GNaz, *Ep.* 193–94 and identifies the addressee of both those letters as a man named Vitalianus (or, less likely, Vitalius). Gallay (1964–1967) 2:163, then identifies this Vitalianus with the Vitalianus for whom Gregory composed *Carm.* II.2.3. In *Ep.* 193.1 Gregory complimented Vitalianus for the wedding of "your golden Olympias." Gallay suggests that this Olympias was Vitalianus' daughter; Delmaire (1989a) 89–92, identifies this Olympias with the heiress Olympias at Constantinople (cf. *PLRE* 1:642–43, "Olympias 2"), and Vitalianus as her guardian. Regali (1988), dates *Carm.* II.2.3 to 374; Demoen (1997) 5n.18, questions this date; McLynn (1998) 240, suggests the mid-380s.

15. GNys, *Vita Macrinae* 4, assistance from Macrina's fiancé, 21, father's reputation in Pontus.

16. Cappadocian rhetorician: Libanius, *Ep.* 1222.2, mentioning Palladius in the mid-360s. Studies at Constantinople: GNaz, *Orat.* 43.14; student of Libanius: GNys, *Ep.* 13.4. Libanius taught at Constantinople from 349 to 354: Libanius, *Orat.* 1.74–86, 94. Studies with Proaeresius and Himerius: Socrates, *HE* 4.26, Sozomen, *HE* 6.17. Eunapius, *Vitae sophistarum* 489, Proaeresius and Hermes, 495, Libanius. Himerius: Libanius, *Ep.* 469.1. For the influence of grammarians on their students, see Kaster (1988) 205: "their loyalty to the grammarian, a more distant figure from their earlier years, was more attenuated and remote."

17. Basil the Elder died at the same time that his son Peter was born: GNys, *Vita Macrinae* 12, with Chapter 3, for the date. The age difference between Macrina the Younger, the oldest child, and Peter, the youngest child, was about fifteen, perhaps almost twenty years (see Chapter 6), and young men from aristocratic families typically married in their later twenties: see Saller (1994) 41. At his death Basil the Elder was hence in his forties, perhaps almost fifty, and died at an expected age; according to GNaz, *Orat.* 18.38, forty-five years was "the measure of a man's life."

18. Saller (1994) 229: "perhaps a third of Roman children lost their fathers before reaching puberty and another third became fatherless before the age of twenty-five." For a possible hint at familiarity with the Roman notion of *patria potestas*, note B, *Ep.* 276, to a father about his son: "with regard to his body he is liable [to you] both by the law of nature and by that civil law according to which we are governed, but with regard to his soul . . .'"; with Arjava (1998), on the survival of paternal power even in the later Roman empire and even in the provinces.

19. GNaz, *Orat.* 43.4, pedigrees of horses, 12, Basil as colt. Reminder: GNys, *Vita Macrinae* 21. Unbroken colt: B, *Ep.* 244.4, used to describe Eustathius.

20. Disdain: GNys, *Vita Macrinae* 6. Young man: GNys, *Vita Gregorii Thaumaturgii*, *PG* 46.937C. Prestige: B, *Ep.* 150.1. Embassy from Neocaesarea: B, *Ep.* 210.1. For the suggestion that Basil became a rhetorician at Caesarea, see Aubineau (1966) 54–55, who also dates his return to 355. One of Basil's students, apparently at Caesarea, was his brother Gregory of Nyssa; since in the mid-350s Gregory was in his late teens or early twenties, Basil was presumably teaching rhetoric and philosophy, not grammar: see Chapter 3. Nightingale: Philostratus, *Vitae sophistarum* 516.

Libanius' ambitions: Eunapius, *Vitae sophistarum* 495. Metropolis of culture: GNaz, *Orat.* 43.13. For a public chair of rhetoric at Caesarea, see Libanius, *Orat.* 31.42, mentioning a sophist who preferred to teach at Caesarea rather than at Antioch, with *PLRE* 1:6, "Acacius 4," 729, "Priscio."

21. Teacher: B, *Ep.* 150.1. Guides: B, *Ep.* 204.6. Teachers as fathers: B, *Ep.* 300. On guardians for fatherless children, see Saller (1994) 181–203.

22. Conversations about Libanius: GNys, *Ep.* 13.4, with Petit (1956) 35–36, for Libanius as a "father" to some of his students. For the dossier of letters between Basil and Libanius, see B, *Ep.* 335–59 = Libanius, *Epistularum commercium* 1–24, 26. Of these letters, Fedwick (1981) 5n.19, accepts only B, *Ep.* 335–41, 344, 346, 358, as authentic, Pouchet (1992a) 151–75, only B, *Ep.* 335–40; for the debate, see Hauschild (1993) 243n.616. Eunapius, *Vitae sophistarum* 486, Proaeresius' family, 487–88, students from Asia Minor, 493, true son. Proaeresius' birthplace: *Suda* Π.2375, "a Cappadocian from Caesarea," with Penella (1990) 83–94, on Proaeresius' life. Himerius from Bithynia: Eunapius, *Vitae sophistarum* 491, 494, with Barnes (1987), and Penella (1990) 97–100, on Himerius' life. His estates in Armenia: Libanius, *Ep.* 469.1. Oration: Himerius, *Orat.* 18.5. The heading of this fragmentary oration claimed that it was delivered to a Cappadocian; Bernardi (1992) 39–40, suggests that it was the "discours d'adieu" that Himerius addressed to Basil and Gregory. Teachers: GNaz, *Orat.* 43.22.

23. Athens as a threat: GNaz, *Orat.* 43.21, "in spiritual affairs Athens was harmful for other [students]"; for additional discussion of Basil at Athens, see Chapter 10.

24. Pilgrimage to East: B, *Ep.* 1, 223.2; Gribomont (1959), Hauschild (1990) 161n.1, and Pouchet (1992a) 87–93, identify the Eustathius to whom Basil sent *Ep.* 1 with Eustathius of Sebasteia. For the intriguing possibility that Basil visited Antioch during this journey, see Beagon (1997). Expulsion from clergy: Socrates, *HE* 2.43, although Sozomen, *HE* 3.14 defended Eustathius' attire. Both Socrates, *HE* 2.43, and Sozomen, *HE* 4.24, identified Eulalius, Eustathius' father, as bishop of Caesarea in Cappadocia; but because there is no other evidence for his episcopacy at Caesarea, Loofs (1898) 94–95, suggests he was bishop of Sebasteia. The young Eustathius was apparently once investigated by bishop Hermogenes of Caesarea: B, *Ep.* 263.3. Cloak, sandals, and conversations: B, *Ep.* 2.6, 223.3–5.

25. Boy: B, *Ep.* 244.1; for "boyhood" lasting until age fourteen or fifteen, see *Anthologia Graeca* 14.126–27. For the end of Basil's relationship with Eustathius, see Chapter 10.

26. Macrina's influence: GNys, *Vita Macrinae* 6, with Maraval (1971) 52, who suggests that Macrina introduced Eustathius' ideas to Basil while he was still at Athens. Visits to mother: B, *Ep.* 223.5, with Chapter 6. Basil's retreat has conventionally been identified with the οἰκία at Annisa that he mentioned in *Ep.* 3.2; and modern scholars have conventionally located Annisa at the modern village of Uluköy or Sonusa, near the confluence of the Iris and Lycus rivers: see Gallay (1943) 68, Maraval (1971) 38–44, and Rousseau (1994) 62. Although Basil's retreat was certainly in Pontus, it is not obvious that it should be identified with the settlement of Annisa, or that ancient Annisa should be identified with Uluköy. Olshausen and Biller (1984) 119, have suggested that Uluköy/Sonusa can be identified with ancient Boenasa, and Huxley (1989), has proposed identifying Annisa with an ancient settlement in Cappadocia about fifteen miles northeast of Caesarea called Hanisa (or Anisa, modern

Kültepe): see Hild and Restle (1981) 193, with *Kingdom of Snow*, Chapter 1. Given these alternatives, Basil's family estate in Pontus should remain unnamed, and the precise location of his retreat is still uncertain: see Van Dam (1996) 44–45.

27. GNys, *Vita Macrinae* 6, daughters' marriages, 13, Emmelia's funeral. Amisus: *Studia Pontica* 3.1:26, no. 15. Shoulders: Artemidorus, *Onirocritica* 1.40, with Bannon (1997) 91–135, on assistance among brothers.

Although his married sisters most likely had children, Basil did not mention any nephews or nieces. The anonymous recipient of B, *Ep.* 155, was a native of Cappadocia who was apparently serving in the army in Scythia. Basil asked him to send "the relics of the martyrs" to his native land. This correspondent was most likely Junius Soranus, the *dux* of Scythia who was credited with recovering the remains of St. Sabas after his martyrdom in April 372 and sending them to Cappadocia: see *Passio Sabae* 8.1–2, with Hauschild (1973) 168n.157, *PLRE* 1:848, "Junius Soranus 2," and Zuckerman (1991) 473–79. Pouchet (1992a) 458, 599–600, has in addition claimed that Soranus was related to Basil by marriage as a nephew-in-law. As reassurance that his correspondent was being included in his prayers Basil mentioned various reminders. According to the text in *PG* 32.613A and in Deferrari (1926–1934) 2:382, these reminders included "a sister (ἀδελφὴν) and nephews." But Courtonne (1957–1966) 2:81, emended the text to read "a niece (ἀδελφιδῆν) and nephews," and went on to translate the sentence in such a way that the correspondent's relatives also became "our," i.e., Basil's, relatives. Pouchet then identified this niece as both Soranus' wife and a daughter of one of Basil's sisters. In fact, the textual emendation is speculative (other manuscripts apparently have ἀδελφικὴν, "brother's wife"?), as is the suggestion about Soranus' marriage; and Heather and Matthews (1991) 122n.47, noted that Courtonne anyway mistranslated the sentence to suggest that Soranus' relatives were Basil's too.

Gaudentius of Brescia, *Tractatus* 17.15, mentioned meeting some elderly nuns at Caesarea who had once received some relics from Basil, "their maternal uncle." Although these women may have been daughters of Basil's sisters, it is more likely that they were merely spiritual nieces. Since the nuns in Macrina's convent in Pontus called her "mother," nuns in Cappadocia may also have thought of Basil as their spiritual uncle: see GNys, *Vita Macrinae* 26, with Chapter 6. For the possibility that Basil addressed his treatise on Greek literature, *Ad adulescentes*, to his nephews, see *Kingdom of Snow*, Chapter 10.

28. Amaseia: *Studia Pontica* 3.1:121, no. 99, dated to 376/377.

29. Eulogy of Musonius: B, *Ep.* 28.3, dated to early 371 by Hauschild (1990) 178n.153. Atarbius as relative: B, *Ep.* 210.4. First letter to Atarbius: B, *Ep.* 65. Nicopolis: B, *Ep.* 126. Public hearing: B, *Ep.* 204. Bishops: B, *Ep.* 203. Clerics at Neocaesarea: B, *Ep.* 207. Visit to Peter: B, *Ep.* 216. Warning: B, *Ep.* 210.3. Governor: B, *Ep.* 63, addressed to the "hegemon of Neocaesarea," whom *PLRE* 1:1024, "Anonymus 122," identifies as the governor of Pontus Polemoniacus; for the heading to this letter, see Fedwick (1993) 515, and for the date, Fedwick (1981) 12. Appeal to Anthimus: B, *Ep.* 210.5.

30. Blood relations: B, *Ep.* 204.2.

31. B, *Ep.* 204.2, spiritual fathers, 6, Macrina. Seclusion of Gregory Thaumaturgus: GNys, *Vita Gregorii Thaumaturgii*, *PG* 46.908B–C. Basil's retreat in Pontus: B, *Ep.* 210.1.

32. Warning: B, *Ep.* 207.4. Verification: B, *De spiritu sancto* 29.74. Friend's embarassment: B, *Ep.* 208, "Neocaesarea seems to be the reason for your silence toward us."

33. Cappadocian saints: B, *Ep.* 252, dated to 376 by Fedwick (1981) 17, to 377 by Hauschild (1993) 222n.389. For Eupsychius, martyred during Julian's reign, see *Kingdom of Snow*, Chapter 10. Basil as Cappadocian: GNaz, *Ep.* 2.1.

34. Epitaph of immigrant from Phrygia, found in the territory of Amaseia: Merkelbach and Stauber (2001) 384, no. 11/09/01.

35. Uncle Gregory as father: B, *Ep.* 59.1. For the role of maternal uncles, see Bremmer (1976), and Patlagean (1977) 121–24.

36. Dianius as bishop by early 341: Athanasius, *Apologia contra Arianos* 21.1, ed. Opitz (1935–1941) 102, with Barnes (1993) 59. Baptism and ordination from "a man who served for a long time in the ministry of God": B, *De spiritu sancto* 29.71, with Aubineau (1966) 55n.5, on the date of Basil's baptism. Basil as reader: GNaz, *Orat.* 43.27. Basil as deacon and council of Constantinople: Philostorgius, *HE* 4.12, with *Becoming Christian*, Chapter 1. Clergy and kinship: B, *Ep.* 54. Affection: B, *Ep.* 51.1.

37. Dianius' theology and confession: B, *Ep.* 51.2, with Lipatov (2001), for a possible statement of Basil's doctrines at the time. A survey of councils composed in the late ninth century claimed that Basil eventually anathematized Dianius: see *Synodicon vetus* 66.

38. Opposition from bishops in Cappadocia: GNaz, *Orat.* 43.37. Old mistakes: B, *Ep.* 59.1. Relatives: B, *Ep.* 60. Since uncle Gregory was not mentioned with a specific see, perhaps he was one of the "rural bishops" in Cappadocia: see *Becoming Christian*, Chapter 2.

39. Support from monks: GNaz, *Orat.* 43.28. Selection of Eusebius: GNaz, *Orat.* 18.33, with Hauser-Meury (1960) 75–77; Eusebius was bishop by the time the emperor Julian traveled through Cappadocia in mid-362. Ordination as priest in 362: GNaz, *Ep.* 8; for the date, see Fedwick (1981) 7, and Pouchet (1992a) 129–35, correcting Fedwick (1979) 140. Recruitment of teachers, and career of Apollinarius the Elder: Kaster (1988) 125, 242–43.

40. Meletius' sermon: Sozomen, *HE* 4.28, Theodoret, *HE* 2.31; Epiphanius, *Panarion* 73.29–33, included the text of the sermon. For the larger debate over Proverbs 8:22, see Pelikan (1993) 218–19, with van Parys (1970) 364–66, 378, for Basil's "timid" theological interpretation. For the treatise Basil was now writing against the heretic Eunomius, see *Becoming Christian*, Chapter 1. B, *Hom.* 12.1, invitation, 13, milk, 15, steering; with Bernardi (1968) 56–58, who dates this sermon to soon after Basil's ordination as a priest.

41. Hateful envy: *Studia Pontica* 3.1:142, no. 123, a tombstone from Amaseia in Pontus, with Maraval (1971) 154n.3, for other references. B, *Hom.* 11.2, young man, 5, oratory.

42. B, *Hom.* 11.5, being second. Departure for Pontus: GNaz, *Orat.* 43.29. Bernardi (1968) 58–60, argues that Basil's *Hom.* 11 contributed to the break with Eusebius; Gribomont (1981) 30, is reluctant to associate sermons with specific events in Basil's career.

43. Origen's eloquence: Jerome, *Ep.* 33.5. Eusebius' behavior: GNaz, *Ep.* 16.6–7. Insolence: GNaz, *Ep.* 17.1. For Origen's reputation in Pontus, note B, *Ep.* 17, addressed

to a man named Origen. Pouchet (1992a) 106–7, suggests that this Origen may have lived at Neocaesarea, and that his name was an indication of lingering veneration in the region for Origen, the teacher of Gregory Thaumaturgus.

44. Letter to Basil: GNaz, *Ep.* 19.3. Smallmindedness, wild beasts: GNaz, *Ep.* 18.2. Liontamer, leader: GNaz, *Orat.* 43.33.

45. Quotation from Hall and Lindzey (1967) 23, in a fine survey of Freud's theory of personality.

46. Advice about priesthood: GNaz, *Ep.* 8. Suspect creed: GNaz, *Orat.* 18.18; for the identification of this creed, see Chapter 2. In a sermon delivered on the occasion of this reconciliation between his father and these schismatics Gregory of Nazianzus noted the anticipation over the arrival of "the most esteemed of shepherds" who was coming to help "the true shepherd," that is, Gregory the Elder: see GNaz, *Orat.* 6.9. Bernardi (1968) 103, (1983) 36–37, identifies this "most esteemed of shepherds" with Basil, while Hauser-Meury (1960) 44n.49, identifies him with one of the schismatics, and Calvet-Sebasti (1995) 17–18, 142–43, with Gregory himself. Recommendation: GNaz, *Ep.* 41.8. Bishops: GNaz, *Ep.* 43. Participation at Basil's consecration: GNaz, *Orat.* 18.36.

47. Gregory the Elder as father for Basil: GNaz, *Orat.* 18.41. For the suggestion that Basil also delivered a panegyric at Gregory the Elder's funeral, see Gallay (1943) 125.

48. For Eusebius' career, see Halkin (1967); for the possibility that he had become bishop of Samosata already in 349, see Devos (1967) 203n.1, 224. Eustathius as "your Eloquence": B, *Ep.* 1, with Gain (1985) 400, on this honorific title. Human wisdom: B, *Hom.* 12.4. Eusebius as "your wisdom": B, *Ep.* 27, with Pouchet (1984), for this characterization of their relationship.

49. First letter: B, *Ep.* 27, dated to autumn 368 by Loofs (1898) 50, Forlin Patrucco (1983) 364–68, and Pouchet (1984) 180, to early winter 368 or spring 369 by Hauschild (1990) 177n.150; since the letter begins with a reference to "your prayers," perhaps Eusebius had written first. Meeting: B, *Ep.* 34, dated to 369 by Loofs (1898) 50, and Forlin Patrucco (1983) 396, but to Basil's episcopacy by Fedwick (1981) 13, and Hauschild (1990) 181n.173. Gregory the Elder: GNaz, *Ep.* 42; in *Ep.* 44.7 Gregory of Nazianzus apologized for not having met Eusebius at Caesarea. Visit: B, *Ep.* 48. Mother's death: B, *Ep.* 30, dated to 371 by Loofs (1898) 50n.2, and Hauschild (1990) 179n.161; for other possibilities, see Forlin Patrucco (1983) 382. Gregory of Nyssa: B, *Ep.* 100, dated to August 373 by Hauschild (1973) 157n.26. Address of Eusebius as "father": B, *Ep.* 98.2, 128.2, 181, with Pouchet (1984) 194, "une relation typique de fils à père."

50. Epitaph: GNaz, *Epitaph.* 103 = *Anthologia Graeca* 8.131, on Amphilochius the Elder. Julian's success: Libanius, *Orat.* 13.5. Basil the Elder: GNaz, *Orat.* 43.10, with Schouler (1980), on the theme of surpassing a father.

51. Beardless boyhood: GNaz, *Orat.* 43.25. Care for parents: Parkin (1997) 135, "The duty of caring for elderly parents lay primarily with the children, whether naturally, morally, or in strict legal terms."

52. Fevers: B, *Ep.* 193, sent to a doctor; the fundamental problem was apparently a liver ailment, his "longstanding plague" (B, *Ep.* 138.1). For Basil's illnesses, see Hauschild (1973) 14, and Gain (1985) 50–53, 397–98; Drecoll (1997), attempts to

identify his ailment as Crohn's disease, a chronic inflammation of the bowels. Old men: B, *Ep.* 176, with Demos (1986) 114–38, for the history of midlife. Phases of life: B, *Hom. in psalmos* 44.1, *PG* 29.388B–C; cf. *Hom.* 21.2, boy, adult, old man.

53. Constantius' threat: Theodoret, *HE* 2.32. Eusebius may have been exiled earlier if he was the Eusebius who had attended the council at Constantinople in early 360: see Philostorgius, *HE* 5.3. For Gregory the Elder and Julian, see Chapter 2, and *Kingdom of Snow*, Chapter 6.

54. GNaz, *Orat.* 43.31, Tetrarchs, 80, funeral; also 57, a description of Basil as "a bloodless martyr." B, *Ep.* 139.2, martyrs' crowns (a reaction to the death of Athanasius in 373); *Ep.* 240.1, past events; *Ep.* 242.2, more afflictions.

55. Basil's relatives: B, *Ep.* 31, mentioning Hypatius, "of the same blood"; *Ep.* 37, "I admit to having many friends and relatives in my fatherland"; *Ep.* 109, mentioning a widow "related to me"; *Ep.* 280, "my family relatives"; *Ep.* 310, "my relatives"; *Ep.* 315, mentioning a woman "related by kinship." Fatherly standing: B, *Ep.* 37. Widows and orphans: GNaz, *Orat.* 43.81. Substitute son: B, *Ep.* 280. Complaint: B, *Ep.* 289.

56. Mistakes: B, *Ep.* 210.5, with Crouzel (1963), (1969) 30–31, on this so-called "Dialogue with Aelianus." Refutation: B, *Adversus Eunomium* 2.20, with Pelikan (1993) 224. Obelisk: B, *Hom. in Hexaemeron* 4.5. Basil's comments on the Hebrew text of Genesis 1:9 were certainly disingenuous, since he could not read Hebrew: see Giet (1950) 264n.2. Most likely he was following the lead of Origen in his (now lost) commentary on Genesis: see Amand de Mendieta and Rudberg (1997) 64. For Basil's ideas about an education in classical literature, see *Kingdom of Snow*, Chapter 10.

Chapter 2. Gregory of Nazianzus and Gregory the Elder

1. Improve: Eusebius, *HE* 6.27, describing a visit by Firmilianus, bishop of Caesarea in Cappadocia. Gregory Thaumaturgus, *Oratio panegyrica in Origenem* 5.49–50, father's death, 5.65–69, brother-in-law, 16.189, father's house, with Crouzel (1969) 14–22, on Gregory and Origen, 74–78, on Gregory's estimation of Origen's teaching, Van Dam (1982) 272–73, on Gregory's early life, and *Becoming Christian*, Chapter 3.

2. Models: GNaz, *Orat.* 7.5.

3. Undistinguished family of Gregory the Elder: GNaz, *Orat.* 18.5, "he was the sprout of an unexceptional stem." Family's wealth: GNaz, *Orat.* 18.20–21, 39, with Coulie (1985) 9–28, and Van Dam (1995) 128–31. Second to none: GNaz, *Orat.* 18.6, with the supporting arguments of Kopecek (1973) 454–56. Since Gregory also mentioned that his father had not enriched himself from public revenues, perhaps Gregory the Elder had administered municipal funds; note Holman (2001) 107–8, for the suggestion that Gregory the Elder had been a local imperial tax assessor. The speculation of Vanderspoel (1999) 437–38, that Gregory the Elder may have held a provincial governorship is unwarranted. Wanderer: GNaz, *Carm.* II.1.11.55. Hypsistarians: GNaz, *Orat.* 18.5, "Greek error and legalistic posturing," with Trebilco (1991) 127–44, 163–64, and Mitchell (1993) 2:49–51, (1999a), on the various cults of the Highest God. GNys, *Refutatio confessionis Eunomii* 38, distinguished the "Hypsistians"

from both Jews and Christians: they "agree that there is a God whom they call *Hypsistos*, 'Most High,' and All-Powerful, but they do not accept him as Father." Christians also referred to God as "Most High": see B, *Ep.* 161.2.

4. Marriage: GNaz, *Orat.* 18.7–10. The date for his marriage assumes that the episodes in *Orat.* 18 are in correct chronological sequence. Unless his Hypsistarian convictions had imposed celibacy, age discrepancy permits the suggestion that Gregory the Elder had been married before. At the time of their marriage Nonna was still young (see Chapter 5), while Gregory the Elder would have been in his (late?) forties, about fifteen to twenty years older than the usual age at which men first married; for ages at first marriage, see Saller (1994) 25–41. In his writings Gregory of Nazianzus often mentioned "relatives": see the list in Hauser-Meury (1960) 185–86. The exact relationships are sometimes unclear, but the further suggestion that Gregory the Elder had had children by a first marriage might imply that some of Gregory of Nazianzus' relatives were half-siblings or their children.

5. Local family: the home town of Amphilochius the Elder, Nonna's brother, was Diocaesarea, i.e., Nazianzus: see GNaz, *Epitaph.* 105–6 = *Anthologia Graeca* 8.134–35. Nonna's family's Christianity: GNaz, *Orat.* 7.4, 18.11. Gregory the Elder's marriage to a Christian may perhaps explain the vague reference to his temporary alienation from his mother and his possessions that followed the rejection of his previous religious beliefs: see GNaz, *Orat.* 18.5. Nonna's vow about Gregory: GNaz, *Orat.* 2.77, *Carm.* II.1.11.68–73, II.1.12.805. Raised at home: GNaz, *Epitaph.* 72 = *Anthologia Graeca* 8.32, a description of himself as "a child of my [mother's] breast." Teaching: GNaz, *Orat.* 2.103. Drops of her prayers: GNaz, *Orat.* 18.11; for more discussion of Nonna, see Chapter 5. If the episodes in *Orat.* 18 are in correct chronological order, then the sequence implies that Gregory was born before the Council of Nicaea in 325; if so, he was a few years older than Basil. In *Carm.* II.1.11.512–13, however, Gregory recalled an observation by his father: "the length of your life does not yet match the tenure of my sacrificial service." If Gregory the Elder was referring to his episcopal tenure, then his comment seemed to imply that he had become bishop before his son's birth. Gallay (1943) 25–7, (1964–1967) 1:VIII n.1, and Wittig (1981) 3, suggest that Gregory was born in 329 or 330, which would make him about the same age as Basil; but see the counter arguments of Jungck (1974) 231–33, who concludes that Gregory was born in ca. 326. For the implications of the comparison of Gregory's and Basil's ages, see Chapter 10.

6. Dream: GNaz, *Orat.* 18.12, referring to Psalms 122:1. History and the future: B, *Hom. in psalmos* 1.1, PG 29.212A.

7. For the participants at the council of Antioch, see *Epistula synodica* 3 = Urkunde 18 in Opitz (1934–1935) 37, with Schwartz (1959) 148–54, on the identities of the bishops, and Hanson (1988) 146–51, on the doctrinal disputes. Barnes (1981) 212, (1982) 76, dates Constantine's visit to Antioch to December 324-January 325, Lane Fox (1987) 638–43, to April 325. Friend of Christ: GNaz, *Carm.* II.1.11.55. GNaz, *Orat.* 18.12, Leontius, 13, baptism, 15, episcopacy. For the date of his consecration, see GNaz, *Orat.* 18.38: when Gregory the Elder died in 374, he had served as bishop for forty-five years.

8. Rustic church: GNaz, *Orat.* 18.16. Celestial church: GNaz, *Orat.* 1.6. Birdcage: *Passio Athenogenis* 13, mentioning an octagonal church known as κλωβός at

Pedachthoe, near Sebasteia, thought to have been built in the early fourth century. Memorial: GNaz, *Orat.* 18.39, with the architectural comments of Mango (1972) 26–27; for possible reconstructions of this church, based in part on comments in Byzantine *scholia*, see Birnbaum (1907), (1913) 191–202, with Nimmo Smith (2000), on the *scholia*. For verses from Psalms inscribed on lintels, see Grégoire (1909) 42–43, no. 17, and Roueché (1989) 247. At the dedication of new churches orators commonly cited Psalms 122:1, the verse that Gregory the Elder had recited in his dream: see Eusebius, *HE* 10.4.7, in a panegyric about a new church at Tyre.

9. Smalltown bishop: GNaz, *Orat.* 18.34, "the work of this micropolitan bishop"; *Orat.* 19.11, a concession that the see of Nazianzus was insignificant; *Ep.* 41.1, Gregory the Elder's description of himself as an "insignificant shepherd and the leader of a small flock"; with Bernardi (1978) 249n.6, for other references. Bethlehem: GNaz, *Orat.* 18.17. Father of orthodoxy: GNaz, *Orat.* 18.16. Love for children: GNaz, *Orat.* 1.6.

10. Comparisons: GNaz, *Orat.* 18.17, 41. GNaz, *Ep.* 79.1, on the assumption that "our common father" refers to Gregory the Elder, as suggested by Gallay (1964–1967) 1:100n.1, and not Basil, as suggested by Gallay (1943) 131n.5.

11. GNaz, *Orat.* 43.13, Caesarea as "the guide and teacher of my eloquence," 14, meeting Basil. At Caesarea in Palestine one of Gregory's teachers was the rhetorician Thespesius: see GNaz, *Epitaph.* 4, Jerome, *De viris illustribus* 113, with Kaster (1988) 435. Chair at Athens: GNaz, *Carm.* II.1.11.254–56, with the analysis of Jungck (1974) 163. Superiority in rhetoric: GNaz, *Carm.* II.1.11.265–74, 400–4. For the suggestion that Gregory taught as a rhetorician, see GNaz, *Ep.* 3, with Gallay (1943) 65–66.

12. GNaz, *Orat.* 18.16, father's oratory, 23, his demeanor. One of Gregory's first teachers at Nazianzus may have been Carterius, who later accompanied him on his overseas studies and then became a cleric or monk: see GNaz, *Carm.* II.2.1.139–42, *Epitaph.* 111, 115–18 = *Anthologia Graeca* 8.148, 142 +143, 144–46, with Gallay (1943) 31, 46, and Hauser-Meury (1960) 52.

13. Solitude: GNaz, *Orat.* 18.37. Old age: GNaz, *Carm.* II.1.11.262. Laws: GNaz, *Ep.* 1.2, with Chapter 10 for additional discussion of Gregory and Basil in Pontus. Lover and son: with grateful apologies to Gibbon (1984) 208.

14. Consecration and flight: GNaz, *Carm.* II.1.11.337–56. Trust and respect: GNaz, *Ep.* 205.1. For the chronology, see Gallay (1943) 73n.3, and Bernardi (1978) 11–17.

15. Tyranny: GNaz, *Orat.* 1.1, delivered on Easter 362; *Orat.* 3.1, delivered a week later; cf. *Orat.* 2.6, an apology composed before Easter 362 but not delivered as a public sermon: see Bernardi (1978) 236n.3. Hesitation: GNaz, *Orat.* 1.1–2. Longing: GNaz, *Orat.* 2.102. Scolding audience: GNaz, *Orat.* 3. Duty for parents: GNaz, *Orat.* 2.103. Gregory the Elder: GNaz, *Carm.* II.1.11.357–64.

16. Gregory as staff: GNaz, *Orat.* 2.103. Basil as staff for Eusebius: GNaz, *Orat.* 43.33. Sturdy aid: GNaz, *Carm.* II.1.1.111–12.

17. GNaz, *Orat.* 15.1, Maccabees, 3, Eleazar, sons, 4, mother, 5–6, speech, 12, imitation, based on II Maccabees 6:18–31, 7, and the version in IV Maccabees. Gregory delivered this sermon on a festival of the Maccabees most likely on August 1 or perhaps in December, probably in 362, less likely in 363: see Gallay (1943) 76–77, Bernardi (1968) 101–2, who also suggests the comparisons with Gregory's family, and

Vinson (1994) 187–89, who also surveys the development of Christian traditions about the Maccabees. For Julian's visit, see Chapter 3, and *Kingdom of Snow*, Chapters 6, 9.

18. Unity: GNaz, *Orat.* 3.6. For the Council of Constantinople, see *Becoming Christian*, Chapter 1. Creed from council of Antioch: Socrates, *HE* 3.25, Sozomen, *HE* 6.4. Hauser-Meury (1960) 88n.174, Kurmann (1988) 6–12, Brennecke (1988) 60, McLynn (1996) 206–8, and Elm (2000) 88–89, suggest that Gregory the Elder had signed the creed from the council at Constantinople, Bernardi (1983) 27–31, (1995) 135, and Calvet-Sebasti (1995) 29–31, the creed from the council at Antioch.

19. Intimidation: GNaz, *Orat.* 21.24, with Mossay and Lafontaine (1980) 158n.2, suggesting that Gregory had his father in mind. Fervent faction, clever words: GNaz, *Orat.* 18.18. Group: GNaz, *Orat.* 4.10. Monks: although in *Orat.* 6 Gregory often addressed "brothers," only the heading to this oration mentioned a reconciliation of monks. In *Orat.* 21.25, a sermon delivered during his tenure at Constantinople in 379–381, Gregory referred back to the secession of "those attached to philosophy," who may have been these monks: see Mossay and Lafontaine (1980) 103, for the date, 162n.1, for the identification. For the suggestion that these schismatics were instead lesser clerics at Nazianzus, see McLynn (1996) 209–10.

20. GNaz, *Orat.* 6.1, philosophy, 2, characteristics of "the brothers," 3, silence, 14, earth and air, 21, common father and children. Whichever creed his father had endorsed, Gregory delivered *Orat.* 6 in 364: see Gallay (1943) 84, and Bernardi (1968) 103.

21. End of schism: GNaz, *Orat.* 18.18.

22. GNaz, *Ep.* 7.1, embarrassment, 3–4, gossip, 6–7, parents; this letter was written to Caesarius in 362: see Gallay (1964–1967) 1:8, (1969) XIV.

23. GNaz, *Ep.* 29, to Sophronius, the *magister officiorum*, dated to 369: see Van Dam (1995) 123n.18. For more context, see Chapter 3, and *Becoming Christian*, Chapter 10. GNaz, *Carm.* II.1.1.183, dogs, 192, pain; *Carm.* II.1.11.378–79, father.

24. Rejection of earlier offer: GNaz, *Orat.* 43.39. Old age and friendship: GNaz, *Orat.* 10.1. The sequence both of events and of Gregory's orations between his consecration in spring and his return to Nazianzus in autumn is uncertain; for reconstructions, see Gallay (1943) 108–21, and Calvet-Sebasti (1995) 88–99. For Gregory's friendship with Basil, see Chapter 10.

25. GNaz, *Carm.* II.1.11.465, mud, 494–96, settlement at Sasima and father's anger, 502–17, father's request, 518–19, soul and sun. GNaz, *Orat.* 12.4, tranquillity, 5, eagle.

26. Consecration of new bishop: GNaz, *Orat.* 13. The heading for *Orat.* 13 identified this see as Doara: see Hild and Restle (1981) 171–72. Although the heading also mentioned Eulalius, he was not this new bishop but instead a later bishop of Nazianzus and the editor of this oration: see n. 42 in this chapter. For another ordination that Gregory shared with his father, see GNaz, *Ep.* 79, with Hauser-Meury (1960) 154–55. GNaz, *Orat.* 16.4, chief shepherd, 5–6, destruction of harvest, 18–19, criticism. Gallay (1943) 122, and Bernardi (1968) 118–20, date *Orat.* 16 to the late summer or autumn of 372, soon after Gregory returned to Nazianzus. Magistrate: GNaz, *Orat.* 17.8–9; for discussion, see *Kingdom of Snow*, Chapter 5.

27. GNaz, *Carm.* II.1.11.533–37, pressure, 538–44, request to bishops, 545–49, St. Thecla. Hint: GNaz, *Orat.* 19, with *Kingdom of Snow*, Chapter 5, for discussion.

28. Despair: GNaz, *Ep.* 80.1, citing Psalms 27:10.

29. Happiness: GNaz, *Orat.* 43.14. For the Parthenon during the fourth century, see Frantz (1979). In the early 370s Jerome likewise visited the "Acropolis of Athens" and the "statue of Athena": see Jerome, *In Zachariam* 3, on Zechariah 12:1–3. St. Thecla: GNaz, *Carm.* II.1.11.547–49, with Jungck (1974) 175–76, on the meaning of παρθενών, and Dagron (1978) 56, on Seleucia as Gregory's "Christian Athens," 84–85, comparisons between Athena and Thecla. Mother: GNaz, *Epitaph.* 71.1–2 = *Anthologia Graeca* 8.30.

30. Long time: GNaz, *Carm.* II.1.11.551. For Gregory's service in Constantinople, see *Kingdom of Snow*, Chapter 8.

31. Amphilochius the Elder and Libanius: Libanius, *Ep.* 670.3. Teacher: GNaz, *Epitaph.* 104 = *Anthologia Graeca* 8.132–33. Advocate: GNaz, *Epitaph.* 106–7 = *Anthologia Graeca* 8.135–36. For the possibility that Amphilochius the Elder had held an office in the imperial administration, see Hauser-Meury (1960) 29–30. Sons and Libanius: Libanius, *Ep.* 634, 670–71. Euphemius: GNaz, *Epitaph.* 29–35 = *Anthologia Graeca* 8.122–28, with Hauser-Meury (1960) 71, who suggests that Euphemius died in the 360s, and Chapter 4, for his tomb. Amphilochius as advocate: GNaz, *Ep.* 9, 13, with Holl (1904) 6–15, and Datema (1978) ix–xi, on Amphilochius' early life. Accusation: GNaz, *Ep.* 22.3, "something despicable involving money"; also *Ep.* 23–24.

32. Basil's recommendation: B, *Ep.* 161.1. Earlier invitation: B, *Ep.* 150.4. Amphilochius the Elder: GNaz, *Ep.* 63, with Hauser-Meury (1960) 31n.22, on the date of Amphilochius' homecoming, and Gallay (1943) 124n.6, on the date of his selection as bishop. Pouchet (1988), (1992a) 405–6, suggests that Basil discussed the selection of a successor in *Ep.* 81 to bishop Faustinus of Iconium.

33. GNaz, *Ep.* 63.3, prop, 6, common friends.

34. Death of Amphilochius the Elder: GNaz, *Epitaph.* 104, 107 = *Anthologia Graeca* 8.132, 136. For the oration on Basil, see Chapter 10; for the retrospective poems, *Becoming Christian*, Chapter 10. For the dates of Gregory's tenure as acting bishop, see Gallay (1943) 219–20, and Van Dam (1996) 23n.34.

35. Complaints: GNaz, *Ep.* 138.4. Respect: GNaz, *Ep.* 182.5.

36. Household: GNaz, *Orat.* 26.17, with Mossay and Lafontaine (1981) 28–31. Theodosia: GNaz, *Carm.* II.2.6.97–102: "Most beloved [Olympias], Theodosia [or Theodosis] stands beside you. Let her be your living exemplar of all eloquence and behavior. At the beginning of a marriage she is the female equivalent of Chiron [the teacher of Achilles]. She received you from your father and molded your wonderful disposition. She is the sister of the most blameless bishop Amphilochius." Gregory composed this poem in honor of Olympias' marriage in late 384 or 385: see Gallay (1943) 230. Bernardi (1984), (1995) 177–79, suggests that Theodosia had married Olympias' (unnamed) older brother. If so, then her son was perhaps the Seleucus who received a poem from Amphilochius, in which he identified Olympias as "your aunt": see Amphilochius, *Iambi ad Seleucum* 337. This Seleucus might then be identified with the Seleucus who served as prefect in the early fifth century: see *PLRE* 2:987–88. For the debate over whether the Olympias who received Gregory's poem was in fact the heiress Olympias, see Gallay (1964–1967) 2:163, Delmaire (1989a) 90–92, Demoen (1997) 8–9, and McLynn (1998) 228–30. In the mid-380s Gregory wrote to bishop Nectarius of Constantinople on behalf of an unnamed female

cousin who was apparently living in the capital and who may have been Theodosia: see GNaz, *Ep.* 186.2.

37. Amphilochius: GNaz, *Ep.* 171, 184. Assistance for relatives: GNaz, *Ep.* 103, for Euphemius, with Hauser-Meury (1960) 72, and Van Dam (1995) 146n.104; *Ep.* 106, for Eustratius, with Hauser-Meury (1960) 79; *Ep.* 159, for Amazonia, with Van Dam (1996) 69–70; *Ep.* 186, for a woman, "our most distinguished cousin"; *Ep.* 198, for Valentinianus, with Hauser-Meury (1960) 177–78; *Testamentum, PG* 37.392B, "my relative" Russiana. Estate: GNaz, *Ep.* 203, with Gallay (1943) 240–41.

38. GNaz, *Ep.* 12.7, a reminder for Nicobulus to cherish his marriage; Gallay (1964–1967) 1:19, dated this letter to ca. 365. For Nicobulus' life, see Hauser-Meury (1960) 128–31. Military service and family: GNaz, *Carm.* II.2.4.118–21: "I know that you attended great emperors and were honored with the brave men, if ever [anyone] was, when you brandished your eager spear at the Achaemenids [Persians]. You are noted for your wealth and ancestry and intelligence"; *Ep.* 196.4, "a good father who served the emperors for a long time with his weapons, and this not in anonymity but with great distinction, and who assisted you magistrates for a long time." Assistance: GNaz, *Ep.* 13, to Amphilochius, 21, 67.1. Premature widow: GNaz, *Ep.* 195.5, with Van Dam (1996) 51–52, for the date.

39. Reward: GNaz, *Epitaph.* 102 = *Anthologia Graeca* 8.76. Amphilochius as brother: GNaz, *Ep.* 63.3; as son: GNaz, *Testamentum, PG* 37.393A. Nicobulus as brother: GNaz, *Ep.* 67.1; as son: GNaz, *Ep.* 126.3, 127.2, 147.2, 157.2, 174.4. Alypiana as daughter: GNaz, *Testamentum, PG* 37.392C. Note that Gallay (1964–1967) 2:87, (1969) 142, emended the text of *Ep.* 196.4 to have Gregory refer to Alypiana as ἀδελφιδῆν, "niece," rather than ἀδελφήν, "daughter," the reading accepted by Hauser-Meury (1960) 25. Other relatives as daughter: GNaz, *Ep.* 159.1, the virgin Amazonia; *Ep.* 160.1, Eugenia, who is not to be identified with Gregory's niece Eugenia: see Hauser-Meury (1960) 69. For other examples of imprecise indications of affiliation, see Hauser-Meury (1960) 185–86. Nicobulus as staff: GNaz, *Ep.* 147.2.

40. Gregorius: GNaz, *Epitaph.* 125 = *Anthologia Graeca* 8.165. This epitaph identified Gregory as the boy's μήτρως, specifically "maternal uncle," more generally "relative on the mother's side." Hauser-Meury (1960) 94n.189, concluded that this Gregorius was an otherwise unknown nephew; he would then be a son of Alypius and Gorgonia. But unless he had died by 381, it is difficult to understand why in his will Gregory did not mention him with his sisters. It is more likely that this Gregorius was a grandnephew, one of the elsewhere unnamed sons of Nicobulus the Elder and Alypiana: see GNaz, *Ep.* 157.2, 195.5. Gregorius the deacon: GNaz, *Testamentum, PG* 37.389B, 392A, with Van Dam (1995) 128–29. Eulalius as adjunct bishop: GNaz, *Ep.* 152.5, "my distinguished fellow priest Eulalius, a *chorepiskopos*, 'rural bishop.'" Eulalius as bishop: GNaz, *Ep.* 182.4. Consecration: Jerome, *De viris illustribus* 117, "episcopum in loco suo ordinans." Although Gregory had once described Eulalius and his brother Helladius as "my distinguished cousins" (*Ep.* 15.4), perhaps they were sons of an older half-sibling.

41. Parents' intention: GNaz, *Testamentum, PG* 37.392D. Epitaph: GNaz, *Epitaph.* 58 = *Anthologia Graeca* 8.15. Church: GNaz, *Ep.* 57.3, on the assumption that "the enclosure of the building" refers to this church, with Gallay (1964–1967) 1:72n.1, for the attribution of the letter; note also GNaz, *Ep.* 141.8, "the temple that we built for God."

42. GNaz, *Ep.* 52.3, father and writings; *Ep.* 53.1, collection of letters. For Eulalius' edition of orations, see the heading to GNaz, *Orat.* 13 (*PG* 35.852), εἰς τὴν χειροτονίαν Δοαρῶν ὁμιλία ἐκδοθεῖσα Εὐλαλίῳ ἐπισκόπῳ. Gallay (1943) 123n.3, and Hauser-Meury (1960) 71, 182n.4, interpret ἐκδοθεῖσα to mean that this oration about the consecration at Doara had been "published" by bishop Eulalius; less likely is the suggestion of Scholten (1992) 157n.29, that the oration had been "delivered" for Eulalius on the occasion of his consecration as bishop of Doara. Gallay (1943) 243–44, Nautin (1961), and Bernardi (1995) 236–37, suggest that Gregory died in ca. 390.

Chapter 3. Forgotten Brothers

1. Most important: GNaz, *Ep.* 167.1. Study with father and Gregory: GNaz, *Ep.* 176.6. GNaz, *Carm.* II.2.4.58, desire, 89–93, mother's uncle. Alexandria, Beirut, Athens: GNaz, *Carm.* II.2.5.226–29. Athens and eloquence: GNaz, *Orat.* 43.14. *Carm.* II.2.5 was a response from Nicobulus the Elder to his son's plea in *Carm.* II.2.4. Gregory himself presumably composed *Carm.* II.2.4 in the name of Nicobulus the Younger. But since Nicobulus the Elder was noted for his "sharp thinking in every form of expression equally, both bound and unbound" (*Carm.* II.2.4.115–16), that is, in both prose and verse, perhaps he himself composed *Carm.* II.2.5. Demoen (1997) 5–6, suggests that both poems were simply rhetorical exercises.

2. Rhetoric, assemblies: GNaz, *Carm.* II.2.4.59–60. Shorthand: GNaz, *Ep.* 157.2. For the contours of this new vocational education, note Theodoret, *HE* 4.18.8–9, mentioning a priest from Edessa exiled during Valens' reign to Egypt, where he established a school in which he taught "fast writing" and biblical studies. These younger brothers are unnamed, but one may have been Gregorius: see Chapter 2.

3. Caesarius was born before 329, on the assumption that his father practiced celibacy after becoming a bishop, or a few years later, on the assumption that Gregory was born soon after his father's consecration (see Chapter 2). GNaz, *Orat.* 7.6, separation, workshop, 7, curriculum. Zenon: Julian, *Ep.* 17, with *PLRE* 1:992. Magnus as healer: *Anthologia Graeca* 11.281; as teacher: Eunapius, *Vitae sophistarum* 497–98, with *PLRE* 1:534, and Penella (1990) 111–12.

4. Gregory at Alexandria: GNaz, *Carm.* II.1.11.128.

5. GNaz, *Orat.* 7.8, enticements, 9, preference, with *Kingdom of Snow*, Chapter 3, for the recruitment of provincials. Throughout this funerary oration Gregory did not name the emperors, although he did use singular and plural references. The emperor who received this delegation was most likely Constantius, who resided primarily at Milan and Sirmium during the 350s before moving to Constantinople in autumn 359: see Barnes (1993) 221–23. Jungck (1974) 231–33, dates Gregory's return to 356, Gallay (1943) 65, 243–44, and Calvet-Sebasti (1995) 48n.2, 197n.4, to ca. 358/359.

6. GNaz, *Orat.* 7.9, ambition and glory, 10, honors; *Ep.* 7.3, complaints, 9–10, choice.

7. For the suggestion that Caesarius was still in Julian's entourage in Cappadocia, see Bernardi (1983) 12, 17–18. GNaz, *Orat.* 7.13, declaration, 15, new office, earthquake, death. For the identification of Caesarius as a *comes thesaurorum* in Bithynia, see Delmaire (1989b) 186–87, 271, and Van Dam (1995) 121–22. Earthquake:

GNaz, *Carm.* II.1.1.172–73, *Epitaph.* 15 = *Anthologia Graeca* 8.94; the date of the earthquake was October 11, 368: see Socrates, *HE* 4.11. Letters: GNaz, *Ep.* 20, B, *Ep.* 26. Date of death: when Gregory delivered his funeral oration for his brother, the earthquake was still "recent" (*Orat.* 7.15); the suggestion of Fedwick (1981) 13n.78, that Caesarius survived into the early 370s, should be ignored.

In 362 when he assumed his priesthood at Nazianzus, Gregory had described clerical duty as "medicine for souls": GNaz, *Orat.* 2.16, with Chapter 2, and Elm (2000) 94–97. In addition to justifying his own new responsibilities, perhaps Gregory had been hinting how his brother might use his medical training to make a similar transition.

8. Morning star: GNaz, *Carm.* II.1.1.177–78. Patronage: GNaz, *Orat.* 7.11.

9. GNaz, *Orat.* 7.1, enjoyment, 9, ranks, second life, 10, doctor's fees, 11, philosophy at court, 13, refutation, 15, philosophic soul. Possessions left to poor: B, *Ep.* 32.1. In *Orat.* 7.11, Gregory stated that Caesarius had acted like a philosopher "even in a χλανίς." A χλανίς was a wool tunic often contrasted to the thin cloak of a philosopher; Hauser-Meury (1960) 27n.14, 49n.61, equates this garment with a χλαμύς, in Latin *paludamentum*, the short cloak worn by civil magistrates and soldiers. For discussion of philosophy and the "second life," see Malingrey (1961) 256–57, and Calvet-Sebasti (1995) 51–53.

10. For the dispute over Caesarius' possessions, see Van Dam (1995) 122–26. GNaz, *Carm.* II.1.1.63–101, ambitions, 102–39, parents, 108, only child, 183, dogs, 229, soul, 247, laughable, 601–6, consolation, with *Becoming Christian*, Chapter 10, on Gregory's self-indulgence. Gallay (1943) 92n.1, dated the composition of *Carm.* II.1.1 to the late 360s, Meehan (1987) 20, to ca. 371.

11. Gregory as father for Caesarius: GNaz, *Carm.* II.1.1.220. For his friendship with Basil, see Chapter 10.

12. GNaz, *Orat.* 7.15, shrine, 19, vanity, 20, envy, with Miller (1994) 233, on the ending of this oration: "the dreams of his brother are as much about Gregory as they are about his brother."

13. Description of Naucratius: GNys, *Vita Macrinae* 8. Sickness: B, *Ep.* 203.1; also GNaz, *Orat.* 43.10, for a roundabout description complimenting Basil on his robustness before he ruined his health by adopting an ascetic lifestyle.

14. GNys, *Vita Macrinae* 8, early life, 9, death. GNaz, *Epitaph.* 1–3 = *Anthologia Graeca* 8.156–58, claimed that Naucratius had died while fishing. For a chronology of Naucratius' life, see Maraval (1971) 165n.3: birth in ca. 330, rejection of secular affairs in ca. 352, death in ca. 357.

15. Strabo, *Geographia* 12.3.15, wild animals in a plain next to the Iris River; for the game parks, see *Kingdom of Snow*, Chapter 6, and *Becoming Christian*, Chapter 4. Tombstones at Neoclaudiopolis: *Studia Pontica* 3.1:64, no. 52, hunter; *Studia Pontica* 3.1:66, no. 56 = *IGR* 3:60, no. 143 = Merkelbach and Stauber (2001) 364, no. 11/05/05, distinction.

16. Basil's education: GNaz, *Orat.* 43.12. GNaz, *Ep.* 4.3, wild animals, 12, visits. Quotation about hunter and ascetic from Patlagean (1987) 630.

17. Naucratius and Macrina: GNys, *Vita Macrinae* 10. Rousseau (1994) 76, suggests that Naucratius too may have been influenced by the teachings of Eustathius of Sebasteia.

18. GNys, *Vita Macrinae* 5, mother's distractions, 12, Peter as orphan, Macrina's care. Date of Peter's birth: Aubineau (1966) 36, argues that he was born in ca. 341, Maraval (1971) 48, between 341 and 345; Bernardi (1992) 135n.6, suggests that Basil the Elder died in ca. 342, Fedwick (1979) 133–34, (1981) 1:5n.18, less plausibly, that he did not die before 345 or 346.

19. GNys, *Vita Macrinae* 12, education, distribution of food, 13, mother's death, 14, priesthood, 37, head of men's community. Peter's letter: [GNys,] *Ep.* 30.5; the suggestion of Pouchet (1992a) 519–25, that Peter composed B, *Ep.* 197.2, is unlikely: see McLynn (1997) 77–78. Small house: B, *Ep.* 216.

20. Emmelia's death: when Gregory visited Macrina on her deathbed, he admitted that he had not seen her for many years, eight years according to GNys, *Vita Macrinae* 15, nine years according to GNys, *Ep.* 19.10. For the date of Macrina's death, see Chapter 6; the interval of eight or nine years suggests that Gregory had last visited about the time of their mother's death. Teaching by grammarians: GNys, *De beneficentia* = *De pauperibus amandis* 1, PG 46.453A. Festival: GNys, *Encomium in XL martyres* 2, PG 46.784D–785A, with *Becoming Christian*, Chapter 7. Date of Gregory's birth: Aubineau (1966) 29, 38, suggests after 331, Maraval (1980) 163, between 331 and 335, May (1971) 52–53, between 335 and 340, and Gribomont (1967) 250, perhaps ca. 340.

21. Macrina as teacher and mother: GNys, *Ep.* 19.6, 10; as teacher: GNys, *Dialogus de anima et resurrectione*, PG 46.12A. Gregory's reputation: Theodoret, *HE* 4.30, mentioning "outside culture," presumably referring to non-Christian classical literature and not study overseas. Study with Basil, "my father and my teacher," guardian: GNys, *Ep.* 13.4, 6. For other references to Basil as Gregory's father and teacher, see Aubineau (1966) 31n.2, and Maraval (1990) 199n.3.

22. Native language: GNys, *Contra Eunomium* 3.10.54; for the context, see *Becoming Christian*, Chapter 1. For Gregory's familiarity with classical culture and Greek philosophy, see Aubineau (1966) 45–49, and Ladner (1958).

23. Joining Basil: B, *Ep.* 14.1. Reader and rhetorician: GNaz, *Ep.* 11, with Gallay (1964–1967) 1:16, for the confusion in the manuscripts over the addressee of this letter. Maraval (1997) 384, suggests that Gregory may have kept his clerical readership despite his interest in rhetoric. Libanius' writings: GNys, *Ep.* 13.4.

24. Forged letters and complaints: B, *Ep.* 58, with Daniélou (1965) 32–34. Basil's insistence: see B, *Ep.* 225, "the man [Gregory of Nyssa] compelled by every necessity to accept the office." Councils: B, *Ep.* 100, with May (1966) 107–9, on Gregory's attempt to reach out to heterodox Christians. Rome: B, *Ep.* 215.

25. Macrina's evaluation: GNys, *Vita Macrinae* 21.

26. GNys, *De virginitate* praef. 2, our father, 2.3, Basil's request, 3.1, choice, 23.4, blunders, with Chapter 7. Aubineau (1966) 31, and Daniélou (1956) 72, (1966) 159–60, argue that Gregory composed this treatise in 371, May (1971) 55, and Rist (1981) 217, sometime during Basil's episcopacy, and Gribomont (1967) 249–52, in ca. 378.

The significance of Gregory's comments about marriage in a treatise on virginity is certainly contested. Because he did not insist that complete renunciation of marriage was necessary to achieve freedom from human passions, Hart (1990) 477, argues that Gregory's complaint about his own marriage "is thus to be read as ironic." Burrus (2000) 90, disagrees: "I do not . . . take Gregory's extended lament as ironic or dissimulative, pabulum for the simpleminded." As a result, Gregory's marriage is itself contested. Gregory of Nazianzus once consoled Gregory of Nyssa for the death of Theosebia, "our blessed sister" and "the companion of a priest": see GNaz, *Ep.* 197.2, 6. He also composed an epitaph for Theosebia, "child of Emmelia and companion of the great Gregory": see GNaz, *Epitaph.* 123 = *Anthologia Graeca* 8.164. For the arguments over whether Gregory of Nyssa married, whether the Theosebia of the letter should be identified with the Theosebia of the epitaph, and whether Theosebia was Gregory of Nyssa's wife or sister, see Hauser-Meury (1960) 171–72, Aubineau (1966) 65–76, and Devos (1983). For the unlikely possibility that Gregory of Nyssa had a son, see Chapter 7.

27. Painting of Abraham and Isaac: GNys, *De deitate filii et spiritus sancti, PG* 46.572B–D.

28. Mirror: GNaz, *Ep.* 76.5, with May (1966) 111–24, on Gregory's activities after Basil's death. Appeal: GNys, *Ep.* 7.2, on behalf of Synesius, who was "not outside my family," with Van Dam (1996) 56–57, on the governor Hierius. For the sermons on creation, see *Becoming Christian*, Chapter 6; Eunomius, *Becoming Christian*, Chapter 1. For the possibility of Gregory as a mediator in Pontus, see Mitchell (1999b) 108–16. Ibora and Sebasteia: GNys, *Ep.* 19.12–13, with Torres (1997), on Gregory's participation in episcopal selections. Orthodoxy: *CTh* 16.1.3. Arabia and Jerusalem: GNys, *Ep.* 2.12.

29. Peter's letter: [GNys,] *Ep.* 30.1, "our holy father," 5, salt, 6, paradigm. Peter at council of Constantinople: Theodoret, *HE* 5.8.4. For Peter's episcopacy at Sebasteia, see *Becoming Christian*, Chapter 7. "Our father": GNys, *Ep.* 29.4, 6. Rufinus, *HE* 11.9, would claim that each brother, Gregory for his theological treatises and Peter for his good works, had equaled Basil.

30. See Chapter 4, for the final conversation, and Chapter 6, for the biography of Macrina.

31. Athenodorus: Eusebius, *HE* 6.30, 7.14, 28. On the absence of Athenodorus in Gregory Thaumaturgus' own panegyric about Origen, see Crouzel (1969) 14–15. GNys, *Vita Gregorii Thaumaturgii, PG* 46.905C, Firmilianus, 941C–944A, young man.

32. GNys, *In Basilium fratrem* 2, genealogy, 25, family, with Daniélou (1955) 351–53, and Bernardi (1968) 313–15, on the date, and Mosshammer (2001) 227, for the inclusion of Basil in "the whole history of salvation." For comparisons with Moses as a means of promoting episcopal authority, see Harl (1984); for differences between the panegyrics by Gregory of Nazianzus and Gregory of Nyssa, see Meredith (1997), and Konstan (2000).

33. Dream: GNys, *In Basilium fratrem* 19.

34. Basil as teacher: GNys, *In Basilium fratrem* 27. Note Momigliano (1985) 449: "While Macrina is brought near by a biography, Basil is made distant by a panegyric."

Chapter 4. "The Father Was Always the Father"

1. Basil, *De spiritu sancto* 1.3, doxology, 10.26, baptism, with Williams (1993), and Wiles (1997), on the theology of baptism.

2. Bishop Leontius: Theodoret, *HE* 2.24.3. GNys, *Contra Eunomium* 1.155–59, abstruse terms, 563, "your father," with *Becoming Christian*, Chapter 1, on the heresiarch Eunomius, and Osborne (1993) 165, on the theological implications: "Just as the orthodox prefer 'Son' because it guarantees the status of the Son, while the Arians object because it compromises the nature of the Father, so the Arians prefer creature because it guarantees the uniqueness of the Father, and the orthodox object because it compromises the status of the Son." Modern discussions of the interplay between abstract theological formulations and aspects of ordinary life are rare: see Pelikan (1993) 237–38, and Burrus (2000) 99, who suggests that Gregory of Nyssa "faithfully reproduces the theological truth about the begotten Son's full divinity as proof of his own legitimacy as an orthodox son."

3. Theodosius and Arcadius: Sozomen, *HE* 7.6; Theodoret, *HE* 5.16, identified this churchman as bishop Amphilochius of Iconium. Begotten and mortal god: GNaz, *Carm.* II.2.3.1–2, a poem written to Vitalianus in the name of his sons: see Chapter 1. Become a god: GNaz, *Carm.* II.2.4.199, a poem written to Nicobulus the Elder in the name of his son Nicobulus the Younger: see Chapter 3.

4. Panegyric: Philostratus, *Vita Apollonii* 4.30. Fatherhood: B, *Ep.* 210.5. For the reluctance to associate theology with personal experiences, see Widdicombe (1994) 256: "It is notable that Origen and Athanasius . . . did not support their picture of God as Father either by drawing on the biological or on the psychological and sociological dimensions of human fatherhood. Contemporary ideas about the family and about adoption play no role in their discussions of the divine being or of the Father's relation to us"; and Garnsey (1996) 234–35 [= (1997) 120]: "It is worth asking whether, for the Church Fathers, slavery and sonship had two more or less independent existences, one metaphorical, in the land of theology, the other physical, in Graeco-Roman society. The two worlds seem . . . to have intersected surprisingly little." In contrast, Van Dam (1993) 110–14, argues for a linkage between doctrines of bodily resurrection and the representations of healings at saints' shrines.

5. Always the Father: Sozomen, *HE* 7.17, with Pelikan (1971) 195, and Vaggione (2000) 247. For an orthodox formulation, see Theodoret, *HE* 1.4.26 = Urkunde 14.26, in Opitz (1934–1935) 23.

6. Entire family: *Studia Pontica* 3.1:66, no. 56 = *IGR* 3:60, no. 143 = Merkelbach and Stauber (2001) 364, no. 11/05/05, a tombstone at Neoclaudiopolis. Father's tomb: *Studia Pontica* 3.1:144, no. 128, at Amaseia. For the pattern of burial, see Patlagean (1981). Son from Bithynia: *Studia Pontica* 3.1:129, no. 103 = *IGR* 3:40, no. 103 = Merkelbach and Stauber (2001) 376, no. 11/07/12. Men from Alexandria: B, *Ep.* 306. For other examples of the retrieval of bodies from abroad, see Mitchell (1993) 2:85.

7. Euphemius and Amphilochius the Elder: GNaz, *Epitaph.* 25–27, 36, 104 = *Anthologia Graeca* 8.118–20, 129–30, 132. Visit by bishop Amphilochius: B, *Ep.* 217, mentioning the οἶκος at Euphemias, which here probably refers not to a house but to the family tomb. Gregory of Nazianzus also visited Euphemias: see GNaz, *Ep.* 197.1. Caesarius' dust: GNaz, *Epitaph.* 14 = *Anthologia Graeca* 8.93. Inheritence: GNaz, *Carm.* II.1.95 = *Anthologia Graeca* 8.84, "I have acquired my hallowed father's name and throne, and also his tomb." Tombstone: GNaz, *Carm.* II.1.91 = *Anthologia Graeca* 8.77.

8. Tomb of ancestors: GNaz, *Epitaph.* 110 = *Anthologia Graeca* 8.147, with

Hauser-Meury (1960) 45, on Bassus, a spiritual adviser from Cappadocia. Macrina's funeral and burial: GNys, *Vita Macrinae* 34–35; location of shrine near Ibora: GNys, *Encomium in XL martyres* 2, PG 46.784B, with *Becoming Christian*, Chapter 7. Note also *Studia Pontica* 3.1:68, no. 58 = Merkelbach and Stauber (2001) 362, no. 11/05/02, mentioning brothers who constructed a tomb for their virgin sister.

9. Basil's "tomb of ancestors," high priest: GNaz, *Orat.* 43.80. Basil and Moses: GNys, *In Basilium fratrem* 23. For the traditional celebration of Basil's death on January 1, the Feast of Jesus' Circumcision a week after Christmas, see Andreas of Crete, *Homilia in circumcisionem et in Basilium*, PG 97.928B. For the debate over the date of Basil's death, see Maraval (1988a), arguing for August 377, Pouchet (1992b), for September 378, Moutsoulas (1997), for early September 378, Hauschild (1993) 27–29, for late 378, possibly January 1, 379, and Barnes (1997), for January 1, 379.

10. GNys, *Vita Macrinae* 14, Basil as τὸ κοινὸν τῆς γενεᾶς καλόν, 17, conversation about Basil; also GNys, *Dialogus de anima et resurrectione*, PG 46.12A, "I sought a companion for my tears." Basilias: B, *Ep.* 94, Sozomen, *HE* 6.34, with *Kingdom of Snow*, Chapter 2.

Mothers and Daughters Introduction

1. The canons of this council survive only in an Armenian translation; for a Latin translation, see Lebon (1938) 106–10, with Barnes (1981) 65, dating the council to the summer or autumn of 314, and Parvis (2001), discussing the authenticity of these canons. For the proximity of the civil wars, note that in 313 the emperor Maximinus, after being defeated by Licinius, tried to raise additional troops in Cappadocia: see Lactantius, *De mortibus persecutorum* 47.6. For some of the difficulties in interpreting "male-authored, male-centred texts" about women's sexuality in the Roman world, see Flemming (1999).

2. For the range of ascetic behavior, see Burns (2001). GNaz, *Ep.* 5.5, manual labor; *Ep.* 14.2, purchase of estate πρὸς ἀναχώρησιν. Adherents of idleness: *CTh* 12.1.63 = *CJ* 10.32.26.

3. On strategies of heirship, see Goody (1983) 48–102. Parents: B, *Ep.* 199, Can. 18, with Elm (1994) 140, on the advantages to families, and Arjava (1996) 166: "asceticism provided a sound method for disposing of extra children in a family, perhaps predominately daughters." For virginity as a form of female emancipation, see Verdon (1988); for the prestige of female ascetics, Cloke (1995) 157–211; for deaconesses, Elm (1994) 166–83: "The creation of a new, well-defined female ministry, the deaconess, served to restrict the potential role of women" (174). On notions of authority, see the analysis of early non-Christian asceticism in Francis (1995) 185: "The conflict over . . . asceticism should . . . be cast . . . in terms of the nature of power in society."

4. Illegitimate children: B, *Ep.* 2.5; also Julian, *Ep.* 59, on tests for illegitimate children. For the interaction between the theology of Christology and discussions of female virginity, see Brakke (1995) 17–79: "The virgin's relationship with Christ was to be exclusive: he alone was permitted to enter the garden and harvest the fruit" (43).

Chapter 5. Nonna and Gorgonia

1. Pleasure: GNaz, *Orat.* 7.8.

2. For the home town of Amphilochius the Elder, Nonna's brother, see Chapter 2. As for Nonna's age, Gregory described his mother as the same age as her husband, and he compared his parents with the Old Testament patriarch Abraham and his wife Sarah, who had given birth to a son in her old age: see GNaz, *Orat.* 8.4–5, 18.41. Hauser-Meury (1960) 134, and Jungck (1974) 154, Zeittafel, hence suggest that Nonna was quite old at Gregory's birth, perhaps almost as old as her husband (for Gregory the Elder's age, see Chapter 2). This suggestion is highly improbable. Non-senatorial women typically married young: see Shaw (1987b), suggesting late teens, and Saller (1994) 37, "The best estimate of median age at first marriage for non-senatorial women . . . is twenty years, give or take a couple of years." Women typically experienced menopause during their forties: see Parkin (1992) 123. Even an imperial constitution considered it remarkable for a woman older than fifty to bear a child: see *CJ* 6.58.12, with Clark (1993) 88–89. For age discrepancies between husbands and wives, see Bradley (1991) 156–76.

3. GNaz, *Orat.* 18.5, estrangement, 10, Nonna's behavior, 11, legacy, with Dölger (1936). In *Orat.* 8.5 Gregory noted that Nonna "never shared salt with idolaters." This odd refusal perhaps reflects a belief in the function of salt as a "safeguard against spiritual corruption": see van der Meer (1961) 356. Leaving family: GNaz, *Orat.* 8.4.

4. GNaz, *Orat.* 18.8, teacher, 11, vow, complaints, dripping, 12, dream (with Chapter 2). Christian and bishop: GNaz, *Epitaph.* 58.2–3 = *Anthologia Graeca* 8.27. Note also GNaz, *Carm.* II.1.12.805: "before I was born, my mother promised me to God," with Cloke (1995) 134–56, for maternal ambitions.

5. GNaz, *Orat.* 18.21, Atlantic Ocean, 28–29, Gregory the Elder's illnesses. For women as benefactors, see van Bremen (1983) 226–30, (1996) 55–81, 194–95.

6. Gorgonia's death: GNaz, *Orat.* 8.22. In *Orat.* 8.17 Gregory mentioned that "the tears of parents" had not been able to heal Gorgonia's illness; for the possibility that Gregory was referring to their parents, see Calvet-Sebasti (1995) 284n.1.

7. Man's confidence: GNaz, *Carm.* II.1.1.119; also *Carm.* II.1.11.60, "in body a woman, but in character surpassing a man." Weakness and piety: GNaz, *Ep.* 7.7, with Harrison (1990) 453–65, for Gregory's ideas about gender, and Chapter 3, on Caesarius' career. GNaz, *Orat.* 7.15, funeral, 20, gift.

8. Prayer for son and vision: GNaz, *Carm.* II.1.1.424–30, II.1.11.68–81. GNaz, *Carm.* II.1.1.431, Samuel, 438, hand; *Carm.* II.1.11.91, Samuel.

9. Prayer and hand: GNaz, *Carm.* II.1.94.3–4 = *Anthologia Graeca* 8.80. Desire: GNaz, *Carm.* II.1.1.446.

10. In order of composition the three versions are in GNaz, *Carm.* II.1.1.307–21, *Orat.* 18.31, *Carm.* II.1.11.121–210; for discussion, see Coulie (1988). Offering: GNaz, *Carm.* II.1.11.196–97. For the date of this voyage and Gregory's arrival at Athens, see Chapter 10.

11. For Gregory's life, see Chapter 2; Basil and Gregory, Chapter 10.

12. GNaz, *Orat.* 18.30, Nonna's vision, 41, Abraham and Sarah, 43, Isaac and mother's prayers, with Miller (1994) 243: "the dreams of his mother seem to function as images of reassurance."

13. Nonna's death: GNaz, *Carm.* II.1.90.2–3, Nonna died "not long after" her husband. Death in church: GNaz, *Epitaph.* 66–68 = *Anthologia Graeca* 8.25–27. Hugging: *Miracula Theclae* 46, with Davis (2001) 55–64, on the formation of a monastic community for women at St. Thecla's shrine.

14. Intention: GNaz, *Testamentum*, PG 37.392D. Family tombs: see Chapter 4. Preference: GNaz, *Epitaph.* 71 = *Anthologia Graeca* 8.30.

15. Gorgonia's age: according to GNaz, *Orat.* 8.21, at her death Gorgonia was "not yet full of the days of men." Gallay (1943) 25n.5, Hauser-Meury (1960) 87, and Calvet-Sebasti (1995) 58, suggest that Gorgonia was the oldest of the siblings, Jungck (1974) 154, that Gregory was the oldest. Her husband, Alypius, was mentioned by name only in GNaz, *Epitaph.* 24 = *Anthologia Graeca* 8.103. This Alypius cannot be identified with any of the other men named Alypius mentioned in Gregory's writings: see Van Dam (1996) 24–27. Children and grandchildren: GNaz, *Orat.* 8.8. The three daughters of Alypius and Gorgonia were Alypiana, Eugenia, and Nonna. Alypiana was married to Nicobulus the Elder by ca. 365, and their children included Nicobulus the Younger and other sons, among them possibly Gregorius: see Van Dam (1995) 136n.74, and Chapters 2–3. The "pair of children dedicated to God" mentioned in *Orat.* 8.11 were not sons of Alypius and Gorgonia: see Hauser-Maury (1960) 87n.168, 133 "Nicomedes," and Calvet-Sebasti (1995) 60n.4. Gorgonia's death: in his panegyric for his sister Gregory noted that he had already delivered a panegyric in honor of Caesarius, which implies that his brother had died before Gorgonia: see *Orat.* 8.23, with Chapter 3, for the date of Caesarius' death. Gallay (1943) 92, suggests that Gorgonia died in 370, Hauser-Meury (1960) 87, between 369 and 374.

16. GNaz, *Orat.* 8.19, posturing, 21, loved her husband.

17. The connection between Alypius and Iconium was mentioned only in the annotations of Elias, a bishop on Crete during the twelfth century: see Hauser-Meury (1960) 28n.15.

18. Husband: GNaz, *Orat.* 8.20. Alypius' death: GNaz, *Epitaph.* 24 = *Anthologia Graeca* 8.103. The concession that his audience was already familiar with his sister's life suggests that Gregory was speaking in her town of residence: see GNaz, *Orat.* 8.7, 15. Bernardi (1968) 108–9, suggests that Gregory delivered *Orat.* 8 in 371 on the anniversary of Gorgonia's death. Gregory did once visit "the cities in the mountains of Pamphylia" (GNaz, *Ep.* 28), and Iconium was on the road between Nazianzus and Pamphylia.

19. Reprimand: GNaz, *Ep.* 12, dated to ca. 365 by Gallay (1964–1967) 1:19. My son: GNaz, *Ep.* 13.3, 21.3. For more on Nicobulus the Elder, see Chapters 2–3.

20. Deaths: GNaz, *Ep.* 80.1. Father, mother, brother: GNaz, *Ep.* 222.5.

21. GNaz, *Orat.* 8.15–16, accident, 16–18, illness, 21–22, deathbed. If Gorgonia and Alypius had lived at Iconium, then this bishop was most likely Faustinus, whom Amphilochius would succeed as bishop: see B, *Ep.* 138.2, with Holl (1904) 14, and Calvet-Sebasti (1995) 60n.4.

22. GNaz, *Orat.* 8.4, husband as lord, 8, head and master, 11, woman's limits (using the alternative reading in Calvet-Sebasti (1995) 269n.5). For a survey of Christian ideas of the virtues of women, see Calvet-Sebasti (1995) 61–82.

23. GNaz, *Orat.* 8.11, patronage, 14, feminine nature, 20, baptism.

24. Dedication at Neoclaudiopolis: *Studia Pontica* 3.1:99, no. 80 = Merkelbach

and Stauber (2001) 353, no. 11/03/01. Praise for Basilissa: GNaz, *Ep.* 244.10, with Hauser-Meury (1960) 38, on the similarity to pagan virtues, and Evans Grubbs (1995) 87, on the "adoption of a pre-Christian marital ethos by late antique Christians." GNaz, *Orat.* 8.8, married and unmarried, 19, Lover.

25. GNaz, *Orat.* 8.4–5, parents, 11, goodness.

26. This count of epitaphs is based on the edition in *PG* 38. In *Anthologia Graeca* 8 some of the longer epitaphs were divided into shorter poems. Mother's blood: GNaz, *Epitaph.* 71.4–6 = *Anthologia Graeca* 8.30.

Chapter 6. Emmelia and Macrina

1. Macrina and Peter: GNys, *Vita Macrinae* 12.

2. GNys, *Vita Macrinae* 3. Only Gregory of Nazianzus mentioned Emmelia by name: see GNaz, *Orat.* 43.10, *Epitaph.* 54, 120, 123 = *Anthologia Graeca* 8.161–62, 163, 164.

3. GNys, *Vita Macrinae* 2, marriage, 3, Macrina's nurse and education. Note the clear distinction in GNaz, *Orat.* 43.3, between the "father's family" in Pontus and the "mother's family" in Cappadocia. For nurses, see Chapter 1; bride theft, *Becoming Christian*, Chapter 2. Influence on Basil: B, *Ep.* 223.3.

4. On the comparative probability of widows and widowers, note that mortality levels were about the same, if not tilted in favor of men: see Parkin (1992) 103: "That . . . males on average lived longer than females in antiquity, is quite likely." But the significant difference in the ages of husbands and wives would have produced more widows: see McGinn (1999) 625, "Sub-élite Roman society had a vast number of unmarried, and quite unmarriageable, widows, many of them young and burdened with minor-age children." Widow, daughter, mother: B, *Ep.* 269.2. Simplicia: GNaz, *Ep.* 207.2, ornament, 3, orphans and magnitude; *Ep.* 208.2, defender of orphans; with Van Dam (1996) 24–27, on her husband, Alypius, 57–58, on the recipients of these letters. Alypiana: GNaz, *Ep.* 195.5, distinguished family, 6, misfortunes; *Ep.* 196.4, wretched family; with Gallay (1964–1967) 2:88n.1, for the suggestion about the imperial treasury, and Van Dam (1996) 51–53, on the recipients of these letters. Widows: GNaz, *Ep.* 162.1, with Van Dam (1996) 69–73, for the date of the letter and the identification of the recipient Theodorus as the bishop of Tyana. Relative: GNaz, *Testamentum*, *PG* 37.392B–C, with Van Dam (1995) 145n.101, for the suggestion that Russiana was a widow. Julitta: B, *Ep.* 107–9.

5. Enemies: GNys, *De virginitate* 3.8, with McGinn (1999) 619, "Widows were more exposed than most to the depredations of tax-collectors and other public officials." GNys, *Vita Macrinae* 5, wealth, 20, distinguished family; with Maraval (1971) 160n.1, for attempts to identify these three provinces, and Arjava (1996) 89–94, for widows as guardians. Support for Basil: GNaz, *Ep.* 5.4, with Chapter 10. For the confusing information about the number of children in the family, see GNys, *Vita Macrinae* 5, "four sons and five daughters," 13, Emmelia's description of Peter, her youngest child, as her "tenth," 20, division of property "into nine parts, according to the number of children." Pfister (1964), and Aubineau (1966) 35n.6, argue for ten total children by suggesting there had been a child who died in infancy. Their

argument is similar to the distinction of demographers between living and ever-born children: see Parkin (1992) 116–33. Maraval (1971) 186n.1, (1980) 162–63, argues for nine children by suggesting that Emmelia was describing Peter as her "tithe" to God. Note also that the sequence of events in the *Vita Macrinae* implies that Emmelia divided the property after Naucratius' death.

6. GNys, *Encomium in XL martyres* 2, *PG* 46.784B, shrine was near Ibora, 784D–785B, Gregory's complaints. For additional discussion of the cult of the Forty Martyrs, see *Becoming Christian*, Chapter 7.

7. For Naucratius, Gregory of Nyssa, and Peter, see Chapter 3; for Basil, Chapter 1. Other daughters: GNys, *Vita Macrinae* 6. Maraval (1980) 165, and Hauschild (1990) 193nn.232, 234, suggest that Basil sent *Ep.* 46, addressed to "a lapsed virgin," to one of his sisters; Pouchet (1992a) 583–84, 589, agrees that the recipient was a sister, but argues that the author was Gregory of Nyssa; Rudberg (1981) 55, is skeptical about the authenticity of the letter.

8. Epigram: *Anthologia Graeca* 14.127; for mortality rates, see Saller (1994) 12–25.

9. GNys, *Vita Macrinae* 11, division of property, 20, surpass ancestors. Village near Ibora: GNys, *Encomium in XL martyres* 2, *PG* 46.784B. Estate in Galatia: B, *Ep.* 313; also *Ep.* 137, mentioning "my house," apparently in Cappadocia: see Van Dam (1996) 40–41, "Antipater."

10. For the debate over the date of Macrina's birth, see Maraval (1971) 45, who suggests ca. 327. GNys, *Vita Macrinae* 3, Psalter, 4, wool, maturity, 5, bread. Quotation from Dixon (1992) 62; also Weber (1976) 168: "One married a family, not a woman or a man."

11. Marriage: GNys, *Vita Macrinae* 4. *Sermo de virginitate* 2.10, chase, 12, daughter, 4.58, "let men not delay to be persuaded to sanctify their bodies." Amand and Moons (1953) 238, dates this anonymous sermon to the fourth or early fifth centuries; Amand de Mendieta (1955) 818, suggests that it was composed in the early fourth century by an author in Syria or a nearby region.

12. Groom: GNys, *Vita Macrinae* 4, with Evans Grubbs (1995) 167–69, on waiting for an absent fiancé, 172–83, on the bonds of betrothal.

13. Secret name: GNys, *Vita Macrinae* 2. For the apocryphal traditions about Thecla, see *Acta Pauli et Theclae*, with Albrecht (1986) . Footsteps: *Sermo de virginitate* 8.100. Common name: see GNaz, *Ep.* 56, 57, 222–23, with Hauser-Meury (1960) 158–60, and Berges and Nollé (2000) 1:273–74, no. 112, for women named Thecla.

14. Raising Peter: GNys, *Vita Macrinae* 12. Note that other virgins would later address Macrina as "mother": GNys, *Vita Macrinae* 26. For the impact of ascetic vows, see Harvey (1996) 51: "the ascetic life provided women a means to remain together as mother and daughter rather than being separated into different households by fathers and husbands."

15. GNys, *Vita Macrinae* 6, Basil, 10, mother's soul.

16. Although Maraval (1971) 48, dates Macrina's retreat to an ascetic life soon after her father's death, the timing remains debatable. Gregory himself located the moment in different contexts: see GNys, *Vita Macrinae* 5, after her fiancé's death Macrina resolved "never to be separated from her mother"; 7, after her confrontation with Basil, Macrina "persuaded her mother to abandon her usual life"; 11, after

Naucratius' death "the life of the virgin [Macrina] directed her mother toward a philosophical and spiritual lifestyle." Since Macrina remained with her mother, and since Emmelia had maintained her customary life, Macrina too had most likely lived in Neocaesarea until the mid-350s. Maraval (1971) 53, dates Emmelia's decision to adopt an ascetic life to ca. 357. For the possible influence of Eustathius, see Elm (1994) 135: "even Macrina . . . can be seen as responding directly to some of Eustathius' ideas."

17. Other retreat: GNaz, *Ep.* 222.7, entourage; *Ep.* 223.2, children, "you have secluded yourself with the holy martyrs near whom you live." In these letters Gregory wrote to Thecla about the death of Sacerdos, "your most blessed brother" (*Ep.* 222.1). Hauser-Meury (1960) 158–59, identifies this Thecla as Sacerdos' sister, Gallay (1964–1967) 2:168, as his wife. GNys, *Vita Macrinae* 8, remote spot, 11, other virgins, 16, other men, 37, convent and monastery, Peter. For the shrine to the Forty Martyrs, see Chapter 4, and *Becoming Christian*, Chapter 7; for Basil's retreat and its presumed location at "Annisa," Chapters 1, 10. Emmelia's support: GNaz, *Ep.* 5.4. Opposite village: B, *Ep.* 223.5.

18. Emmelia's death: B, *Ep.* 30, GNys, *Vita Macrinae* 13; for the date, see Maraval (1971) 56–57, 185n.4.

19. GNys, *Vita Macrinae* 11, lifestyle, 16, boards, 24, prayer, 30, necklace.

20. GNys, *Vita Macrinae* 1, human virtue, 17–18, discussion, with Miller (1994) 236–42, on Gregory's association of asceticism with identity. For Gregory's use of "philosophy," see Maraval (1971) 90–103; more generally, Malingrey (1961) 257–61. Hand: GNys, *Dialogus de anima et resurrectione*, PG 46.17A. On Macrina's reputation as a philosopher and theologian, see Beagon (1995) 170–71, and Pelikan (1993) 8–9.

21. GNys, *Vita Macrinae* 14, mourning Basil, 20, memories, 21, evaluation of Gregory, with Geary (1994) 48–73, on the role of women in preserving family memories.

22. GNys, *Vita Macrinae* 30, necklace, 31, scar, 36–38, soldier's story, 39, more stories; Luck (1984) 26, suggests that Gregory used a more colloquial Greek in recounting the soldier's story. Macrina died almost a year after Basil's death: see Maraval (1971) 57–66, and for the debate over the date of Basil's death, Chapter 4.

23. Account, virgin: GNys, *Vita Macrinae* 1, with Krueger (2000), on the tension between Macrina's memories and Gregory's memories, and Cardman (2001), on Gregory's use of stories about himself and his family.

24. GNys, *Vita Macrinae* 28–29, discussion over clothing, 30, servants, 32, like a bride.

25. Bridegroom: GNys, *Vita Macrinae* 22–23.

26. GNys, *Vita Macrinae* 11, souls and angels, 22, angel in human form. Impassibility: GNys, *Hom. in Canticum canticorum* 8, PG 44.948A–B, commenting on Song of Songs 4:9. For discussion, see Daniélou (1954) 92–103, on the absence of passions, 310, "Il y a de curieuses analogies entre le rôle de Macrine . . . et celui qu'il attribue à l'Épouse dans le Cantique"; and Maraval (1971) 90–98. Daniélou (1966) 168, dated the composition of the *Hom. in Canticum canticorum* to the early 390s, near the end of Gregory's life.

27. In the preface to the *Vita Macrinae* Gregory noted that he was now sending this work as a response to a request from a friend. While on his way to Jerusalem

Gregory had met this friend at Antioch, where they had talked about Macrina: "you thought that a history of her virtues would have some usefulness." Different manuscripts provided various identities for this recipient: bishop Euprepius, bishop Eutropius, Hierius, Olympus the ascetic; for texts and discussion, see Maraval (1971) 134–35. The date of Gregory's visit to Antioch and Jerusalem is debatable; for discussion, see Maraval (1971) 67. For the chronological perspective in the *Vita*, see Momigliano (1985) 453, "The arch of time is built in such a way that adolescence is in direct contact with death."

28. For the ubiquity of "ventriloquism," male authors speaking through female characters, see Burrus (2000) 120, on Gregory of Nyssa's portrait of his sister: "Macrina . . . is the reflection of a masculine erotics."

29. GNys, *Vita Macrinae* 33–36, funeral. Location of family's shrine: GNys, *Vita Macrinae* 34, Macrina's ascetic community was seven or eight stades (i.e., about a mile) from a shrine to the Forty Martyrs; GNys, *Encomium in XL martyres* 2, *PG* 46.784B, shrine was near Ibora; with *Becoming Christian*, Chapter 7, on the cult of the Forty Martyrs. Gregory identified the bishop who presided as Araxius, who was most likely bishop of Ibora: see Maraval (1971) 250n.1.

30. Scar and heart: GNys, *Vita Macrinae* 31, with Frank (2000), on a possible Homeric allusion for the story of Macrina's scar.

31. GNys, *Vita Macrinae* 32, cloak, 35, prayer.

Chapter 7. Virginity and Social Extinction

1. GNys, *Vita Macrinae* 12, reputation, 26, women, with additional discussion in *Kingdom of Snow*, Chapter 2.

2. Definition of virgin: B, *Ep.* 199, Can. 18. Vetiana, daughter of Araxius and husband of Agilo: GNys, *Vita Macrinae* 28, with *PLRE* 1:28–29, 94, 954.

3. *Sermo de virginitate* 2.29–37, daughters, 5.63, sons.

4. Basil of Ancyra, *De virginitate* 3, woman's body, 5, seeds, 36, bride and friends. Medical training: Jerome, *De viris illustribus* 89, with Vaggione (2000) 161–66, on Basil's use of medical terminology in his theology. Basil became bishop of Ancyra in 336, was deposed in 360, but either returned or just remained active into the reign of Jovian: see Socrates, *HE* 3.25, with Cavallera (1905), who identifies Basil as the author of this treatise about virginity, and Barnes (1996), for his deposition. For discussion of his treatise, see Aubineau (1966) 137–42, on its influence on Gregory of Nyssa, Elm (1994) 113–24, and Shaw (1998) 82–92, 184–87, on its ideas about fasting. Quotation about Galen from Foucault (1986) 100; see also Malina (1995), on asceticism and the concept of self.

5. GNys, *De virginitate* 3.2, attractions, 15.1, success, 16.1, adultery, 18.2, house, 21.2, pleasures, 22.1, severity, with Chapter 3, for the date and context.

6. Quotation about rhetoric from Gleason (1995) xxii. Gymnastics of silence: B, *Regulae fusius tractatae* 13. Athlete: GNys, *Vita Macrinae* 14, with Cooper (1996) 58: "even self-denial could signal an antisocial self-assertion."

7. On options for women, see Arjava (1996) 158: "for well-born women there had been no career outside marriage." Woman and grandfather: B, *Ep.* 315

8. GNys, *Vita Macrinae* 5, extended pregnancy, with Harrison (1990) 465–71, for Gregory's speculations about gender.

9. GNys, *Vita Macrinae* 1, virgin, woman, 12, Peter. In *Ep.* 19.6 Gregory discussed "my sister," who was clearly Macrina even though he did not mention her name. Basil of Ancyra, *De virginitate* 18, appearance and voices, 51, equal to men.

10. See Forlin Patrucco (1976) 178–79, on monasticism and families, and Clark (1995), on the renunciation of gender by women.

11. See Chapter 2, for Amphilochius and Amphilochius the Elder; *Becoming Christian*, Chapter 2, for sees as wives; and Elm (1994) 184–223, for an excellent discussion of monasticism and hierarchy.

12. Zeus, immortality: Menander Rhetor, *Treatise* II.401, ed. Russell and Wilson (1981) 138–39. Marriage, death: GNaz, *Carm.* I.2.1.124–27, with Ruether (1969) 129–55, for Gregory's ideas about asceticism, Van Eijk (1972), for a fine survey of ideas of virginity and immortality, and Cooper (1996) 92–115, on lingering Christian support for marriage.

13. Marriage and death: Artemidorus, *Onirocritica* 2.49. St. Thecla and resurrection: *Acta Pauli et Theclae* 12, 14.

14. Parents: GNys, *Vita Macrinae* 35. GNys, *De virginitate* 3.3, graves, 14.1, birth and death, with Brown (1988) 291–304, on Gregory's fear of death, although Hart (1990) 465, suggests that Gregory nevertheless conceded that husbands and wives might still benefit: "the lessons of separation and detachment which characterize a life in retirement from the world are in fact present in marriage as well." Quotation about realized eschatology from Van Eijk (1972) 235.

15. Father and Son: Hilary of Poitiers, *In Constantium imperatorem* 13, "ad generandum naturalis machinula," with Rocher (1987) 242, for the identification of this bishop at Antioch as Eudoxius. For Eudoxius' career and theology, see Hanson (1988) 583–88, and *Becoming Christian*, Chapter 1.

16. Paradox: GNys, *De virginitate* 2.1. God's sexuality remained a topic that was both intriguing and confusing. Note that in his account of the martyrdom of St. Theodorus, Gregory invented a dialogue about God's passion: see GNys, *De Theodoro*, PG 46.741C–D. Theodorus' confession in Christ as God's only-begotten Son had supposedly baffled his persecutors. "Does your God have a son? And does that God procreate like a man, with passion?" Theodorus' innocent reply perhaps reflected Gregory's own embarrassment. "My God did not procreate with passion. But I confess a Son, and I say that His begatting was worthy of God." For an excellent discussion of the difficulties in imagining God's sexual anatomy within ancient Jewish thought, see Eilberg-Schwartz (1994).

17. Quotation from Brown (1988) 286. B, *Ep.* 5.1, heir; *Ep.* 6.1, collapse. These letters were sent to Nectarius and his wife; for the possibility that this correspondent can be identified with the Nectarius who succeeded Gregory of Nazianzus as bishop of Constantinople, see Hauschild (1990) 165n.41. See you: B, *Ep.* 211. Bereft of heirs: B, *Ep.* 84, with Van Dam (1996) 32–33, for the date. For the tradition of consolatory letters and orations, see Gregg (1975).

18. Parents' estate: Cyril of Scythopolis, *Vita Sabae* 2, with Hild and Restle (1981) 259, for this monastery near Caesarea. Of the other brothers, since Naucratius died in his late twenties and Caesarius in his mid- to late thirties, they were still

young enough that it is uncertain whether they had committed themselves to remaining unmarried.

In a letter to Libanius written after 378 or 379, Gregory of Nyssa requested a favor for "my son Cynegius": GNys, *Ep.* 13.3. Daniélou (1956) 76–77, suggests that this Cynegius might be Gregory's natural son, born in the early 360s. But since Gregory commonly referred to acquaintances as sons, he was more likely designating Cynegius as another of his spiritual offspring: see Aubineau (1966) 76–77, who also points out that one important manuscript omitted υἱός in this letter, and Maraval (1990) 196n.2.

19. Emmelia: GNaz, *Orat.* 43.10. Grandmother Gorgonia, married to Philtatius: GNaz, *Epitaph.* 107 = *Anthologia Graeca* 8.136. Alypiana, Eugenia, Nonna: GNaz, *Testamentum, PG* 37.392C, with Chapters 2–3 on Nicobulus the Elder. Gregory also composed epitaphs for "hallowed Nonna" and for a young man named Philtatius: GNaz, *Epitaph.* 121, 124 = *Anthologia Graeca* 8.150, 149. Their names suggest that this Philtatius and this Nonna were members of his extended family, presumably on his mother's side: see Hauser-Meury (1960) 135, 147. For the importance of names in preserving family memories, see Geary (1994) 73–79.

20. Peter as common name: Eusebius, *HE* 7.25.14.

21. Secret name: GNys, *Vita Macrinae* 2. Gorgon: Eunapius, *Fragmenta historica* 65.1 = *Suda* E.3776. For the etymological connection between Gorgonia and Gorgon, see Zgusta (1964) 137, and Chantraine (1968–1980) 1:233–34, s.v. γοργός.

22. Wedding orations: Menander Rhetor, *Treatise* II.402–4, ed. Russell and Wilson (1981) 140–44. Macrina's wealth: GNys, *Vita Macrinae* 20.

Friendship Introduction

1. GNys, *De virginitate* 3.3, uncertainty, 5, mother's death, 6, traveling, 4.8, one escape, with Barnes (2001), on Gregory's ambivalence about the delights and burdens of marriage, and the excellent summation of Hart (1990) 466: "Amid the impermanence of the world, the pure of heart rest in the permanence of God."

Chapter 8. The Emotional Life of Letters

1. Diary: B, *Ep.* 231, to Amphilochius, with Devos (1992) 251–52, on ἐφημερίς.

2. Verses: GNaz, *Carm.* II.1.39.22–24, with Milovanovic-Barham (1997). Good letters: GNaz, *Ep.* 51, with Mullett (1981), (1997) 148–61, and Dennis (1986), on the characteristics of early Byzantine letters. The editor of Gregory's letters was certainly impressed at their liveliness: see Gallay (1964–1967) 1:xviii, "Ses lettres sont vivantes."

3. Most correspondents were mentioned by name only in the heading (or address, title, superscription) to each letter. The reliability of these headings needs more investigation; see Hauser-Meury (1960) 18, for warnings about the letters of Gregory of Nazianzus, and Van Dam (1996) 14–17, for discussion and examples. Circle: B, *Ep.* 112.2. Water: B, *Ep.* 222. Pretext: GNaz, *Ep.* 106.1. Note that the editor of Gregory's letters wondered whether he had followed his own advice about good

letters: see Gallay (1964–1967) 1:68n.1, "ses lettres sont très travaillées, parfois même trop."

4. Lifeless: B, *Ep.* 212.2; note the dismissive comment of Jones (1964) 1009, on Symmachus' letters: "elegant nothings."

5. For the debate over the utilitarian and altruistic nature of friendship in the ancient world, see Konstan (1997) 12–14; also Mullett (1988) 16, on Byzantine society: "the pure type of emotional friendship . . . is not characteristic of Byzantine friendship. . . . it is arguable that instrumental friendship and patronage were more characteristic."

6. Quotation from Trexler (1980) 132; also Mullett (1997) 17: "the formality of Byzantine letters . . . coexists with the intimacy."

7. Exchange: B, *Ep.* 317. Unites: GNaz, *Ep.* 229.1, with Maraval (1988b), for the identification of the recipient as Pansophius, bishop of Ibora. Widely separated: B, *Ep.* 197.1; cf. B, *Ep.* 185. Shadow: GNaz, *Ep.* 93.2, 201.2. Soul: B, *Ep.* 163. Flowers: B, *Ep.* 13. Fantasizing: B, *Ep.* 207.1. Long interval: GNaz, *Ep.* 128.1. Salutations: GNys, *Ep.* 1.13, for Gregory of Nyssa's amazement when these greetings were not used. For letters representing "une lutte pour obtenir la présence et l'union, indépendamment de la distance," see Karlsson (1959) 57.

8. Gift: GNys, *Ep.* 4.3. Testimonials: GNaz, *Ep.* 121.1. Dried fruit and candles: B, *Ep.* 232. Herbs and gold: GNaz, *Ep.* 26. Love this letter: B, *Ep.* 57, with Mullett (1981) 85, arguing that letter writers of the fourth century finally realized the "emotional force" of the genre.

9. Demonstration: GNaz, *Ep.* 92.3.

10. Without letters: B, *Ep.* 218. Reminder: GNaz, *Ep.* 134.3. First letter: GNaz, *Ep.* 82.1.

11. Pure friendship: GNaz, *Ep.* 230.2. Whip: GNaz, *Ep.* 174.1. First and second: B, *Ep.* 191. Silence: GNaz, *Ep.* 73. Regard: GNaz, *Ep.* 240.4. Be a friend: B, *Ep.* 330; cf. B, *Ep.* 12, "only write to me."

12. Remembrance: GNaz, *Ep.* 234, to Olympianus; for the name and identification of this correspondent, see Van Dam (1996) 63–64. Basil's disposition: Photius, *Bibliotheca* 143.

13. Quotation from Brain (1976) 18–19. Tyrannize us: GNaz, *Ep.* 86.1.

14. Reluctance: B, *Ep.* 162.

15. GNaz, *Ep.* 139.2–3, not accuse; *Ep.* 187.2, limits.

16. GNaz, *Ep.* 17.1, Eusebius of Caesarea; *Ep.* 240.4, care.

Chapter 9. The Friends of Basil and Gregory of Nazianzus

1. Parents: B, *Ep.* 112. Early boyhood: B, *Ep.* 274, on behalf of Hera, whom Hauschild (1993) 235n.521, identifies as a cleric in Cappadocia; for other petitions on behalf of Hera, see B, *Ep.* 273, 275. The recipient of B, *Ep.* 274, was Himerius, described in the heading as a *magister* and identified by *PLRE* 1:437, "Himerius 5," as the *magister officiorum* in ca. 378.

2. School lessons: B, *Ep.* 212.1, with Hauschild (1973) 183n.325. One home: B, *Ep.* 271. Comrades at Athens: GNaz, *Orat.* 43.20. Armenian students: GNaz, *Orat.*

43.17. Hellenius: GNaz, *Carm.* II.2.1.285–86, "old friendship," 295–96, introduction by Basil, 359, "pride of Armenia," with Van Dam (1996) 54–56, for Hellenius' tenure as an assessor at Nazianzus in 372. Hellenius as courier: B, *Ep.* 71.1, 98.1. In *Ep.* 290 Basil mentioned that he had known Nectarius "from boyhood." In this case he was not referring to his own boyhood, but noting that he had watched Nectarius grow up.

3. Habit: B, *Ep.* 273. Questions at Athens: GNaz, *Orat.* 43.17.

4. Deserve to suffer: B, *Ep.* 112. Return to youth: B, *Ep.* 271.

5. Intimacy: B, *Ep.* 272.1. Titles: B, *Ep.* 32, 76, 96, 177. Favor: B, *Ep.* 180; cf. *Ep.* 192.

6. B, *Ep.* 272.1, flattery, early youth, 3, never sinned; with *Kingdom of Snow*, Chapter 3, for Sophronius' career, Chapter 7, for the context of the appeal.

7. Family affairs: B, *Ep.* 30, 100, 237. Reconciliation: B, *Ep.* 128. The estranged bishop was Euippius: see B, *Ep.* 68, 239.1, 244.6–7, 251.2–3, with Hauschild (1990) 205n.310, who suggests that Euippius was perhaps bishop of Amaseia.

8. Defense: B, *Ep.* 266.2. Letter to West: B, *Ep.* 92.1. For Meletius' family and connections, see *Kingdom of Snow*, Chapter 7. Man of God: B, *Ep.* 210.5, 214.2.

9. B, *Ep.* 150, is a letter to Amphilochius, written by Basil in the name of Heraclides, Amphilochius' friend: see Hauschild (1973) 167n.147. Christian philosophy: GNaz, *Ep.* 25.2. For Amphilochius' life, see Holl (1904) 5–42, Datema (1978) IX–XI, and Chapter 2.

10. Preaching and order: B, *Ep.* 161.1. Advice: B, *Ep.* 190.1, discussing affairs at Isaura, a city in Lycaonia: see Hauschild (1973) 176n.239, and Belke (1984) 180–81. Martyrs' festivals: B, *Ep.* 176, 200. Isauria: B, *Ep.* 190.3, mentioning Sympius, bishop of Seleucia in Isauria: see Hauschild (1973) 176n.247. Lycia: B, *Ep.* 218. Pisidia: B, *Ep.* 260, a reply to Optimus, metropolitan bishop of Antioch in Pisidia. Amphilochius may have introduced Optimus to Basil, since both had once studied with Libanius: see Libanius, *Ep.* 1544. Questions: B, *Ep.* 188, 190.3, 199, 201, 232–36. Appreciation: B, *De spiritu sancto* 1.1.

11. Nyssa: B, *Ep.* 190.2, 231, 232. Advice: B, *Ep.* 201, 202. Token: B, *Ep.* 217. B, *De spiritu sancto* 1.1, dedication, 30.79, stateliness.

12. Father's heart: B, *Ep.* 161.2, with Drecoll (1996) 268–69, on the importance of friendship with Amphilochius for expanding Basil's theological influence.

13. Philagrius and Caesarius: GNaz, *Epitaph.* 21 = *Anthologia Graeca* 8.100. Studies and teachers: GNaz, *Ep.* 30.2. Meetings: GNaz, *Ep.* 34.1. Explanation: GNaz, *Ep.* 87. Praise for Hellenius: GNaz, *Carm.* II.2.1.7–9.

14. GNaz, *Ep.* 189.1, Alexander, 2, culture, Athens, fathers; *Ep.* 190.5, Demosthenes, Homer. For Himerius' influence on Gregory, see Bernardi (1992) 38–40.

15. GNaz, *Ep.* 190.3, complaints, Athens; *Ep.* 191.1, Eustochius as sophist, 2, like a friend. For Gregory and his grandnephew Nicobulus the Younger, see Chapters 2–3. In *Ep.* 192 Gregory asked Stagirius to share Nicobulus the Younger with Eustochius. Hauschild (1990) 207n.332, and Pouchet (1992a) 294, suggest that this rhetorician Eustochius can be identified with the "most eloquent Eustochius" involved in a local feud that Basil tried to mediate: see B, *Ep.* 72. Hauser-Meury (1960) 78–79, suggests that Gregory's friend Eustochius should be identified with the Cappadocian sophist Eustochius who wrote a life of the emperor Constans: see *PLRE* 1:313, "Eustochius 2," and the introduction to "Empire and Province" in *Kingdom of Snow*.

Gregory's friend might also be identified with the Eustochius whom the emperor Julian invited to attend the celebration of his consulship on January 1, 363, at Antioch: see Julian, *Ep.* 54, with *PLRE* 1:313, "Eustochius 5." This Eustochius whom Julian invited might instead be another Eustochius, an advocate from Palestine: see Hauser-Meury (1960) 79, and *PLRE* 1:313, "Eustochius 3."

16. Philagrius: GNaz, *Ep.* 30.2, Homer; *Ep.* 31.2, education, 4, Plato, 7, Demosthenes; *Ep.* 32.5–6, Aristotle; *Ep.* 34, Psalm.

17. GNaz, *Ep.* 29.4, friend of Caesarius; *Ep.* 21.2, goodness, 5, most beautiful; *Ep.* 37.4, eloquence. Fatherland: GNaz, *Ep.* 37.1, 4, 39.4. Complaint: GNaz, *Ep.* 93.1. Prefect: Ammianus Marcellinus, *Res gestae* 26.7.2, with *PLRE* 1:847, for the suggestion that Sophronius was prefect of Constantinople briefly in 382. In the later 380s Sophronius was splitting his time between Caesarea (Libanius, *Ep.* 883.1) and Constantinople (Libanius, *Ep.* 924): see *Kingdom of Snow*, Chapter 3.

18. For Basil as broker, see B, *Ep.* 14.1: Gregory of Nyssa informed Basil about the plans of Gregory of Nazianzus. Chiding: GNaz, *Ep.* 11, with further discussion in Chapter 3. GNaz, *Orat.* 11.1, true friend, 2, name and soul, Moses and Aaron, 3, pilot and remedy, embarrassment or annoyance, brothers.

19. Heretics: GNaz, *Ep.* 72; also *Ep.* 73–74. Condolence: GNaz, *Ep.* 76.5. Journey: GNaz, *Ep.* 81. Companion: GNaz, *Ep.* 197; for the relationship between Gregory of Nyssa and the deceased Theosebia, see Chapter 3.

20. New bishop: GNaz, *Ep.* 182.5.

21. Fathers: GNaz, *Ep.* 13.2. Pindar: GNaz, *Ep.* 9.1. Old men: Libanius, *Ep.* 1543.3; the authenticity of this letter is accepted by Holl (1904) 8n.4, but doubted by Seeck (1906) 496, and not cited in Hauser-Meury (1960) 30–32, and *PLRE* 1:58, "Amphilochius 4." Poet on friendship: GNaz, *Ep.* 13.1. Philosopher: GNaz, *Ep.* 24.2. Short notes: GNaz, *Ep.* 25–28. Christian and Greek: GNaz, *Ep.* 62.

22. GNaz, *Ep.* 63.3, advisor, 6, tyranny. Care for father: B, *Ep.* 150.4; for additional discussion of Amphilochius, see Chapter 2. Letters: GNaz, *Ep.* 171.2.

23. Great Paul: GNys, *Ep.* 25.1, referring to Acts of the Apostles 14:1–6. Mediation: GNaz, *Ep.* 184. St. Thecla: GNaz, *Carm.* II.2.6.102–3.

24. Messenger and prince: GNaz, *Epitaph.* 58 = *Anthologia Graeca* 8.15; this description referred to Gregory, not to his father, as suggested by Holl (1904) 39.

25. My letters: GNaz, *Ep.* 52.2, with Gallay (1957) 9–14, (1964–1967) 1:xxi–xxiii, on collections of Gregory's letters; for additional discussion, see Chapter 10. Coppola (1923), discusses the possible publication of letters by Basil, Pouchet (1992a) 45–72, the various collections of Basil's letters. Important examinations of the manuscripts for Basil's letters include Bessières (1923), Cavallin (1944), Rudberg (1953), Gribomont (1983), and Fedwick (1993).

26. Foremost friend: GNaz, *Ep.* 29.4.

27. With God: B, *Ep.* 96.

28. More critical: B, *Ep.* 66.2, with Batiffol (1922), and Krivochéine (1969) 93–102, on Basil's connections with Antioch and Alexandria.

29. Gregory once criticized an "Armenian" as "an outright barbarian, far from being worthy of my veneration": see GNaz, *Ep.* 62. Gallay (1964–1967) 1:81n.1, suggests that this Armenian may have been Eustathius; Hauser-Meury (1960) 184–85, remains skeptical. Eusebius of Samosata: GNaz, *Ep.* 42, in the name of Gregory the

Elder; *Ep.* 44.7, failure to meet; *Ep.* 64.1, illness, 2, patron. Meletius: GNaz, *Carm.* II.1.11.1514–24, 1574–82, with Hauser-Meury (1960) 121–23. Factions: GNaz, *Ep.* 135.3. Alexandria: GNaz, *Carm.* II.1.11.576–78.

    30. Mount Argaeus: Strabo, *Geographica* 12.2.7.

    31. For Basil's travels, see Chapter 1; for Gregory's, Chapter 2.

Chapter 10. The Friendship of Basil and Gregory of Nazianzus

    1. Shadows: GNaz, *Ep.* 16.7, with Hanriot-Coustet (1983), on Gregory's deference, and Halperin (1990), for the inherent unevenness between heroes and their pals. Giet (1941), provides a perceptive and nuanced analysis of their friendship; for a general survey, see White (1992) 61–84.

    2. GNaz, *Orat.* 43.13, studies at Caesarea, 15, "Athens received me a bit earlier, Basil immediately after me," 16, hazing, 17, interrogation.

    3. GNaz, *Orat.* 43.18, cheering up, 22, Basil as leader, pair.

    4. GNaz, *Orat.* 43.14, source of culture, 17, empty happiness. Basil's departure: B, *Ep.* 1. Basil had arrived at Athens after studying at Constantinople with Libanius, who taught there between 349 and 354: see Barnes (1987) 211, for Libanius' chronology, and Chapter 1. Basil had left Athens before the future emperor Julian arrived in summer 355; Gregory finally left Athens when he was "almost thirty": see GNaz, *Carm.* II.1.11.239. He had arrived in Athens in about 350 and stayed possibly until late 358 or 359: see Gallay (1943) 36–37, Wittig (1981) 13, and Bernardi (1992) 178n.1.

    5. On Eustathius and Basil's travels, see Chapter 1. Decision at Athens: GNaz, *Ep.* 1.1.

    6. GNaz, *Ep.* 1.2, parents, 3, half the time; *Ep.* 2, mud. B, *Ep.* 14.1, empty hopes; *Ep.* 2.2, separation, distractions. For the sequence of both extant and missing letters, see Forlin Patrucco (1983) 313–14.

    7. Scrutiny: B, *Ep.* 2.3. Smile: GNaz, *Ep.* 4.1.

    8. Tree: GNaz, *Ep.* 6.5–6. On the arguments over the composition of the *Philocalia*, see Junod (1972), (1988), and Harl (1983) 20–24.

    9. Equal honor: GNaz, *Ep.* 1.3.

    10. B, *Ep.* 2.5, no jesting; *Ep.* 14.2, Calypso's island. GNaz, *Ep.* 4.1, teasing or serious, 5, desert; *Ep.* 5.3, bread, 4, mother; *Ep.* 6.8, breathe you; *Ep.* 235.5, joking. The Lord never laughed: B, *Regulae fusius tractatae* 17.1.

    11. On Basil's and Gregory's ordinations, see Chapters 1–2. GNaz, *Ep.* 8.1, Basil's letter, praiseworthy, 2, philosophy. Criticism of clerics: GNaz, *Orat.* 2.8.

    12. For Basil and bishop Eusebius, see Chapter 1; Basil and Eunomius, *Becoming Christian*, Chapter 1. Heretics: GNaz, *Ep.* 8.4. Short letters: B, *Ep.* 19, dated before 365 by Hauschild (1990) 173n.117.

    13. Letters to Eusebius: GNaz, *Ep.* 16.4, insult, doubt, 6, honor; *Ep.* 17, annoyance; *Ep.* 18, offer to help. Letter to Basil: GNaz, *Ep.* 19.2, conciliation, 7, not refuse.

    14. Illness: GNaz, *Ep.* 40.2. Basil may well have been ill, since Gregory the Elder would brush aside Basil's poor health as an obstacle to his selection: see GNaz, *Ep.* 43.4.

    15. GNaz, *Ep.* 40.4, surprise, piety, 5, complaints. If B, *Ep.* 313, referred to his

selection as bishop, then Basil claimed that he had summoned friends to support him against insulting treatment: see Hauschild (1993) 241n.590.

16. Gregory the Elder's letters: GNaz, *Ep.* 41–43. GNaz, *Ep.* 44.4, worthy bishop; *Ep.* 45, misgivings.

17. GNaz, *Ep.* 5.5, vintager; *Ep.* 46.1, small grapes, 2, fortress, 5, eloquence.

18. GNaz, *Ep.* 41.6, mother; *Ep.* 44.4, widow's weeds; *Ep.* 46.2, Athens.

19. Offer of episcopacy: GNaz, *Orat.* 43.39.

20. Advice: GNaz, *Ep.* 47.3.

21. GNaz, *Ep.* 48.7, seclusion; *Ep.* 49.1, τὰ σὰ Σάσιμα.

22. GNaz, *Ep.* 48.1, accusations, 2, weariness, 10, one lesson; *Ep.* 49.1, lazy.

23. B, *Ep.* 154, spiritual love; *Ep.* 56, forgetting friends.

24. For their differing notions of friendship, see Vischer (1953), who explains Basil's austerity by his commitment to an ascetic life that Gregory could not understand; Treu (1961), who contrasts Basil's biblical perspective with Gregory's more traditional classical outlook; and, for additional background, Treu (1972), Malunowicz (1985), and Van Dam (1986) 70–73.

25. GNaz, *Ep.* 50.2, Basil's annoyance, 3–5, visit from bishop Anthimus.

26. GNaz, *Ep.* 50.8, insult, 9, bishops. For the interpretation of πρεσβυτέρους in GNaz, *Ep.* 50.8 as "older," see Jungck (1974) 231–32.

27. GNaz, *Ep.* 58.2, advantage, 9–10, Holy Spirit, with Kustas (1981) 221–24, for the rhetorical figures, and the introduction to "Preachers and Audiences" in *Becoming Christian*, for the date and context of the letter. In *Orat.* 43.68–69, Gregory offered a similar explanation for Basil's reticence about his theology of the Holy Spirit.

28. Love, same disposition: B, *Ep.* 71.1. Mask: GNaz, *Ep.* 59.2. For the suggestion that B, *Ep.* 71, was a reply to GNaz, *Ep.* 58, see Gallay (1964–1967) 1:77n.1, and Hauschild (1990) 207n.324. Equal to talent: B, *Ep.* 98.2; for the identification of "brother Gregory" as Gregory of Nazianzus, see Hauschild (1973) 156n.13.

29. B, *Ep.* 71.2, living together. GNaz, *Ep.* 59.4, join Basil; *Ep.* 60.2, mother. Compliment for Eulalius: GNaz, *Carm.* II.2.1.135–38, with Van Dam (1996) 54–56, for the dating of this poem to 372. For the correspondence between Basil and Gregory about the deacon Glycerius, see *Becoming Christian*, Chapter 2.

30. GNaz, *Orat.* 18.15, father's consecration, 17, smallness of see, 24–26, virtues, 25, grudges, 34, micropolitan bishop, 35, Basil's selection.

31. GNaz, *Orat.* 18.2–3, reasons for Basil's presence, 35, companion, 37, reproach, 40, tyranny.

32. Fathers and consecration: GNaz, *Carm.* II.1.11.391–94. Sudden departure: B, *Ep.* 217, dated to late summer 376 by Hauschild (1993) 188n.27. The Gregory, "our brother and fellow cleric," mentioned in B, *Ep.* 225, was Gregory of Nyssa, not Gregory of Nazianzus, as suggested by Deferrari (1926–1934) 3:323n.1.

33. Monastic retreats: Egeria, *Itinerarium* 23.4. For the amenities of the shrine, see Dagron (1978) 55–73. Description of Seleucia: *Vita Theclae* 27, with Dagron (1978) 129–30, on the rhetoricians, and the survey in Hild and Hellenkemper (1990) 1:402–6. Friend of culture: *Miracula Theclae* 38.

34. On aristocratic retirement, see Marrou (1964), and Matthews (1975) 1–12. For Gregory's association of the shrine with Athens, see Chapter 2.

35. Bishop of Seleucia: B, *Ep.* 190.3. For Basil's father and teachers, see Chapter

1; his relationship with Eunomius, *Becoming Christian*, Chapter 1; Gregory and Constantinople, *Kingdom of Snow*, Chapter 8.

36. GNaz, *Orat.* 43.59, afterthought; *Ep.* 48.3, scaffolding; *Ep.* 49.1, bone.

37. GNaz, *Ep.* 16.4, companion; *Ep.* 58.1, guide.

38. Marriage and haze: Libanius, *Orat.* 1.12. Epitaph: GNaz, *Epitaph.* 119.35 = *Anthologia Graeca* 8.8.1.

39. Living library: Eunapius, *Vitae sophistarum* 456, with Marrou (1956) 270: "Learning to speak properly meant learning to think properly, and even to live properly." GNaz, *Orat.* 43.20, one soul, 23, curriculum, educating character; *Ep.* 165.4, books, with Hauser-Meury (1960) 157–58, on the sophist Stagirius.

40. Heavy accent: Philostratus, *Vitae sophistarum* 594, on the sophist Pausanias. For the protocol of exchanging letters, see Chapter 8.

41. B, *Ep.* 1, departure; *Ep.* 74.3, example from Athenian history; *Ep.* 223.2, youthful studies. Banquet: GNaz, *Ep.* 58.4.

42. B, *Ep.* 79, assistance; *Ep.* 119, pretense.

43. B, *Ep.* 99.3, suspicions, conjecture; *Ep.* 119, constant love.

44. B, *Ep.* 125, declaration of faith; *Ep.* 128.2, confirmation; *Ep.* 130.1, true disciple; *Ep.* 244.1, become someone else. For Basil's correspondence with Apollinarius during the early 360s, see B, *Ep.* 361–64, with Drecoll (1996) 21–42.

45. B, *Ep.* 223.1, three years of silence, 3, wandering opinions; *Ep.* 224.2, boyhood; *Ep.* 226.3, creed, innovations; *Ep.* 236.1, boyhood; *Ep.* 244.9, clouds.

46. B, *Ep.* 251.4, always the same; with Drecoll (1996) 199–212, for a survey of this breakup, and Rousseau (1990), for suggestive comments on Basil's search for a consistent past.

47. GNaz, *Carm.* II.1.1.97, Athens; *Carm.* II.1.12.78, cannot say; with *Kingdom of Snow*, Chapter 8, on Gregory at Constantinople. For Gregory's reevaluation of his life after his episcopacy at Constantinople, see Van Dam (1995) 137–43, and *Becoming Christian*, Chapter 10.

48. GNaz, *Carm.* II.1.11.17–18, without falsehood, 94, exemplars, 112–13, passion, 211, Athens, 225, great prize, 228–32, pair, one soul, 345, tyranny. Jungck (1974) 169, dates this poem to early 382.

49. GNaz, *Carm.* II.1.11.405–7, questions, law, 415–16, Basil, 432–34, Pontus, 476–82, Athens.

50. GNaz, *Carm.* II.1.11.425, kick.

51. GNaz, *Carm.* II.1.11.560–61, indictment, 792–93, same character, 808, Proteus.

52. GNaz, *Carm.* II.1.11.1043, overcome. Quotation from Spacks (1976) 308.

53. Reactions: GNaz, *Ep.* 53. For the dating, see Gallay (1964–1967) 1:126–27; also McLynn (2001) 186, suggesting that in his collection "Gregory paired each letter from Basil with one or more of his own."

54. For Gregory's intrusion of himself into this panegyric about Basil, note Konstan (2000) 161: "Biography threatens to dissolve into autobiography." The enormous length of the panegyric has raised questions about its public performance. Gallay (1943) 214, suggests it would have taken Gregory at least two and a half hours to deliver, Bernardi (1992) 27–28, that Gregory delivered this oration in 382, and that the published text was an expansion and revision of the public oration, and Bernardi (1995) 274, that the panegyric originally did not include the criticisms of Basil or the account of their education in Athens.

55. GNaz, *Orat.* 43.1, oration, 2, friendship, 14, my affairs, friendship, 17, spark, blaze, 19, desire, with Børtnes (2000), on Gregory's appropriation of the theme of Platonic eros.

56. GNaz, *Orat.* 43.24, accusation, betrayal, splitting.

57. GNaz, *Orat.* 43.29, Pontus, 31, return, 39, contact, 59, innovation.

58. GNaz, *Orat.* 43.25, discomfort, 59, confusion.

59. In *Carm.* II.1.11.388, Gregory mentioned Basil, "whom I recently stopped eulogizing." For the identification of this eulogy with *Orat.* 43, see Jungck (1974) 169. Norris (2000), provides a fine survey of the main themes in the panegyric; McLynn (2001) 179–83, suggests that Gregory was claiming Basil's legacy.

60. GNaz, *Orat.* 43.13, priest, 27, from God, 33, power in church, 59, increase.

61. GNaz, *Orat.* 43.59, ideas, 64, vanity.

62. GNaz, *Orat.* 43.17, lover of Athens, 59, Jerusalem.

63. Comrade and same rank: GNaz, *Orat.* 43.82. Note that when a later poet celebrated Basil's virtues, he insisted that Gregory's virginity and wisdom had been identical: see *Anthologia Graeca* 1.86.

64. Mythological friendships: GNaz, *Orat.* 43.22, with Brain (1976) 122–44, on friends as twins. Scipio and Laelius: Julian, *Orat.* 8.244c. My tongue: Severus of Antioch, *Ep.* 4.7, tr. Brooks (1903–1904) 2:266. Bishop and friend: *Suda* B.150, Γ.450. Michael Psellus would use the rift between Gregory and Basil as an analogy for one of his friendships: see Tinnefeld (1973) 166–67.

65. Our friendship: GNaz, *Ep.* 58.4.

66. GNaz, *Orat.* 43.20, crying, 80, dreams.

67. Bodies and soul: GNaz, *Carm.* II.1.11.229–30. Epitaphs: GNaz, *Epitaph.* 119 = *Anthologia Graeca* 8.2–11; quotation from *Epitaph.* 119.26–27 = *Anthologia Graeca* 8.6.2–3.

68. Friendship in heaven: GNaz, *Epitaph.* 119.30 = *Anthologia Graeca* 8.6.6.

Epilogue

1. Amphilochius' treatise on Holy Spirit: Jerome, *De viris illustribus* 133. List: Jerome, *Ep.* 70.4. Council at Side: Photius, *Bibliotheca* 52, with Elm (1994) 189–94. Basil's authority: Amphilochius, *Epistula synodalis* 1, referring probably to Basil's *De spiritu sancto*: see Datema (1978) xxiii. For the debate on Amphilochius' suitability for inclusion among the great Cappadocian Fathers, see Holl (1904) 263: 'Ein Bahnbrecher ist Amphilochius auf keinem Punkt gewesen"; Gstrein (1966) 135: "der vierte im Bunde der großen Kappadokier"; and Datema (1978) xxx: "nous ne croyons pas que ce théologien foncièrement traditionnel mérite l'épithète de 'quatrième grand Cappadocien.'" Note that Holl's book on Amphilochius in fact provides one of the best synthetic surveys of the theological doctrines of the other Cappadocian Fathers.

2. For the importance of Macrina, note Pelikan (1993) 9: "it does seem to be at least permissible, if perhaps not obligatory, . . . to link her name with those of her two brothers and Gregory of Nazianzus as the Fourth Cappadocian." For the hesitation of churchmen regarding women's achievements, see Cloke (1995) 220: "feminine spirituality as a concept had no currency in the eyes of the patristic writers."

Editions and Translations

In this book all translations from Greek and Latin texts are by the author. In this list of editions and translations full references for books and articles already cited in the notes are in the Bibliography.

The Cappadocian Fathers

Basil of Caesarea

Ad adulescentes (= *Hom.* 22): ed. and tr. R. J. Deferrari and M. R. P. McGuire, in Deferrari (1926–1934), vol. 4, pp. 378–435—ed. F. Boulenger, in N. G. Wilson, *Saint Basil on the Value of Greek Literature* (London, 1975), pp. 19–36.

Adversus Eunomium: ed. and tr. [French] B. Sesboüé, G.-M. de Durand, and L. Doutreleau, *Basile de Césarée, Contre Eunome suivi de Eunome, Apologie*, 2 vols. SChr. 299, 305 (1982–1983).

De iudicio Dei (= *Prologus 7*): ed. *PG* 31.653–76—tr. W. K. L. Clarke, *The Ascetic Works of Saint Basil* (London, 1925), pp. 77–89—tr. M. M. Wagner, *Saint Basil: Ascetical Works*. FC 9 (1950), pp. 37–55.

De spiritu sancto: ed. and tr. [French] B. Pruche, *Basile de Césarée, Traité du Saint-Esprit*. SChr. 17 (1947; 2nd ed., 1968)—tr. B. Jackson, in *St. Basil: Letters and Select Works*. NPNF, 2nd series, 8 (1895; reprint, 1978), pp. 2–50.

Epistulae: ed. and tr. Deferrari (1926–1934)—ed. and tr. [French] Courtonne (1957–1966)—tr. [German] Hauschild (1973), (1990), (1993)—*Ep.* 1–46, ed. and tr. [Italian] Forlin Patrucco (1983).

Homilia 11: ed. *PG* 31.372–85—tr. M. M. Wagner, *Saint Basil: Ascetical Works*. FC 9 (1950), pp. 463–74.

Homilia 12: ed. *PG* 31.385–424.

Homiliae in Hexaemeron: ed. Amand de Mendieta and Rudberg (1997)—ed. and tr. [French] Giet (1950)—tr. B. Jackson, in *St. Basil: Letters and Select Works*. NPNF, 2nd series, 8 (1895; reprint, 1978), pp. 52–107—tr. A. C. Way, *Saint Basil: Exegetic Homilies*. FC 46 (1963), pp. 3–150.

Homiliae in psalmos: ed. *PG* 29.209–494—tr. A. C. Way, *Saint Basil: Exegetic Homilies*. FC 46 (1963), pp. 151–359.

Regulae fusius tractatae: ed. *PG* 31.901–1052—tr. W. K. L. Clarke, *The Ascetic Works of Saint Basil* (London, 1925), pp. 152–228—tr. M. M. Wagner, *Saint Basil: Ascetical Works*. FC 9 (1950), pp. 232–337.

Gregory of Nazianzus

Carmina:
I.2.1–40 = *Carmina moralia*: ed. *PG* 37.521–968.
II.1.1–99 = *Carmina de se ipso*: ed. *PG* 37.969–1452—*Carm.* II.1.1, 11, 12: tr. Meehan
(1987)—*Carm.* II.1.11: ed. and tr. [German] Jungck (1974)—*Carm.* II.1.11, 19, 34,
39, 92: tr. C. White, *Gregory of Nazianzus: Autobiographical Poems*. Cambridge
Medieval Classics 6 (Cambridge, 1996)—*Carm.* II.1.12: ed. and tr. [German] B.
Meier, *Gregor von Nazianz: Über die Bischöfe (Carmen 2,1,12). Einleitung, Text,
Übersetzung, Kommentar*. Studien zur Geschichte und Kultur des Altertums,
Neue Folge, 2. Reihe: Forschungen zu Gregor von Nazianz 7 (Paderborn, 1989).
II.2.1–8 = *Carmina quae spectant ad alios*: ed. *PG* 37.1451–1600.
Epistulae: ed. Gallay (1969)—*Ep.* 1–100, 103–201, 203–42, 244–49: ed. and tr. [French]
Gallay (1964–1967); *Ep.* 101–2, 202: ed. and tr. [French] P. Gallay and M. Jourjon,
Grégoire de Nazianze: Lettres théologiques. SChr. 208 (1974)—tr. [German] Wittig
(1981)—selections tr. C. G. Browne and J. E. Swallow, in *S. Cyril of Jerusalem.
S. Gregory Nazianzen*. NPNF, 2nd series, 7 (1894; reprint, 1978), pp. 437–82.
Epitaphia: ed. *PG* 38.11–82—*Epitaph.* 1–3, 6–78, 80–128 are included in *Anthologia
Graeca* 8: ed. and tr. W. R. Paton, *The Greek Anthology*, vol. 2. LCL (1917), pp.
400–73 (see *CPG* 2:191–92, for a concordance).
Orationes: *Orat.* 1–3: ed. and tr. [French] Bernardi (1978)—*Orat.* 4–5: ed. and tr.
[French] Bernardi (1983)—*Orat.* 6–12: ed. and tr. [French] Calvet-Sebasti
(1995)—*Orat.* 7: ed. and tr. [French] F. Boulenger, *Grégoire de Nazianze: Discours
funèbres en l'honneur de son frère Césaire et de Basile de Césarée* (Paris, 1908), pp.
2–57—*Orat.* 13–19: ed. *PG* 35.852–1064—*Orat.* 20–23: ed. and tr. [French] Mossay
and Lafontaine (1980)—*Orat.* 24–26: ed. and tr. [French] J. Mossay and G.
Lafontaine, *Grégoire de Nazianze: Discours 24–26*. SChr. 284 (1981)—*Orat.* 42–43:
ed. and tr. [French] Bernardi (1992)—*Orat.* 43: ed. and tr. [French] F. Boulenger,
*Grégoire de Nazianze: Discours funèbres en l'honneur de son frère Césaire et de
Basile de Césarée* (Paris, 1908), pp. 58–231—*Orat.* 1–3, 7–8, 12, 16, 18, 21, 27–31,
33–34, 37–43, 45: tr. C. G. Browne and J. E. Swallow, in *S. Cyril of Jerusalem. S.
Gregory Nazianzen*. NPNF, 2nd series, 7 (1894; reprint, 1978), pp. 203–434.
Testamentum: ed. *PG* 37.389–96—ed. J. B. Pitra, *Iuris ecclesiastici graecorum historia
et monumenta iussu Pii IX. pont. max.* (Rome, 1864–1868), Vol. 2, pp. 155–159—
tr. [French] F. Martroye, "Le testament de saint Grégoire de Nazianze,"
Mémoires de la Société nationale des antiquaires de France 76 (1924), pp. 219–25;
translation reprinted in H. Leclercq, "Nazianze," in *Dictionnaire d'archéologie
chrétienne et de liturgie*, ed. F. Cabrol and H. Leclercq, vol.12.1 (Paris, 1935), col.
1057–59—tr. Van Dam (1995), pp. 143–48.

Gregory of Nyssa

Contra Eunomium: ed. W. Jaeger, *Gregorii Nysseni Contra Eunomium libri, Pars prior:
Liber I et II (vulgo I et XIIB)*, and *Gregorii Nysseni Contra Eunomium libri, Pars
altera: Liber III (vulgo III-XII). Refutatio confessionis Eunomii (vulgo Lib. II)*.
GNO 1–2 (2nd ed., 1960)—tr. W. Moore, H. A. Wilson, H. C. Ogle, and M. Day,

in *Select Writings and Letters of Gregory, Bishop of Nyssa*. NPNF, 2nd series, 5 (1893; reprint, 1976), pp. 35–100, 250–314, 135–248 [in that order]—*Contra Eunomium* 1: tr. S. G. Hall, in *El "Contra Eunomium I" in la producción literaria de Gregorio de Nisa. VI Coloquio internacional sobre Gregorio de Nisa*, ed. L. F. Mateo-Seco and J. L. Bastero (Pamplona, 1988), pp. 35–135.

De beneficentia (= *De pauperibus amandis* 1): ed. A. Van Heck, in *Gregorii Nysseni Sermones*. GNO 9 (1967), pp. 93–108; reference numbers from *PG* 46.453–69.

De deitate filii et spiritus sancti: ed. *PG* 46.553–76.

De Theodoro: ed. J. P. Cavarnos, in *Gregorii Nysseni Sermones, pars II*. GNO 10.1 (1990), pp. 59–71; reference numbers from *PG* 46.736–48.

De virginitate: ed. J. P. Cavarnos, in *Gregorii Nysseni opera ascetica*. GNO 8.1 (1952), pp. 248–343—ed. and tr. [French] Aubineau (1966)—tr. V. W. Callahan, *Saint Gregory of Nyssa: Ascetical Works*. FC 58 (1967), pp. 6–75.

Dialogus de anima et resurrectione: ed. *PG* 46.12–160—tr. W. Moore, in *Select Writings and Letters of Gregory, Bishop of Nyssa*. NPNF, 2nd series, 5 (1893; reprint, 1976), pp. 430–68—tr. V. W. Callahan, *Saint Gregory of Nyssa: Ascetical Works*. FC 58 (1967), pp. 198–272.

Encomia in XL martyres 1A, 1B, 2: ed. O. Lendle, in *Gregorii Nysseni Sermones, pars II*. GNO 10.1 (1990), pp. 135–69; reference numbers from *PG* 46.749–88.

Epistulae: ed. G. Pasquali, *Gregorii Nysseni Epistulae*. GNO 8.2 (2nd ed., 1959)—ed. and tr. [French] Maraval (1990)—*Ep.* 29–30, 2, 4–18, 20, 25, 3, 1 [in that order]: tr. W. Moore, H. C. Ogle, and H. A. Wilson, in *Select Writings and Letters of Gregory, Bishop of Nyssa*. NPNF, 2nd series, 5 (1893; reprint, 1976), pp. 33–34, 382–83, 527–48.

Homiliae in Canticum canticorum: ed. H. Langerbeck, *Gregorii Nysseni In Canticum canticorum*. GNO 6 (1960); reference numbers from *PG* 44.756–1120.

In Basilium fratrem: ed. and tr. J. A. Stein, *Encomium of Saint Gregory Bishop of Nyssa on His Brother Saint Basil Archbishop of Cappadocian Caesarea*. Catholic University of America Patristic Studies 17 (Washington, D. C., 1928)—ed. O. Lendle, in *Gregorii Nysseni Sermones, pars II*. GNO 10.1 (1990), pp. 107–34.

Refutatio confessionis Eunomii: ed. W. Jaeger, *Gregorii Nysseni Contra Eunomium libri, Pars altera: Liber III (vulgo III-XII). Refutatio confessionis Eunomii (vulgo Lib. II)*. GNO 2 (1960), pp. 312–410—tr. H. C. Ogle and H. A. Wilson, in *Select Writings and Letters of Gregory, Bishop of Nyssa*. NPNF, 2nd series, 5 (1893; reprint, 1976), pp. 101–34.

Vita Gregorii Thaumaturgii: ed. G. Heil, in *Gregorii Nysseni Sermones, pars II*. GNO 10.1 (1990), pp. 1–57; reference numbers from *PG* 46.893–957—tr. M. Slusser, *St. Gregory Thaumaturgus: Life and Works*. FC 98 (1998), pp. 41–87.

Vita Macrinae: ed. V. W. Callahan, in *Gregorii Nysseni opera ascetica*. GNO 8.1 (1952), pp. 370–414—tr. V. W. Callahan, *Saint Gregory of Nyssa: Ascetical Works*. FC 58 (1967), pp. 163–91—ed. and tr. [French] Maraval (1971).

Ancient Authors and Texts

Ammianus Marcellinus, *Res gestae*: ed. and tr. J. C. Rolfe, *Ammianus Marcellinus*, 3 vols. LCL (1935–1940).

Amphilochius of Iconium, *Epistula synodalis*: ed. Datema (1978), pp. 219–21.

———, *Iambi ad Seleucum* (= [GNaz,] *Carm.* II.2.8): ed. *PG* 35.1577–1600—ed. E. Oberg, *Amphilochii Iconiensis Iambi ad Seleucum.* Patristische Texte und Studien 9 (Berlin, 1969).

Anthologia Graeca: ed. and tr. W. R. Paton, *The Greek Anthology*, 5 vols. LCL (1916–1918).

Artemidorus, *Onirocritica*: ed. R. A. Pack, *Artemidori Daldiani Onirocriticon libri V.* Teubner (1963)—tr. R. J. White, *The Interpretation of Dreams: Oneirocritica by Artemidorus* (Park Ridge, N.J., 1975).

Basil of Ancyra, *De virginitate*: ed. *PG* 30.669–809.

Callinicus, *Vita Hypatii*: ed. and tr. [French] Bartelink (1971).

CJ = Codex Justinianus: ed. P. Krueger, *Codex Iustinianus.* Corpus Iuris Civilis 2 (11th ed., 1954; reprint, Hildesheim, 1989).

CTh = Codex Theodosianus: ed. Th. Mommsen, *Codex Theodosianus 1.2: Theodosiani libri XVI cum Constitutionibus Sirmondi[a]nis* (Berlin, 1905)—tr. C. Pharr et al., *The Theodosian Code and Novels and the Sirmondian Constitutions* (1952; reprint, Westport, Conn., 1969), pp. 3–486.

Cyprian, *Epistulae*: ed. G. Hartel, *S. Thasci Caecilii Cypriani opera omnia*, vol. 2. CSEL 3.2 (1871)—ed. G. F. Diercks, *Sancti Cypriani episcopi epistularium*, 2 vols. CChr., Series latina 3B–C (1994–1996)—tr. Clarke (1984–1989).

Cyril of Scythopolis, *Vita Sabae*: ed. E. Schwartz, *Kyrillos von Skythopolis.* Texte und Untersuchungen 49.2 (Leipzig, 1939), pp. 85–200—tr. R. M. Price, *Cyril of Scythopolis: The Lives of the Monks of Palestine.* Cistercian Studies Series 114 (Kalamazoo, Mich., 1991), pp. 93–209.

Egeria, *Itinerarium*: ed. A. Franceschini and R. Weber, in *Itineraria et alia geographica*, vol. 1. CChr., Series latina 175 (1965), pp. 37–90—ed. and tr. [French] P. Maraval, *Egérie: Journal de voyage (Itinéraire).* SChr. 296 (1982)—tr. J. Wilkinson, *Egeria's Travels to the Holy Land* (rev. ed., Jerusalem, 1981), pp. 91–147.

Epiphanius, *Panarion*: ed. K. Holl, *Epiphanius (Ancoratus und Panarion)*, 3 vols. GCS 25, 31, 37 (1915–1933)—tr. F. Williams, *The Panarion of Epiphanius of Salamis*, 2 vols. Nag Hammadi and Manichaean Studies 35–36 (Leiden, 1987–1994)—selections tr. P. R. Amidon, *The Panarion of St. Epiphanius, Bishop of Salamis: Selected Passages* (New York and Oxford, 1990).

Eunapius, *Fragmenta historica*: ed. and tr. R. C. Blockley, *The Fragmentary Classicising Historians of the Later Roman Empire: Eunapius, Olympiodorus, Priscus and Malchus, II: Text, Translation and Historiographical Notes.* ARCA Classical and Medieval Texts, Papers and Monographs 10 (Liverpool, 1983), pp. 6–127.

———, *Vitae sophistarum*: ed. and tr. W. C. Wright, *Philostratus and Eunapius: The Lives of the Sophists.* LCL (1921), pp. 342–565.

Eusebius of Caesarea, *HE = Historia ecclesiastica*: ed. E. Schwartz, *Eusebius Werke 2: Die Kirchengeschichte. Die lateinische Übersetzung des Rufinus*, 3 vols. GCS 9.1–3 (1903–1909)—tr. K. Lake, J. E. L. Oulton, and H. J. Lawlor, *Eusebius: The Ecclesiastical History*, 2 vols. LCL (1926–1932).

Gaudentius of Brescia, *Tractatus*: ed. A. Glueck, *S. Gaudentii episcopi Brixiensis Tractatus.* CSEL 68 (1936).

Gregory Thaumaturgus, *Oratio panegyrica in Origenem*: ed. and tr. [French] Crouzel

(1969), pp. 94–183—tr. M. Slusser, *St. Gregory Thaumaturgus: Life and Works*. FC 98 (1998), pp. 91–126.

Hilary of Poitiers, *In Constantium imperatorem*: ed. and tr. [French] Rocher (1987).

Himerius, *Orationes*: ed. A. Colonna, *Himerii declamationes et orationes cum deperditarum fragmentis* (Rome, 1951).

Jerome, *De viris illustribus*: ed. E. C. Richardson, *Hieronymus: Liber de viris inlustribus. Gennadius: Liber de viris inlustribus*. Texte und Untersuchungen 14.1 (Leipzig, 1896), pp. 1–56—tr. T. P. Halton, *Saint Jerome: On Illustrious Men*. FC 100 (1999).

————, *Epistulae*: ed. I. Hilberg, *Sancti Eusebii Hieronymi Epistulae*, 3 vols. CSEL 54–56 (1910–1918)—ed. and tr. [French] J. Labourt, *Jérôme: Correspondance*, 8 vols. Budé (1949–1963)—selections tr. W. H. Fremantle, *St. Jerome: Letters and Select Works*. NPNF, 2nd series, 6 (1892; reprint, 1954), pp. 1–295.

————, *In Zachariam*: ed. M. Adriaen, *S. Hieronymi presbyteri opera 1: Opera exegetica 6: Commentarii in prophetas minores*. CChr., Series latina 76A (1970), pp. 747–900.

Julian, *Epistulae*: ed. and tr. W. C. Wright, *The Works of the Emperor Julian*, vol. 3. LCL (1923), pp. 2–303.

Lactantius, *De mortibus persecutorum*: ed. and tr. J. L. Creed, *Lactantius: De Mortibus Persecutorum*. Oxford Early Christian Texts (Oxford, 1984).

Libanius, *Epistulae* and *Epistularum commercium*: ed. R. Foerster, *Libanii opera*, vols. 10–11. Teubner (1921–1922)—selections ed. and tr. A. F. Norman, *Libanius: Autobiography and Selected Letters*, 2 vols. LCL (1992).

————, *Orationes*: ed. R. Foerster, *Libanii opera*, vols. 1–4. Teubner (1903–1908)—*Orat.* 1: ed. and tr. A. F. Norman, *Libanius: Autobiography and Selected Letters*, vol. 1. LCL (1992), pp. 52–337—*Orat.* 2, 12–24, 30, 33, 45, 47–50: ed. and tr. A. F. Norman, *Libanius: Selected Works*, 2 vols. LCL (1969–1977)—*Orat.* 3, 11, 31, 34, 36, 42–43, 58, 62: tr. A. F. Norman, *Antioch as a Centre of Hellenic Culture as Observed by Libanius*. TTH 34 (2000).

Menander Rhetor, *Treatises* I-II: ed. and tr. Russell and Wilson (1981), pp. 2–225.

Miracula Theclae: ed. and tr. [French] Dagron (1978), pp. 284–412.

Palladius, *Historia Lausiaca*: ed. C. Butler, *The Lausiac History of Palladius, II: The Greek Text Edited with Introduction and Notes*. Texts and Studies 6.2 (Cambridge, 1904)—tr. R. T. Meyer, *Palladius: The Lausiac History*. ACW 34 (1964).

Passio Athenogenis: ed. and tr. [French] P. Maraval, *La passion inédite de S. Athénogène de Pédachthoé en Cappadoce (BHG 197b)*. Subsidia Hagiographica 75 (Brussels, 1990), pp. 30–85.

Passio Sabae: ed. G. Krüger, *Ausgewählte Märtyrerakten: Neubearbeitung der Knopfschen Ausgabe*. 4th ed. by G. Ruhbach. Sammlung ausgewählter kirchen- und dogmengeschichtlicher Quellenschriften, Neue Folge 3 (Tubingen, 1965), pp. 119–24—tr. Heather and Matthews (1991), pp. 111–17.

Paulinus of Nola, *Epistulae*: ed. G. de Hartel, *Sancti Pontii Meropii Paulini Nolani Epistulae*. CSEL 29 (1894)—tr. P. G. Walsh, *Letters of St. Paulinus of Nola*, 2 vols. ACW 35–36 (1966–1967).

Philostorgius, *HE* = *Historia ecclesiastica*: ed. J. Bidez, *Philostorgius Kirchengeschichte: Mit dem Leben des Lucian von Antiochien und den Fragmenten eines arianischen*

Historiographen. GCS 21 (1913); rev. F. Winkelmann, 2nd ed. (1972), 3rd ed. (1981)—tr. E. Walford, *The Ecclesiastical History of Sozomen, Comprising a History of the Church, from A.D. 324 to A.D. 440. Translated from the Greek: with a Memoir of the Author. Also the Ecclesiastical History of Philostorgius, as Epitomised by Photius, Patriarch of Constantinople*. Bohn's Ecclesiastical Library (London, 1855), pp. 429–521.

Philostratus, *Vita Apollonii*: ed. and tr. F. C. Conybeare, *Philostratus: The Life of Apollonius of Tyana. The Epistles of Apollonius and the Treatise of Eusebius*, 2 vols. LCL (1912).

———, *Vitae sophistarum*: ed. and tr. W. C. Wright, *Philostratus and Eunapius: The Lives of the Sophists*. LCL (1921), pp. 2–315.

Photius, *Bibliotheca*: ed. and tr. [French] R. Henry, *Photius: Bibliothèque*, 8 vols., and Index, ed. J. Schamp. Budé (1959–1991).

Pliny the Younger, *Epistulae*: ed. and tr. B. Radice, *Pliny: Letters and Panegyricus*, 2 vols. LCL (1969).

Rufinus, *HE = Historia ecclesiastica*: ed. T. Mommsen, in *Eusebius Werke 2: Die Kirchengeschichte. Die lateinische Übersetzung des Rufinus*, ed. E. Schwartz, vols. 1–2. GCS 9.1–2 (1903–1908)—*HE* 10–11: tr. P. R. Amidon, *The Church History of Rufinus of Aquileia: Books 10 and 11* (New York, 1997).

Sermo de virginitate: ed. and tr. [French] Amand and Moons (1953), pp. 34–69—tr. T. M. Shaw, "Homily: On Virginity," in *Ascetic Behaviour in Greco-Roman Antiquity: A Sourcebook*, ed. V. L. Wimbush (Minneapolis, Minn., 1990), pp. 30–43.

Severus of Antioch, *Epistulae*: tr. Brooks (1903–1904).

Socrates, *HE = Historia ecclesiastica*: ed. G. C. Hansen, with M. Sirinian, *Sokrates: Kirchengeschichte*. GCS, Neue Folge 1 (1995)—tr. A. C. Zenos, in *Socrates, Sozomenus: Church Histories*. NPNF, 2nd series, 2 (1890; reprint, 1973), pp. 1–178.

Sozomen, *HE = Historia ecclesiastica*: ed. J. Bidez, *Sozomenus: Kirchengeschichte*. GCS 50 (1960); rev. G. C. Hansen. GCS, Neue Folge 4 (2nd ed., 1995)—tr. C. D. Hartranft, in *Socrates, Sozomenus: Church Histories*. NPNF, 2nd series, 2 (1890; reprint, 1973), pp. 236–427.

Strabo, *Geographia*: ed. and tr. H. L. Jones, *The Geography of Strabo*, 8 vols. LCL (1917–1932).

Suda: ed. A. Adler, *Suidae Lexicon*, 5 vols. (1928–1938; reprint, Stuttgart, 1967–1971).

Synodicon vetus: ed. and tr. J. Duffy and J. Parker, *The Synodicon Vetus: Text, Translation, and Notes*. Corpus Fontium Historiae Byzantinae 15 (Washington, D.C., 1979), pp. 2–143.

Tertullian, *Ad Scapulam*: ed. E. Dekkers, in *Quinti Septimi Florentis Tertulliani opera, II: Opera Montanistica*. CChr., Series latina 2.2 (1954), pp. 1125–32.

Themistius, *Orationes*: ed. G. Downey and A. F. Norman, *Themistii Orationes quae supersunt*, 2 vols. Teubner (1965–1971)—*Orat.* 17, 20–34: tr. R. J. Penella, *The Private Orations of Themistius* (Berkeley, Calif., 2000)—*Orat.* 1, 3, 5–6, 14–17, 34: tr. P. Heather and D. Moncur, *Politics, Philosophy, and Empire in the Fourth Century: Select Orations of Themistius*. TTH 36 (2001).

Theodoret of Cyrrhus, *HE = Historia ecclesiastica*: ed. L. Parmentier, *Theodoret:*

Kirchengeschichte. GCS 19 (1911); 2nd ed. rev. F. Scheidweiler. GCS 44 (1954); 3rd ed. rev. G. C. Hansen. GCS, Neue Folge 5 (1998)—tr. B. Jackson, in *Theodoret, Jerome, Gennadius, Rufinus: Historical Writings, Etc.* NPNF, 2nd series, 3 (1892; reprint, 1989), pp. 33–159.

Vita Theclae: ed. and tr. [French] Dagron (1978), pp. 168–283.

Vitruvius, *De architectura*: ed. and tr. F. Granger, *Vitruvius: On Architecture*, 2 vols. LCL (1931–1934).

Zachariah Scholasticus, *Vita Severi Antiocheni*: ed. and tr. [French] Kugener (1903)—selections tr. R. A. D. Young, "Zacharias: The Life of Severus," in *Ascetic Behaviour in Greco-Roman Antiquity: A Sourcebook*, ed. V. L. Wimbush (Minneapolis, Minn., 1990), pp. 315–27.

Bibliography

Albrecht, R. (1986). *Das Leben der heiligen Makrina auf dem Hintergrund der Thekla-Traditionem: Studien zu den Ursprüngen des weiblichen Mönchtums im 4. Jahrhündert in Kleinasien*. Forschungen zur Kirchen- und Dogmengeschichte 38. Göttingen.

Alexandre, M. (1984). "Les nouveaux martyrs: Motifs martyrologiques dans la vie des saints et thèmes hagiographiques dans l'éloge des martyrs chez Grégoire de Nysse." In *The Biographical Works of Gregory of Nyssa: Proceedings of the Fifth International Colloquium on Gregory of Nyssa (Mainz, 6–10 September 1982)*, ed. A. Spira, pp. 33–70. Patristic Monograph Series 12. Cambridge, Mass.

Amand [de Mendieta], E., and M. C. Moons (1953). "Une curieuse homélie grecque inédite sur la virginité adressée aux pères de famille." *Revue bénédictine* 63:18–69, 211–38.

Amand de Mendieta, E. (1955). "La virginité chez Eusèbe d'Emèse et l'ascétisme familial dans la première moitié du IVe siècle." *Revue d'histoire ecclésiastique* 50:777–820.

Amand de Mendieta, E., and S. Y. Rudberg, ed. (1997). *Basilius von Caesarea: Homilien zum Hexaemeron*. GCS, Neue Folge 2. Berlin.

Arjava, A. (1996). *Women and Law in Late Antiquity*. Oxford.

———. (1998). "Paternal Power in Late Antiquity." *Journal of Roman Studies* 88:147–65.

Aubineau, M., ed. and tr. (1966). *Grégoire de Nysse: Traité de la virginité*. SChr. 119. Paris.

Bannon, C. J. (1997). *The Brothers of Romulus: Fraternal Pietas in Roman Law, Literature, and Society*. Princeton, N.J.

Barnes, M. R. (2001). "'The Burden of Marriage' and Other Notes on Gregory of Nyssa's *On Virginity*." In *Studia Patristica Vol. XXXVII: Papers Presented at the Thirteenth International Conference on Patristic Studies Held in Oxford 1999. Cappadocian Writers, Other Greek Writers*, ed. M. F. Wiles and E. J. Yarnold, with P. M. Parvis, pp. 12–19. Leuven.

Barnes, T. D. (1971). *Tertullian*. Oxford.

———. (1981). *Constantine and Eusebius*. Cambridge, Mass.

———. (1982). *The New Empire of Diocletian and Constantine*. Cambridge, Mass.

———. (1987). "Himerius and the Fourth Century." *Classical Philology* 82:206–25. Reprinted in T. D. Barnes, *From Eusebius to Augustine: Selected Papers 1982–1993*, Chapter 16. Aldershot, 1994.

———. (1993). *Athanasius and Constantius: Theology and Politics in the Constantinian Empire*. Cambridge, Mass.

————. (1996). "The Crimes of Basil of Ancyra." *Journal of Theological Studies* n.s. 47:550–54.

————. (1997). "The Collapse of the Homoeans in the East." In *Studia Patristica Vol. XXIX: Papers Presented at the Twelfth International Conference on Patristic Studies Held in Oxford 1995. Historica, Theologica et Philosophica, Critica et Philologica*, ed. E. A. Livingstone, pp. 3–16. Leuven.

Bartelink, G. J. M., ed. and tr. (1971). *Callinicos: Vie d'Hypatios*. SChr. 177. Paris.

Batiffol, P. (1922). "L'ecclésiologie de saint Basile." *Echos d'Orient* 21:9–30.

Beagon, P. M. (1995). "The Cappadocian Fathers, Women and Ecclesiastical Politics." *Vigiliae Christianae* 49:165–79.

————. (1997). "Some Cultural Contacts of St. Basil at Antioch." In *Studia Patristica Vol. XXXII: Papers Presented at the Twelfth International Conference on Patristic Studies Held in Oxford 1995. Athanasius and His Opponents, Cappadocian Fathers, Other Greek Writers After Nicaea*, ed. E. A. Livingstone, pp. 67–71. Leuven.

Belke, K. (1984). *Galatien und Lykaonien. = Tabula Imperii Byzantini*, ed. H. Hunger, Bd. 4. Österreichische Akademie der Wissenschaften, philosophisch-historische Klasse, Denkschriften 172. Vienna.

Berges, D., and J. Nollé (2000). *Tyana: Archäologisch-historische Untersuchungen zum südwestlichen Kappadokien*, 2 vols. Inschriften griechischer Städte aus Kleinasien 55.1–2. Bonn.

Bernardi, J. (1968). *La prédication des Pères Cappadociens: La prédicateur et son auditoire*. Paris.

————, ed. and tr. (1978). *Grégoire de Nazianze: Discours 1–3*. SChr. 247. Paris.

————, ed. and tr. (1983). *Grégoire de Nazianze: Discours 4–5, Contre Julien*. SChr. 309. Paris.

————. (1984). "Nouvelles perspectives sur la famille de Grégoire de Nazianze." *Vigiliae Christianae* 38:352–59.

————, ed. and tr. (1992). *Grégoire de Nazianze: Discours 42–43*. SChr. 384. Paris.

————. (1995). *Saint Grégoire de Nazianze: Le théologien et son temps (330–390)*. Paris.

Bessières, M. (1923). *La tradition manuscrite de la correspondance de s. Basile*. Oxford. Reprinted from *Journal of Theological Studies* 21 (1919) 1–50; 21 (1920) 289–310; 22 (1921) 105–37; 23 (1922) 113–33, 225–49, 337–58.

Birnbaum, A. (1907). "De templo Nazianzeno a Gregorio Theologo descripto." *Eos* 13:30–39.

————. (1913). "Die Oktogone von Antiochia, Nazianz und Nyssa: Rekonstruktionsversuche." *Repertorium für Kunstwissenschaft* 36:181–209.

Børtnes, J. (2000). "Eros Transformed: Same-Sex Love and Divine Desire. Reflections on the Erotic Vocabulary in St. Gregory of Nazianzus's Speech on St. Basil the Great." In *Greek Biography and Panegyric in Late Antiquity*, ed. T. Hägg and P. Rousseau, with C. Høgel, pp. 180–93. Berkeley, Calif.

Bradley, K. R. (1991). *Discovering the Roman Family: Studies in Roman Social History*. New York.

————. (2000). "Fictive Families: Family and Household in the *Metamorphoses* of Apuleius." *Phoenix* 54:282–308.

Brain, R. (1976). *Friends and Lovers*. New York.

Brakke, D. (1995). *Athanasius and the Politics of Asceticism.* Oxford.

van Bremen, R. (1983). "Women and Wealth." In *Images of Women in Antiquity,* ed. A. Cameron and A. Kuhrt, pp. 223–42. Detroit, Mich.

————. (1996). *The Limits of Participation: Women and Civic Life in the Greek East in the Hellenistic and Roman Periods.* Amsterdam.

Bremmer, J. (1976). "Avunculate and Fosterage." *Journal of Indo-European Studies* 4:65–78.

Brennecke, H. C. (1988). *Studien zur Geschichte der Homöer: Der Osten bis zum Ende der homöischen Reichskirche.* Beiträge zur Historischen Theologie 73. Tubingen.

Brooks, E. W., tr. (1903–1904). *The Sixth Book of the Select Letters of Severus Patriarch of Antioch in the Syriac Version of Athanasius of Nisibis, Vol. II (Translation),* 2 vols. London and Oxford.

Brown, P. (1988). *The Body and Society: Men, Women, and Sexual Renunciation in Early Christianity.* New York.

Burns, S. K. (2001). "Cappadocian Encratism and the Macarian Community." In *Studia Patristica Vol. XXXVII: Papers Presented at the Thirteenth International Conference on Patristic Studies Held in Oxford 1999. Cappadocian Writers, Other Greek Writers,* ed. M. F. Wiles and E. J. Yarnold, with P. M. Parvis, pp. 27–32. Leuven.

Burrus, V. (2000). *"Begotten, Not Made": Conceiving Manhood in Late Antiquity.* Stanford, Calif.

Calvet-Sebasti, M.-A., ed. and tr. (1995). *Grégoire de Nazianze: Discours 6–12.* SChr. 405. Paris.

Cardman, F. (2001). "Whose Life Is It? The *Vita Macrinae* of Gregory of Nyssa." In *Studia Patristica Vol. XXXVII: Papers Presented at the Thirteenth International Conference on Patristic Studies Held in Oxford 1999. Cappadocian Writers, Other Greek Writers,* ed. M. F. Wiles and E. J. Yarnold, with P. M. Parvis, pp. 33–50. Leuven.

Cavallera, F. (1905). *Le schisme d'Antioche (IVe–Ve siècle).* Paris.

Cavallin, A. (1944). *Studien zu den Briefen des hl. Basilius.* Lund.

Chantraine, P. (1968–1980). *Dictionnaire étymologique de la langue grecque: Histoire des mots,* 4 vols. Paris.

Clark, E. A. (1999). *Reading Renunciation: Asceticism and Scripture in Early Christianity.* Princeton, N.J.

Clark, G. (1993). *Women in Late Antiquity: Pagan and Christian Life-Styles.* Oxford.

————. (1995). "Women and Asceticism in Late Antiquity: The Refusal of Status and Gender." In *Asceticism,* ed. V. L. Wimbush and R. Valantasis, pp. 33–48. New York.

Clarke, G. W., tr. (1984–1989). *The Letters of St. Cyprian of Carthage,* 4 vols. ACW 43–44, 46–47. New York.

Cloke, G. (1995). *"This Female Man of God": Women and Spiritual Power in the Patristic Age, AD 350–450.* London and New York.

Cooper, K. (1996). *The Virgin and the Bride: Idealized Womanhood in Late Antiquity.* Cambridge, Mass.

Coppola, G. (1923). "L'archetipo dell'epistolario di Basilio." *Studi italiani di filologia classica* n.s. 3:137–50.

Coulie, B. (1985). *Les richesses dans l'oeuvre de Saint Grégoire de Nazianze: Etude littéraire et historique.* Publications de l'Institut orientaliste de Louvain 32. Louvain.

———. (1988). "Les trois récits de la tempête subie par Grégoire de Nazianze." In *Versiones orientales, repertorium ibericum et studia ad editiones curandas,* ed. B. Coulie, pp. 157–80. CChr., Series graeca 20 = Corpus Nazianzenum 1. Turnhout.

Courtonne, Y., ed. and tr. (1957–1966). *Saint Basile: Lettres,* 3 vols. Budé. Paris.

Crouzel, H. (1963). "Grégoire le Thaumaturge et le 'Dialogue avec Elien.'" *Recherches de science religieuse* 51:422–31.

———, ed. and tr. (1969). *Grégoire le Thaumaturge: Remerciement à Origène, suivi de la lettre d'Origène à Grégoire.* SChr. 148. Paris.

Dagron, G., ed. and tr. (1978). *Vie et miracles de sainte Thècle: Texte grec, traduction et commentaire.* Subsidia Hagiographica 62. Brussels.

Daniélou, J. (1954). *Platonisme et théologie mystique: Doctrine spirituelle de saint Grégoire de Nysse.* 2nd ed., Aubier.

———. (1955). "La chronologie des sermons de Grégoire de Nysse." *Revue des sciences religieuses* 29:346–72.

———. (1956). "Le mariage de Grégoire de Nysse et la chronologie de sa vie." *Revue des études augustiniennes* 2:71–78.

———. (1965). "Grégoire de Nysse à travers les lettres de saint Basile et de saint Grégoire de Nazianze." *Vigiliae Christianae* 19:31–41.

———. (1966). "La chronologie des oeuvres de Grégoire de Nysse." *Studia Patristica* 7 = *Texte und Untersuchungen* 92:159–69.

Datema, C., ed. (1978). *Amphilochii Iconiensis opera: Orationes, pluraque alia quae supersunt, nonnulla etiam spuria.* CChr., Series graeca 3. Turnhout.

Davis, S. J. (2001). *The Cult of Saint Thecla: A Tradition of Women's Piety in Late Antiquity.* Oxford.

Deferrari, R. J., ed. and tr. (1926–1934). *Saint Basil: The Letters,* 4 vols. LCL. Cambridge, Mass.

Delmaire, R. (1989a). *Les responsables des finances impériales au Bas-Empire romain (IVe–VIe s.): Etudes prosopographiques.* Collection Latomus 203. Brussels.

———. (1989b). *Largesses sacrées et res privata: L'aerarium impérial et son administration du IVe au VIe siècle.* Collection de l'Ecole française de Rome 121. Paris and Rome.

Demoen, K. (1997). "Gifts of Friendship That Will Remain For Ever: Personae, Addressed Characters and Intended Audience of Gregory Nazianzen's Epistolary Poems." *Jahrbuch der österreichischen Byzantinistik* 47:1–11.

Demos, J. (1986). "Towards a History of Mid-Life: Preliminary Notes and Reflections." In J. Demos, *Past, Present, and Personal: The Family and the Life Course in American History,* pp. 114–38. New York.

Dennis, G. T. (1986). "Gregory of Nazianzus and the Byzantine Letter." In *Diakonia: Studies in Honor of Robert T. Meyer,* ed. T. Halton and J. P. Williman, pp. 3–13. Washington, D. C.

Devos, P. (1967). "Le dossier syriaque de s. Eusèbe de Samosate." *Analecta Bollandiana* 85:195–240.

———. (1983). "Grégoire de Nazianze témoin du mariage de Grégoire de Nysse." In

II. Symposium Nazianzenum: Louvain-la-Neuve, 25–28 août 1981, ed. J. Mossay, pp. 269–81. Paderborn.

————. (1992). "Aspects de la correspondance de s. Basile de Césarée avec s. Eusèbe de Samosate et avec s. Amphiloque d'Iconium." *Analecta Bollandiana* 110:241–59.

Dixon, S. (1991). "The Sentimental Ideal of the Roman Family." In *Marriage, Divorce, and Children in Ancient Rome*, ed. B. Rawson, pp. 99–113. Canberra and Oxford.

————. (1992). *The Roman Family*. Baltimore and London.

Dölger, F. J. (1936). "Nonna: Ein Kapitel über christliche Volksfrömmigkeit des vierten Jahrhunderts." In F. J. Dölger, *Antike und Christentum: Kultur- und religions-geschichtliche Studien*, vol. 5, pp. 44–75. Munster.

Drecoll, V. H. (1996). *Die Entwicklung der Trinitätslehre des Basilius von Cäsarea: Sein Weg vom Homöusianer zum Neonizäner*. Forschungen zur Kirchen- und Dog-mengeschichte 66. Göttingen.

————. (1997). "An welcher Krankheit litt Basilius?" *Jahrbuch für Antike und Christentum* 40:147–57.

Eilberg-Schwartz, H. (1994). *God's Phallus and Other Problems for Men and Mono-theism*. Boston, Mass.

Elm, S. (1994). *"Virgins of God": The Making of Asceticism in Late Antiquity*. Oxford.

————. (2000). "The Diagnostic Gaze: Gregory of Nazianzus' Theory of Ortho-dox Priesthood in His Orations 6 *De pace* and 2 *Apologia de fuga sua*," in *Orthodoxie, christianisme, histoire: Orthodoxy, Christianity, History*, ed. S. Elm, E. Rebillard, and A. Romano, pp. 83–100. Collection de l'Ecole française de Rome 270. Rome.

Evans Grubbs, J. (1995). *Law and Family in Late Antiquity: The Emperor Constantine's Marriage Legislation*. Oxford.

Fedwick, P. J. (1979). *The Church and the Charisma of Leadership in Basil of Caesarea*. Toronto.

————. (1981). "A Chronology of the Life and Works of Basil of Caesarea." In *Basil of Caesarea: Christian, Humanist, Ascetic. A Sixteen-Hundredth Anniversary Symposium*, ed. P. J. Fedwick, 1:3–19. Toronto.

————. (1993). *Bibliotheca Basiliana universalis: A Study of the Manuscript Tradition of the Works of Basil of Caesarea, I: The Letters*. Turnhout.

Flemming, R. (1999). "*Quae corpore quaestum facit*: The Sexual Economy of Female Prostitution in the Roman Empire." *Journal of Roman Studies* 89:38–61.

Forlin Patrucco, M. (1976). "Aspetti di vita familiare nel IV secolo negli scritti dei padri cappadoci." In *Etica sessuale e matrimonio nel cristianesimo delle origini*, ed. R. Cantalamessa, pp. 158–79. Studia Patristica Mediolanensia 5. Milan.

————, ed. and tr. (1983). *Basilio di Cesarea: Le lettere*, vol. 1. Turin.

Foucault, M. (1986). *The Care of the Self. = The History of Sexuality*, vol. 3, tr. R. Hurley. New York.

Francis, J. A. (1995). *Subversive Virtue: Asceticism and Authority in the Second-Century Pagan World*. University Park, Pa.

Frank, G. (2000). "Macrina's Scar: Homeric Allusion and Heroic Identity in Gregory of Nyssa's *Life of Macrina*." *Journal of Early Christian Studies* 8:511–30.

Frantz, A. (1979). "Did Julian the Apostate Rebuild the Parthenon?" *American Journal of Archaeology* 83:395–401.

Gain, B. (1985). *L'église de Cappadoce au IVᵉ siècle d'après la correspondance de Basile de Césarée (330–379)*. Orientalia Christiana Analecta 225. Rome.

Gallay, P. (1943). *La vie de saint Grégoire de Nazianze*. Lyon and Paris.

———. (1957). *Les manuscrits des lettres de saint Grégoire de Nazianze*. Paris.

———, ed. and tr. (1964–1967). *Saint Grégoire de Nazianze: Lettres*, 2 vols. Budé. Paris.

———, ed. (1969). *Gregor von Nazianz: Briefe*. GCS 53. Berlin.

Garnsey, P. (1996). *Ideas of Slavery from Aristotle to Augustine*. Cambridge.

———. (1997). "Sons, Slaves—and Christians." In *The Roman Family in Italy: Status, Sentiment, Space*, ed. B. Rawson and P. Weaver, pp. 101–21. Canberra and Oxford.

Geary, P. J. (1994). *Phantoms of Remembrance: Memory and Oblivion at the End of the First Millennium*. Princeton, N.J.

Gibbon, E. (1897–1902). *The History of the Decline and Fall of the Roman Empire*, ed. J. B. Bury, 7 vols. London.

———. (1984). *Memoirs of My Life*, ed. B. Radice. Harmondsworth.

Giet, S. (1941). *Les idées et l'action sociales de saint Basile*. Paris.

———, ed. and tr. (1950). *Basile de Césarée: Homélies sur l'Hexaéméron*. SChr. 26. Paris.

Gleason, M. W. (1995). *Making Men: Sophists and Self-Presentation in Ancient Rome*. Princeton, N.J.

Goody, J. (1983). *The Development of the Family and Marriage in Europe*. Cambridge.

Gregg, R. C. (1975). *Consolation Philosophy: Greek and Christian Paideia in Basil and the Two Gregories*. Patristic Monograph Series 3. Cambridge, Mass.

Grégoire, H. (1909). "Rapport sur un voyage d'exploration dans le Pont et en Cappadoce." *Bulletin de correspondance hellénique* 33:3–169.

Gribomont, J. (1959). "Eustathe le philosophe et les voyages du jeune Basile de Césarée." *Revue d'histoire ecclésiastique* 54:115–24.

———. (1967). "Le panégyrique de la virginité, oeuvre de jeunesse de Grégoire de Nysse." *Revue d'ascétique et de mystique* 43:249–66.

———. (1981). "Notes biographiques sur s. Basile le Grand." In *Basil of Caesarea: Christian, Humanist, Ascetic. A Sixteen-Hundredth Anniversary Symposium*, ed. P. J. Fedwick, 1: 21–48. Toronto.

———. (1983). "La tradizione manoscritta." In *Basilio di Cesarea: Le lettere*, vol. 1, ed. and tr. M. Forlin Patrucco, pp. 50–53. Turin.

Gstrein, H. (1966). "Amphilochios von Ikonion: Der vierte 'Große Kappadokier.'" *Jahrbuch der österreichischen byzantinischen Gesellschaft* 15:133–45.

Halkin, F. (1967). "Une vie grecque d'Eusèbe de Samosate." *Analecta Bollandiana* 85:5–15. Reprinted in F. Halkin, *Martyrs grecs IIe-VIIIe s.*, Chapter 16. London, 1974.

Hall, C. S., and G. Lindzey (1967). "Freud's Psychoanalytic Theory of Personality." In *Personalities and Cultures: Readings in Psychological Anthropology*, ed. R. Hunt, pp. 3–29. Garden City, N.Y.

Halperin, D. M. (1990). "Heroes and Their Pals." In D. M. Halperin, *One Hundred Years of Homosexuality and Other Essays on Greek Love*, pp. 75–87. New York and London.

Hanriot-Coustet, A. (1983). "Grégoire de Nazianze et un agraphon attribué à Barnabé." *Revue d'histoire et de philosophie religieuses* 63:289–92.

Hanson, R. P. C. (1988). *The Search for the Christian Doctrine of God: The Arian Controversy 318–381*. Edinburgh.

Harl, M., ed. and tr. (1983). *Origène: Philocalie, 1–20, Sur les écritures. Et la lettre à Africanus sur l'histoire de Suzanne*, ed. N. de Lange. SChr. 302. Paris.

———. (1984). "Moïse figure de l'évêque dans l'eloge de Basile de Grégoire de Nysse (381): Un plaidoyer pour l'autorité épiscopale." In *The Biographical Works of Gregory of Nyssa: Proceedings of the Fifth International Colloquium on Gregory of Nyssa (Mainz, 6–10 September 1982)*, ed. A. Spira, pp. 71–119. Patristic Monograph Series 12. Cambridge, Mass.

Harrison, V. E. F. (1990). "Male and Female in Cappadocian Theology." *Journal of Theological Studies* n. s. 41:441–71.

Hart, M. D. (1990). "Reconciliation of Body and Soul: Gregory of Nyssa's Deeper Theology of Marriage." *Theological Studies* 51:450–78.

Harvey, S. A. (1996). "Sacred Bonding: Mothers and Daughters in Early Syriac Hagiography." *Journal of Early Christian Studies* 4:27–56.

Hauschild, W.-D., tr. (1973). *Basilius von Caesarea: Briefe, Zweiter Teil*. Bibliothek der griechischen Literatur, Abteilung Patristik, Bd. 3. Stuttgart.

———, tr. (1990). *Basilius von Caesarea: Briefe, Erster Teil*. Bibliothek der griechischen Literatur, Abteilung Patristik, Bd. 32. Stuttgart.

———, tr. (1993). *Basilius von Caesarea: Briefe, Dritter Teil*. Bibliothek der griechischen Literatur, Abteilung Patristik, Bd. 37. Stuttgart.

Hauser-Meury, M.-M. (1960). *Prosopographie zu den Schriften Gregors von Nazianz*. Bonn.

Heather, P., and J. Matthews, tr. (1991). *The Goths in the Fourth Century*. TTH 11. Liverpool.

Helleman, W. E. (2001). "Cappadocian Macrina as Lady Wisdom." In *Studia Patristica Vol. XXXVII: Papers Presented at the Thirteenth International Conference on Patristic Studies Held in Oxford 1999. Cappadocian Writers, Other Greek Writers*, ed. M. F. Wiles and E. J. Yarnold, with P. M. Parvis, pp. 86–102. Leuven.

Hild, F., and H. Hellenkemper (1990). *Kilikien und Isaurien. = Tabula Imperii Byzantini*, ed. H. Hunger, Bd. 5, 2 vols. Österreichische Akademie der Wissenschaften, philosophisch-historische Klasse, Denkschriften, Bd. 215. Vienna.

Hild, F., and M. Restle (1981). *Kappadokien (Kappadokia, Charsianon, Sebasteia und Lykandos). = Tabula Imperii Byzantini*, ed. H. Hunger, Bd. 2. Österreichische Akademie der Wissenschaften, philosophisch-historische Klasse, Denkschriften, Bd. 149. Vienna.

Holl, K. (1904). *Amphilochius von Ikonium in seinem Verhältnis zu den grossen Kappadoziern*. Tubingen and Leipzig.

Holman, S. R. (2001). "Taxing Nazianzus: Gregory and the Other Julian." In *Studia Patristica Vol. XXXVII: Papers Presented at the Thirteenth International Conference on Patristic Studies Held in Oxford 1999. Cappadocian Writers, Other Greek Writers*, ed. M. F. Wiles and E. J. Yarnold, with P. M. Parvis, pp. 103–9. Leuven.

Huxley, G. (1989). "Saint Basil the Great and Anisa." *Analecta Bollandiana* 107:30–32.

Jones, A. H. M. (1964). *The Later Roman Empire 284–602: A Social, Economic and*

Administrative Survey, 2 or 3 vols. (continuous pagination). Oxford and Norman, Okla.

Jungck, C., ed. and tr. (1974). *Gregor von Nazianz: De vita sua.* Heidelberg.

Junod, E., ed. and tr. (1972). *Origène: Philocalie 21–27, Sur le libre arbitre.* SChr. 226. Paris.

———. (1988). "Basile de Césarée et Grégoire de Nazianze sont-ils les compilateurs de la Philocalie d'Origène? Réexamen de la *Lettre* 115 de Grégoire." In *Mémorial Dom Jean Gribomont (1920–1986),* pp. 349–60. Studia Ephemeridis "Augustinianum" 27. Rome.

Karayannopoulos, I. (1981). "St. Basil's Social Activity: Principles and Praxis." In *Basil of Caesarea: Christian, Humanist, Ascetic. A Sixteen-Hundredth Anniversary Symposium,* ed. P. J. Fedwick, 1:375–91. Toronto.

Karlsson, G. (1959). *Idéologie et cérémonial dans l'épistolographie byzantine: Textes du Xe siècle analysés et commentés.* Uppsala.

Kaster, R. A. (1988). *Guardians of Language: The Grammarian and Society in Late Antiquity.* Berkeley, Calif.

Konstan, D. (1997). *Friendship in the Classical World.* Cambridge.

———. (2000). "How to Praise a Friend: St. Gregory of Nazianzus's Funeral Oration for St. Basil the Great." In *Greek Biography and Panegyric in Late Antiquity,* ed. T. Hägg and P. Rousseau, with C. Høgel, pp. 160–79. Berkeley, Calif.

Kopecek, T. A. (1973). "The Social Class of the Cappadocian Fathers." *Church History* 42:453–66.

Krivochéine, B. (1969). "L'ecclésiologie de saint Basile le Grand." *Messager de l'exarchat du patriarche russe en Europe occidentale* 17, no. 65:75–102.

Krueger, D. (2000). "Writing and the Liturgy of Memory in Gregory of Nyssa's *Life of Macrina.*" *Journal of Early Christian Studies* 8:483–510.

Kugener, M.-A., ed. and tr. (1903). *Sévère patriarche d'Antioche 512–518: Textes syriaques publiés, traduits et annotés, Première partie: Vie de Sévère par Zacharie le scholastique. Patrologia Orientalis* 2:7–115. Paris.

Kurmann, A. (1988). *Gregor von Nazianz: Oratio 4, Gegen Julian. Ein Kommentar.* Schweizerische Beiträge zur Altertumswissenschaft 19. Basel.

Kustas, G. L. (1981). "Saint Basil and the Rhetorical Tradition." In *Basil of Caesarea: Christian, Humanist, Ascetic. A Sixteen-Hundredth Anniversary Symposium,* ed. P. J. Fedwick, 1:221–79. Toronto.

Ladner, G. B. (1958). "The Philosophical Anthropology of Saint Gregory of Nyssa." *Dumbarton Oaks Papers* 12:59–94. Reprinted in G. B. Ladner, *Images and Ideas in the Middle Ages: Selected Studies in History and Art.* Storia e Letteratura, Raccolta di Studi e Testi 155 (Rome, 1983), 2:825–76.

Lane Fox, R. (1987). *Pagans and Christians.* New York.

Lebon, J. (1938). "Sur un concile de Césarée." *Le Muséon* 51:89–132.

Lipatov, N. A. (2001). "*The Statement of Faith* Attributed to St. Basil the Great." In *Studia Patristica Vol. XXXVII: Papers Presented at the Thirteenth International Conference on Patristic Studies Held in Oxford 1999. Cappadocian Writers, Other Greek Writers,* ed. M. F. Wiles and E. J. Yarnold, with P. M. Parvis, pp. 147–59. Leuven.

Loofs, F. (1898). *Eustathius von Sebaste und die Chronologie der Basilius-Briefe.* Halle.

Luck, G. (1984). "Notes on the *Vita Macrinae* by Gregory of Nyssa." In *The Biographical Works of Gregory of Nyssa: Proceedings of the Fifth International Colloquium on Gregory of Nyssa (Mainz, 6–10 September 1982)*, ed. A. Spira, pp. 21–32. Patristic Monograph Series 12. Cambridge, Mass.

Malina, B. J. (1995). "Pain, Power, and Personhood: Ascetic Behavior in the Ancient Mediterranean." In *Asceticism*, ed. V. L. Wimbush and R. Valantasis, pp. 162–77. New York.

Malingrey, A.-M. (1961). *"Philosophia": Etude d'un groupe de mots dans la littérature grecque, des Présocratiques au IVe siècle après J.-C.* Etudes et commentaires 40. Paris.

Malunowicz, L. (1985). "Le problème de l'amitié chez Basile, Grégoire de Nazianze et Jean Chrysostome." In *Studia Patristica* 16.2, ed. E. A. Livingstone. = *Texte und Untersuchungen* 129:412–17. Berlin.

Mango, C. (1972). *The Art of the Byzantine Empire, 312–1453: Sources and Documents.* Englewood Cliffs, N.J.

Maraval, P., ed. and tr. (1971). *Grégoire de Nysse: Vie de sainte Macrine.* SChr. 178. Paris.

———. (1980). "Encore les frères et soeurs de Grégoire de Nysse." *Revue d'histoire et de philosophie religieuses* 60:161–66.

———. (1988a). "La date de la mort de Basile de Césarée." *Revue des études augustiniennes* 34:25–38.

———. (1988b). "Un correspondant de Grégoire de Nazianze identifié: Pansophios d'Ibora." *Vigiliae Christianae* 42:24–27.

———, ed. and tr. (1990). *Grégoire de Nysse: Lettres.* SChr. 363. Paris.

———. (1997). "Grégoire de Nysse, évêque et pasteur." In *Vescovi e pastori in epoca teodosiana: In occasione del XVI centenario della consacrazione episcopale di S. Agostino, 396–1996. XXV Incontro di studiosi dell'antichità cristiana, Roma, 8–11 maggio 1996*, 2:383–93. Studia Ephemeridis "Augustinianum" 58. Rome.

Marrou, H. I. (1956). *A History of Education in Antiquity*, tr. G. Lamb. New York.

———. (1964). *MOYCKOC ANHP: Etude sur les scènes de la vie intellectuelle figurant sur les monuments funéraires romains.* Rev. ed., Rome.

Matthews, J. (1975). *Western Aristocracies and Imperial Court A.D. 364–425.* Oxford.

May, G. (1966). "Gregor von Nyssa in der Kirchenpolitik seiner Zeit." *Jahrbuch der österreichischen byzantinischen Gesellschaft* 15:105–32.

———. (1971). "Die Chronologie des Lebens und der Werke des Gregor von Nyssa." In *Ecriture et culture philosophique dans la pensée de Grégoire de Nysse*, ed. M. Harl, pp. 51–66. Leiden.

McGinn, T. A. J. (1999). "Widows, Orphans, and Social History." *Journal of Roman Archaeology* 12:617–32.

McLynn, N. (1996). "Gregory the Peacemaker: A Study of Oration Six." *Kyoyo-Ronso* 101:183–216.

———. (1997). "The Voice of Conscience: Gregory Nazianzen in Retirement." In *Vescovi e pastori in epoca teodosiana: In occasione del XVI centenario della consacrazione episcopale di S. Agostino, 396–1996. XXV Incontro di studiosi dell'antichità cristiana, Roma, 8–11 maggio 1996*, 2:299–308. Studia Ephemeridis "Augustinianum" 58. Rome.

————. (1998). "The Other Olympias: Gregory Nazianzen and the Family of Vital-ianus." *Zeitschrift für Antikes Christentum* 2:227–46.

————. (2001). "Gregory Nazianzen's Basil: The Literary Construction of a Christian Friendship." In *Studia Patristica Vol. XXXVII: Papers Presented at the Thirteenth International Conference on Patristic Studies Held in Oxford 1999. Cappadocian Writers, Other Greek Writers*, ed. M. F. Wiles and E. J. Yarnold, with P. M. Parvis, pp. 178–93. Leuven.

Meehan, D. M., tr. (1987). *Saint Gregory of Nazianzus: Three Poems. Concerning His Own Affairs, Concerning Himself and the Bishops, Concerning His Own Life.* FC 75. Washington, D. C.

van der Meer, F. (1961). *Augustine the Bishop: The Life and Work of a Father of the Church*, tr. B. Battershaw and G. R. Lamb. London and New York.

Meredith, A. (1997). "Gregory of Nazianzus and Gregory of Nyssa on Basil." In *Studia Patristica Vol. XXXII: Papers Presented at the Twelfth International Conference on Patristic Studies Held in Oxford 1995. Athanasius and His Opponents, Cappadocian Fathers, Other Greek Writers After Nicaea*, ed. E. A. Livingstone, pp. 163–69. Leuven.

Merkelbach, R. and J. Stauber (2001). *Steinepigramme aus dem griechischen Osten 2: Die Nordküste Kleinasiens (Marmarameer und Pontos).* Munich and Leipzig.

Miller, P. C. (1994). *Dreams in Late Antiquity: Studies in the Imagination of a Culture.* Princeton, N.J.

Milovanovic-Barham, C. (1997). "Gregory of Nazianzus: Ars Poetica (In suos versus: Carmen 2.1.39)." *Journal of Early Christian Studies* 5:497–510.

Mitchell, S. (1982). "The Life of Saint Theodotus of Ancyra." *Anatolian Studies* 32:93–113.

————. (1988). "Maximinus and the Christians in A.D. 312: A New Latin Inscription." *Journal of Roman Studies* 78:105–24.

————. (1993). *Anatolia: Land, Men, and Gods in Asia Minor.* 2 vols. Oxford.

————. (1999a). "The Cult of Theos Hypsistos Between Pagans, Jews, and Christians." In *Pagan Monotheism in Late Antiquity*, ed. P. Athanassiadi and M. Frede, pp. 81–148. Oxford.

————. (1999b). "The Life and *Lives* of Gregory Thaumaturgus." In *Portraits of Spiritual Authority: Religious Power in Early Christianity, Byzantium and the Christian Orient*, ed. J. W. Drijvers and J. W. Watt, pp. 99–138. Religions in the Graeco-Roman World 137. Leiden.

Momigliano, A. (1985). "The Life of St. Macrina by Gregory of Nyssa." In *The Craft of the Ancient Historian: Essays in Honor of Chester G. Starr*, ed. J. W. Eadie and J. Ober, pp. 443–58. Lanham, Md. Reprinted in A. Momigliano, *On Pagans, Jews, and Christians*, pp. 206–21. Middletown, Conn., 1987.

Mossay, J., and G. Lafontaine, ed. and tr. (1980). *Grégoire de Nazianze: Discours 20–23.* SChr. 270. Paris.

Mosshammer, A. A. (2001). "Gregory of Nyssa as Homilist." In *Studia Patristica Vol. XXXVII: Papers Presented at the Thirteenth International Conference on Patristic Studies Held in Oxford 1999. Cappadocian Writers, Other Greek Writers*, ed. M. F. Wiles and E. J. Yarnold, with P. M. Parvis, pp. 212–39. Leuven.

Moutsoulas, E. (1997). "Le problème de la date de la mort de saint Basile de Césarée." In *Studia Patristica Vol. XXXII: Papers Presented at the Twelfth International Conference on Patristic Studies Held in Oxford 1995. Athanasius and His Opponents,*

Cappadocian Fathers, Other Greek Writers After Nicaea, ed. E. A. Livingstone, pp. 196–200. Leuven.

Mullett, M. (1981). "The Classical Tradition in the Byzantine Letter." In *Byzantium and the Classical Tradition*, ed. M. Mullett and R. Scott, pp. 75–93. University of Birmingham Thirteenth Spring Symposium of Byzantine Studies 1979. Birmingham.

————. (1988). "Byzantium: A Friendly Society." *Past and Present* 118:3–24.

————. (1997). *Theophylact of Ochrid: Reading the Letters of a Byzantine Archbishop.* Birmingham Byzantine and Ottoman Monographs 2. Aldershot.

Nautin, P. (1961). "La date du «De Viris Inlustribus» de Jérôme, de la mort de Cyrille de Jérusalem et de celle de Grégoire de Nazianze." *Revue d'histoire ecclésiastique* 56:33–35.

Nimmo Smith, J. (2000). "The Early Scholia on the Sermons of Gregory of Nazianzus." In *Studia Nazianzenica I*, ed. B. Coulie, pp. 69–146. CChr., Series graeca 41 = Corpus Nazianzenum 8. Turnhout.

Norris, F. W. (2000). "Your Honor, My Reputation: St. Gregory of Nazianzus's Funeral Oration on St. Basil the Great." In *Greek Biography and Panegyric in Late Antiquity*, ed. T. Hägg and P. Rousseau, with C. Høgel, pp. 140–159. Berkeley, Calif.

Olshausen, E., and J. Biller (1984). *Historisch-geographische Aspekte der Geschichte des Pontischen und Armenischen Reiches, Teil 1: Untersuchungen zur historischen Geographie von Pontos unter den Mithradatiden.* Beihefte zum Tübinger Atlas des vorderen Orients, Reihe B (Geisteswissenschaften), Nr. 29/1. Wiesbaden.

Opitz, H.-G., ed. (1934–1935). *Urkunden zur Geschichte des arianischen Streites 318–328. = Athanasius Werke* 3.1. Berlin and Leipzig.

————, ed. (1935–1941). *Athanasius Werke, Zweiter Band, Erster Teil: Die Apologien.* Berlin and Leipzig.

Osborne, C. (1993). "Literal or Metaphorical? Some Issues of Language in the Arian Controversy." In *Christian Faith and Greek Philosophy in Late Antiquity: Essays in Tribute to George Christopher Stead*, ed. L. R. Wickham and C. P. Bammel, assisted by E. C. D. Hunter, pp. 148–70. Supplements to Vigiliae Christianae 19. Leiden.

Parkin, T. G. (1992). *Demography and Roman Society.* Baltimore.

————. (1997). "Out of Sight, out of Mind: Elderly Members of the Roman Family." In *The Roman Family in Italy: Status, Sentiment, Space*, ed. B. Rawson and P. Weaver, pp. 123–48. Canberra and Oxford.

Parvis, S. (2001). "The Canons of Ancyra and Caesarea (314): Lebon's Thesis Revisited." *Journal of Theological Studies* n.s. 52:625–36.

van Parys, M. (1970). "Exégèse et théologie trinitaire: Prov. 8,22 chez les Pères cappadociens." *Irénikon* 43:362–79.

Patlagean, E. (1977). *Pauvreté économique et pauvreté sociale à Byzance 4ᵉ–7ᵉ siècles.* Paris.

————. (1981). "Familles chrétiennes d'Asie Mineure et histoire démographique du IVe siècle." In E. Patlagean, *Structure sociale, famillé, chrétienté à Byzance, IVe–XIe siècle*, Chapter 9. London.

————. (1987). "Byzantium in the Tenth and Eleventh Centuries." In *A History of Private Life, I: From Pagan Rome to Byzantium*, ed. P. Veyne, tr. A. Goldhammer, pp. 551–641. Cambridge, Mass.

Pelikan, J. (1971). *The Christian Tradition: A History of the Development of Doctrine. 1: The Emergence of the Catholic Tradition (100–600)*. Chicago.

———. (1993). *Christianity and Classical Culture: The Metamorphosis of Natural Theology in the Christian Encounter with Hellenism*. New Haven, Conn.

Penella, R. J. (1990). *Greek Philosophers and Sophists in the Fourth Century A.D.: Studies in Eunapius of Sardis*. ARCA Classical and Medieval Texts, Papers and Monographs 28. Leeds.

Petit, P. (1956). *Les étudiants de Libanius*. Etudes prosopographiques 1. Paris.

Pfister, J. E. (1964). "A Biographical Note: The Brothers and Sisters of St. Gregory of Nyssa." *Vigiliae Christianae* 18:108–13.

Pouchet, R. (1984). "Eusèbe de Samosate, père spirituel de Basile le Grand." *Bulletin de littérature ecclésiastique* 85:179–95.

———. (1988). "Essai de décryptage de la Lettre 213 de s. Basile." In *Mémorial Dom Jean Gribomont (1920–1986)*, pp. 487–502. Studia Ephemeridis "Augustinianum" 27. Rome.

———. (1992a). *Basile le Grand et son univers d'amis d'après sa correspondance: Une stratégie de communion*. Studia Ephemeridis "Augustinianum" 36. Rome.

———. (1992b). "La date de l'élection épiscopale de saint Basile et celle de sa mort." *Revue d'histoire ecclésiastique* 87:5–33.

Regali, M. (1988). "La datazione del carme II,2,3 di Gregorio Nazianzeno." *Studi classici e orientali* 38:373–81.

Rist, J. M. (1981). "Basil's 'Neoplatonism': Its Background and Nature." In *Basil of Caesarea: Christian, Humanist, Ascetic. A Sixteen-Hundredth Anniversary Symposium*, ed. P. J. Fedwick, 1:137–220. Toronto.

Rives, J. B. (1999). "The Decree of Decius and the Religion of Empire." *Journal of Roman Studies* 89:135–54.

Rocher, A., ed. and tr. (1987). *Hilaire de Poitiers: Contre Constance*. SChr. 334. Paris.

Roueché, C. (1989). *Aphrodisias in Late Antiquity: The Late Roman and Byzantine Inscriptions Including Texts from the Excavations at Aphrodisias Conducted by Kenan T. Erim*. Journal of Roman Studies Monographs 5. London.

Rousseau, P. (1990). "Basil of Caesarea: Choosing a Past." In *Reading the Past in Late Antiquity*, ed. G. Clarke, B. Croke, A. Emmett Nobbs, and R. Mortley, pp. 37–58. Rushcutters Bay.

———. (1994). *Basil of Caesarea*. Berkeley, Calif.

Rousselle, A. (1988). *Porneia: On Desire and the Body in Antiquity*, tr. F. Pheasant. Oxford.

Rudberg, S. Y. (1953). *Etudes sur la tradition manuscrite de saint Basile*. Lund.

———. (1981). "Manuscripts and Editions of the Works of Basil of Caesarea." In *Basil of Caesarea: Christian, Humanist, Ascetic. A Sixteen-Hundredth Anniversary Symposium*, ed. P. J. Fedwick, 1:49–65. Toronto.

Ruether, R. R. (1969). *Gregory of Nazianzus: Rhetor and Philosopher*. Oxford.

Russell, D. A., and N. G. Wilson, ed. and tr. (1981). *Menander Rhetor*. Oxford.

Saller, R. P. (1994). *Patriarchy, Property and Death in the Roman Family*. Cambridge Studies in Population, Economy and Society in Past Time 25. Cambridge.

Scholten, C. (1992). "Die Chorbischof bei Basilius." *Zeitschrift für Kirchengeschichte* 103:149–73.

Schouler, B. (1980). "Dépasser le père." *Revue des études grecques* 93:1–24.

Schwartz, E. (1959). "Die Dokumente des arianischen Streits bis 325." In E. Schwartz, *Gesammelte Schriften 3: Zur Geschichte des Athanasius*, pp. 117–68. Berlin. Reprinted from *Nachrichten von der königlichen Gesellschaft der Wissenschaften zu Göttingen*, Philologisch-historische Klasse (1905), pp. 257–99.

Seeck, O. (1906). *Die Briefe des Libanius zeitlich geordnet*. Leipzig.

Shaw, B. D. (1987a). "The Family in Late Antiquity: The Experience of Augustine." *Past and Present* 115:3–51.

————. (1987b). "The Age of Roman Girls at Marriage: Some Reconsiderations." *Journal of Roman Studies* 77:30–46.

Shaw, T. M. (1998). *The Burden of the Flesh: Fasting and Sexuality in Early Christianity*. Minneapolis, Minn.

Spacks, P. M. (1976). *Imagining a Self: Autobiography and Novel in Eighteenth-Century England*. Cambridge, Mass.

Spira, A. (1984). "Introduction." In *The Biographical Works of Gregory of Nyssa: Proceedings of the Fifth International Colloquium on Gregory of Nyssa (Mainz, 6–10 September 1982)*, ed. A. Spira, pp. 1–18. Patristic Monograph Series 12. Cambridge, Mass.

Tinnefeld, F. (1973). "'Freundschaft' in den Briefen des Michael Psellos: Theorie und Wirklichkeit." *Jahrbuch des österreichischen Byzantinistik* 22:151–68.

Torres, J. (1997). "Conflictividad de las elecciones episcopales en oriente: el protagonismo de Gregorio de Nisa." In *Vescovi e pastori in epoca teodosiana: In occasione del XVI centenario della consacrazione episcopale di S. Agostino, 396–1996. XXV Incontro di studiosi dell'antichità cristiana, Roma, 8–11 maggio 1996*, 1:255–64. Studia Ephemeridis "Augustinianum" 58. Rome.

Trebilco, P. R. (1991). *Jewish Communities in Asia Minor*. Cambridge.

Treu, K. (1961). "Φιλία und ἀγάπη: Zur Terminologie der Freundschaft bei Basilius und Gregor von Nazianz." *Studii clasice* 3:421–27.

————. (1972). "Freundschaft." In *Reallexikon für Antike und Christentum: Sachwörterbuch zur Auseinandersetzung des Christentums mit der antiken Welt*, ed. E. Dassmann et al., vol. 8, col. 418–34. Stuttgart.

Treucker, B. (1961). *Politische und sozialgeschichtliche Studien zu den Basilius-Briefen*. Munich.

————. (1981). "A Note on Basil's Letters of Recommendation." In *Basil of Caesarea: Christian, Humanist, Ascetic. A Sixteen-Hundredth Anniversary Symposium*, ed. P. J. Fedwick, 1:405–10. Toronto.

Trexler, R. C. (1980). *Public Life in Renaissance Florence*. New York.

Vaggione, R. P. (2000). *Eunomius of Cyzicus and the Nicene Revolution*. Oxford.

Van Dam, R. (1982). "Hagiography and History: The Life of Gregory Thaumaturgus." *Classical Antiquity* 1:272–308.

————. (1986). "Emperor, Bishops, and Friends in Late Antique Cappadocia." *Journal of Theological Studies* n. s. 37:53–76.

————. (1993). *Saints and Their Miracles in Late Antique Gaul*. Princeton, N.J.

————. (1995). "Self-Representation in the Will of Gregory of Nazianzus." *Journal of Theological Studies* n.s. 46:118–48.

————. (1996). "Governors of Cappadocia During the Fourth Century." In *Late*

Antiquity and Byzantium, ed. R. W. Mathisen. = *Medieval Prosopography* 17:7–93.

Vanderspoel, J. (1995). *Themistius and the Imperial Court: Oratory, Civic Duty, and Paideia from Constantius to Theodosius.* Ann Arbor, Mich.

———. (1999). "Correspondence and Correspondents of Julius Julianus." *Byzantion* 69:396–478.

Van Eijk, T. H. C. (1972). "Marriage and Virginity, Death and Immortality." In *Epektasis: Mélanges patristiques offerts au Cardinal Jean Daniélou*, ed. J. Fontaine and C. Kannengiesser, pp. 209–35. Paris.

Verdon, M. (1988). "Virgins and Widows: European Kinship and Early Christianity." *Man* 23:488–505.

Vinson, M. (1994). "Gregory Nazianzen's Homily 15 and the Genesis of the Christian Cult of the Maccabean Martyrs." *Byzantion* 64:166–92.

Vischer, L. (1953). "Das Problem der Freundschaft bei den Kirchenvätern: Basilius der Grosse, Gregor von Nazianz und Chrysostomus." *Theologische Zeitschrift* 9:173–200.

Weber, E. (1976). *Peasants into Frenchmen: The Modernization of Rural France, 1870–1914.* Stanford, Calif.

White, C. (1992). *Christian Friendship in the Fourth Century.* Cambridge.

Widdicombe, P. (1994). *The Fatherhood of God from Origen to Athanasius.* Oxford.

Wiles, M. (1997). "Triple and Single Immersion: Baptism in the Arian Controversy." In *Studia Patristica Vol. XXX: Papers Presented at the Twelfth International Conference on Patristic Studies Held in Oxford 1995. Biblica et Apocrypha, Ascetica, Liturgica*, ed. E. A. Livingstone, pp. 337–49. Leuven.

Williams, R. (1993). "Baptism and the Arian Controversy." In *Arianism After Arius: Essays on the Development of the Fourth Century Trinitarian Conflicts*, ed. M. R. Barnes and D. H. Williams, pp. 149–80. Edinburgh.

Wittig, M., tr. (1981). *Gregor von Nazianz: Briefe.* Bibliothek der griechischen Literatur, Abteilung Patristik, Bd. 13. Stuttgart.

Zgusta, L. (1964). *Kleinasiatische Personennamen.* Prague.

Zuckerman, C. (1991). "Cappadocian Fathers and the Goths." *Travaux et Mémoires* 11:473–86.

Index

Carleton College Library
One North College Street
Northfield, MN 55057-4097

WITHDRAWN

Danube R.
THRACE
Thessalonica
Constantinople
Nicomedia
Cyzicus
Nicaea
AEGEAN
SEA
BITHYNIA
Athens
PHRYGIA
MEDITERRANEAN SEA
Alexandria
EGYPT
0
100
200 Miles
0
100
200 Kilometers